Hugh B. Brown

His Life and Thought

Hugh B. Brown
His Life and Thought

Eugene E. Campbell and Richard D. Poll

BOOKCRAFT, INC.
Salt Lake City, Utah

First Printing, 1975

Library of Congress Catalog Card Number: 75-34834

ISBN 0-88494-293-7

LITHOGRAPHED IN U.S.A. BY
PUBLISHERS PRESS
SALT LAKE CITY, UTAH

Contents

Publisher's Foreword

This book was three years in the writing, to which was necessarily added the months of editorial and production time. President Brown was an interested participant in the several stages, though toward the end he was bedfast and the proofs had to be read to him. It was our hope that we would be able to put a copy of this book in his hands before he passed away, but that was not to be. He breathed his last on December 2, 1975, some five weeks after his ninety-second birthday and while publication was still a few days away. The funeral service was held in the Salt Lake Tabernacle on December 5.

To the end, Hugh B. Brown was a man among men. The strength and courage portrayed by his erect bearing and eloquent address, even his keen sense of humor, were all present despite the breakdown of physical powers. His passing was peaceful. Death came as a friend.

At Bookcraft we have a high admiration and esteem for President Hugh B. Brown. This springs not only from our having published four books he authored but also from having enjoyed a warm and close association with him over the years.

No book could do full justice to the life of this outstanding man, but authors Eugene Campbell and Richard Poll have done what words can do in this respect. To them and to the always cooperative and helpful family of President Brown we express sincere appreciation as we offer to Church members this life story of a man who was early marked for greatness and who amply fulfilled that potential.

MARVIN W. WALLIN
Bookcraft

Preface

"I have fought a good fight, I have finished my course, I have kept the faith." These words of Paul would likewise be a fitting summary to the life of the latter-day apostle, President Hugh B. Brown, who is in his ninety-second year as we write these words.

A man of superlative spiritual and mental powers, President Brown has brought comfort, hope and understanding to millions at home and abroad with his eloquent witness of the divinity of Jesus Christ. Called at seventy to be a General Authority of the Church, he had behind him a life of unusually varied experiences as a cowboy, missionary, farmer, soldier, lawyer, businessman, political leader, public servant, church leader, servicemen's coordinator, and college professor. He has been able to draw on this remarkably broad background for the interesting and inspiring illustrations that have characterized his speeches and writings and made him a favorite with Mormons everywhere. Nor has his influence been limited to LDS circles; his wisdom has a universal quality that transcends denominational lines.

Blessed with a strong, handsome body, a brilliant mind, and an impressive bearing, Hugh B. Brown has long since overcome the lack of formal education by disciplined study of the world's great books, extensive travel, and perceptive interaction with people. A delightful sense of humor and keen powers of observation and description make him always interesting. He is an avid sportsman, but his rugged strength and manliness cloak a tender, thoughtful, sensitive soul. A lover of beauty, he is deeply touched by flowers, fine music and literature, majestic buildings, and the wonders of nature. He is also profoundly spiritual, as is demonstrated by his poetry, prayers, testimony, public addresses, and private counsel.

Despite testing times of separation and disappointed hopes, Hugh B. and Zina Card Brown sustained for sixty-six years a marriage relationship which could well be the pattern for every LDS home. Ever adoring, concerned for, and supportive of each other and their eight children — theirs is surely one of the great love stories of all time.

We were delighted to receive the invitation from the Hugh B. Brown family to write a book on the life and thought of this outstanding man. As former colleagues at Brigham Young University and close friends for twenty years, we have during that time shared an admiration for President Brown. As college professors, we found that he had faced and thought through many of the intellectual challenges of life, and that wide experience and rugged honesty made him a valuable counselor to teachers and students alike.

While geographical and other necessities dictated a division of the assignment as between organizing the work, writing initial drafts, adding the analysis of President Brown's thought, and reworking of drafts, etc., the result is a composite effort for which we share responsibility. For us it has been a fascinating, challenging experience. It is our hope that the book is in some degree worthy of the great man whose life has made it possible.

EUGENE E. CAMPBELL

RICHARD D. POLL

Acknowledgments

We have been assisted in this task by many people. We have spent some delightful hours of conversation with President Brown himself. Of his family, Zina Lou, Zola and Mary have been especially helpful in supplying letters, documents, newspaper clippings, interviews and memorabilia, and in reading the draft chapters to their father for approval and additional information. LaJune, Margaret, Carol, and Charles Manley have also responded willingly to requests for interviews and materials. A series of taped and transcribed interviews with President Brown conducted in 1968-69 by his eldest grandson, Edwin Brown Firmage, have been invaluable, as have Dr. Firmage's own recollections and counsel. Conversations with Ida Archibald Brown, Calvin W. Rawlings, Asael Palmer, and Richard Hodson have provided useful information. President N. Eldon Tanner, Elder Brown's nephew, was interviewed for parts of the story and helpfully reviewed some of the chapters.

Vera Hutchinson, President Brown's secretary, has been most cooperative, supplying the authors with journals, documents, scrapbooks, pictures, letters, speeches and suggestions. Her work has obviously been a labor of love. We have been aided also by our own secretaries who have transcribed our tapes and typed our manuscripts.

Finally we recognize the contribution of our wives, Beth Campbell and Gene Poll, who share our love and admiration for Hugh B. Brown and have read the manuscript and encouraged us in numerous other ways.

The journals of President Brown, kept with varying regularity and detail from 1905, are the primary documents on which this biography is based. Scores of his and Zina Brown's letters, his scrapbooks, and his dictated memoirs have also been extensively used.

In working with the records, the authors have found that, like other good story-tellers, President Brown sometimes embellished a good anecdote for the benefit of his family or a larger audience. Some remembered experiences have also changed shape and texture with the passage of the years, as they do with everyone. We have chosen not to include scholarly textual analyses, but we have tried consistently to indicate whether sources are contemporary with events or are reminiscent. Necessary editorial corrections have been made and, for ease of reading, in most instances formal citations of these documents have been omitted, but every effort has been made to produce a story which is faithful to the sources and to the subject.

1. A Mormon Boy

A young Canadian farmer, exploring his small portion of southern Alberta prairie early in the present century, discovered a currant bush that had grown all to wood, with no sign of either blossom or fruit. Knowing something of pruning, he trimmed the plant down to a much smaller size, and in the course of the task he imagined that the currant bush protested this drastic treatment. He reminded the bush that he was the gardener there, and that he knew what he wanted the bush to be. It was not to be as big as the trees on either side, for its mission was not to provide timber or shade.

"Someday," he said, "when you are laden with currants you will thank me for cutting you down so that you could grow properly and develop the fruit that you were created to produce."

The farmer was Hugh B. Brown, and the story of the currant bush is treasured by thousands of Latter-day Saints who have heard his sermons or read his books. But it is more than a story — it is the key to the life of this much-loved Mormon leader.

"I have had my share of ups and downs," said President Brown, "and to use the words of Rudyard Kipling, have met 'Triumph and Disaster' and have tried to 'treat those two impostors just the same.' "

Favored with a keen mind, a handsome and strong body, a high degree of emotional and spiritual sensitivity, and an unusual talent to influence his fellowmen by his speaking ability, President Brown grew up with a driving ambition to take advantage of his opportunities and "to make his mark" in the world. It led him into wide-ranging agricultural, business, military, legal, political, educational and religious endeavors, with great success often followed by some quirk of fate that seemed to cut him down and force him to change direction. But finally, it led him to be first counselor in the First Presidency of The Church of Jesus Christ of Latter-day Saints and to become one of contemporary Mormonism's greatest speakers and most valued counselors. Nor has his influence been confined to his church, for he has spent much of his long life away from LDS centers and is honored and cherished by thousands of non-Mormon friends and acquaintances.

In a retelling of the currant bush story which appeared on the eve of his ninetieth birthday, Hugh B. Brown stated the moral of his own life in these modest terms: "God is the Gardener here. He knows what he wants you to be. . . . I haven't amounted to very much as it is, but I have done better than I would have done if the Lord had let me go the way I wanted to go." ("The Currant Bush," *The New Era,* January 1973, p. 15.)

Where did it all start, and how did he become the man that he is?

Hugh B. Brown (the B also stands for Brown) was born in Granger, Salt Lake Valley, on October 24, 1883, just 36 years after the Mormon pioneers first entered the region and made it their headquarters. He was the fifth child and second son of Homer Manley Brown and Lydia Jane Brown Brown, who ultimately became the parents of fourteen children. Homer and Lydia had been married in the Salt Lake Endowment House on November 22, 1875.

Hugh's father and mother were both second-generation Mormons, which at that date meant that their parents were among the early converts to the Church. One great-grandfather, Benjamin Brown, was associated with the Mormon Prophet,

HUGH B. BROWN LINE

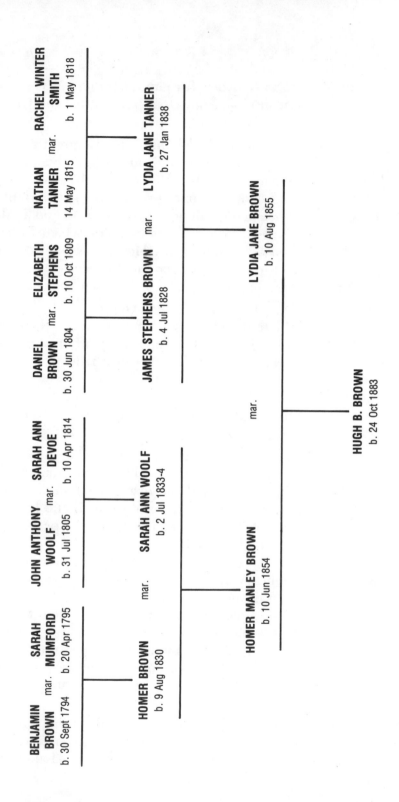

BENJAMIN BROWN
b. 30 Sept 1794

mar.

SARAH MUMFORD
b. 20 Apr 1795

JOHN ANTHONY WOOLF
b. 31 Jul 1805

mar.

SARAH ANN DEVOE
b. 10 Apr 1814

DANIEL BROWN
b. 30 Jun 1804

mar.

ELIZABETH STEPHENS
b. 10 Oct 1809

NATHAN TANNER
14 May 1815

mar.

RACHEL WINTER SMITH
b. 1 May 1818

HOMER BROWN
b. 9 Aug 1830

mar.

SARAH ANN WOOLF
b. 2 Jul 1833-4

JAMES STEPHENS BROWN
b. 4 Jul 1828

mar.

LYDIA JANE TANNER
b. 27 Jan 1838

HOMER MANLEY BROWN
b. 10 Jun 1854

mar.

LYDIA JANE BROWN
b. 10 Aug 1855

HUGH B. BROWN
b. 24 Oct 1883

Joseph Smith, in Nauvoo. Benjamin's father, Asa, participated in Zion's Camp in 1834, only four years after the Church was organized.

Hugh's grandparents and many of his great-grandparents participated in the exodus from Nauvoo, and his parents were born in the Great Salt Lake Valley less than a decade after Brigham Young had pronounced that "this is the right place." It was a rough and demanding environment, and it doubtless helped to shape the patriarchal households which Elder Brown remembers from his childhood. He describes his male fore-bears as "hard-working pioneer stock, sometimes rough and sometimes gruff, but all in all — good men."

Hugh's paternal grandfather, Homer, was as severe and rugged as the Utah wilderness. A polygamist with three wives, he lost the first, Sarah Ann, by divorce, after she had borne ten children, and shortly before his death he was excommuni-cated from the Church after an altercation with his bishop. Homer was a hard worker, a good speaker, an excellent dancer and a good mixer, well liked by many who knew him, but he had an abrasive character.

President Brown believes that this background may have accounted for his own father's harshness, bad temper, and lack of Church activity, although he asserts that his father "had a great faith in the Brethren, was loyal to them and believed them to be prophets of God." His father was especially fond of Wilford Woodruff, his neighbor in Salt Lake Valley for some time. But Homer Manley Brown did not seek church positions, and he was a heavy smoker until the time that Hugh left for his mission to England in 1904. At that time he said that "he would never touch another cigarette," and he kept that promise. Later in his long life he became a more active participant in church work, and in his calling as a stake patriarch he blessed several of his grandchildren. Some of them remember his flow-ing beard, strong hands, and impressive bearing, and see some of his speaking style in their father.

Hugh's principal childhood memory of his father is that he was a stern disciplinarian, quick to anger and sometimes given to physical punishment. The oldest son Homer and Hugh were most frequently subjected to such treatment, and Hugh never forgot one incident in which his sister Lillie stepped between him and his father, held up her hands and said, "Don't you dare touch my little brother." It broke his mother's heart to see her children so treated, but she was reluctant to stand up to her husband because of his "violent temper and sharp tongue." These traits alienated Homer Manley Brown from the members of his family for much of his life.

That the severe, outwardly unloving, family head was a not uncommon type in pioneer Utah is witnessed by a sermon of Brigham Young's which might have been heard but apparently not heeded — by Hugh's father and grandfather: "Kindness, love and affection are the best rod to use upon the refractory. . . . I can pick out scores of men in this congregation who have driven their children from them by using the wooden rod." (*Journal of Discourses*, vol. 9, pp. 195-196.)

Observing this autocratic behavior in many of the homes of his youthful acquaintance, even among LDS leaders, Hugh Brown resolved early that he would try to govern his own family by love rather than fear. Years later he would write:

> There is no room for bossism in married life, or for petty tyranny, where one or the other of the parents exercises unrighteous control or dominion. . . .
>
> To be raised in or to live in an atmosphere of tyranny discourages ambition, saps mental and spiritual vitality, and transforms members of the family into subdued, crushed, and colorless beings. Sometimes harsh discipline leads to hypocrisy, deceit, lying, and trickery in an attempt to escape the tyranny which they do not have the courage or the opportunity to challenge openly. . . .
>
> Both parties to a marriage should understand it to be a partnership, and not a proprietorship. . . . Both partners should agree that neither will be required to "come to heel." It is much easier to meet this tendency in the beginning rather than to correct it after years of cowardly patience. . . . Slavery has no place in the home.
>
> Enforcement of proper discipline need not, should not, and must not lead to the exercise of unrighteous dominion. . . . Love grows best in the atmosphere of freedom, confidence and trust. (Hugh B. Brown, *You and Your Marriage* [Salt Lake City: Bookcraft, Inc., 1960], pp. 157-159.)

President Brown does not remember his childhood with much pleasure because of his father's attitude. "We had to work so hard," he said, "and received no commendation. . . . I would weed two rows of corn and my father would say, 'Why didn't you get to work on the potato patch?'" Yet he admired his father in many ways, remembering him as a large, strong, sinewy man who loved his family sincerely, did everything he could for them in a material way, and generally was a good manager and provider. Homer Manley Brown lived to celebrate his golden wedding anniversary with Lydia, and Hugh was happy to organize the celebration of that event.

Hugh's relationship with his mother was quite different. He remembers her as being kind, generous, sympathetic and understanding — a sweet-spirited woman of deep faith. She had the ability to make each child feel special. In Hugh's case she made him feel from the beginning that he had a great destiny — that if he would behave himself there was nothing he could not have, or do, or become. In their many intimate talks during his childhood and early manhood, she constantly inspired him to do his best, and the memory of her faith proved to be his best safeguard against temptation.

Despite the heavy chores associated with fourteen children, Lydia Brown liked to take each boy and girl alone on occasions for a chat. "The Lord has chosen you to be one of his servants," she would tell Hugh. "I expect big things from you." The barefoot boy who herded Jerseys and Holsteins in the salt grass near Salt Lake Valley's Jordan River never forgot those words. His mother never used a switch on him. When he made an error she would say, "Hugh, I'm surprised at you. I'm disappointed." And the boy would go off and cry as if he had been hit with a stick. A poignant vignette is associated with the arrival of twins in the Brown household: as the family grouped for a photograph, eleven-year-old Hugh asked, "Mother, couldn't you please put your hand on me?"

Like her husband, Lydia Jane Brown Brown had a strong heritage in the Mormon Church. (The appearance of the surname Brown in Hugh's paternal *and* maternal ancestral lines can confuse biographer and reader. See the accompanying genealogical table.)

James Stephens Brown, Lydia's father, joined the Mormon Battalion and made the memorable march from Council Bluffs, Iowa, to San Diego, California, at the age of eighteen. After his military discharge he agreed to work for Captain John Sutter and was one of the six young Mormons who were with Sutter's foreman, James Marshall, at Coloma when the discovery was made that set off the great California gold rush. James Brown participated in the first gold seeking, but he left for the Salt Lake Valley in the early summer of 1848 without having "struck it rich." He ultimately took five wives in plural marriage and fathered forty-five children, and during the anti-polygamy prosecutions of the 1880s he served two months and sixteen days of a three-month sentence in the penitentiary and paid a fine of $100 plus $27.50 in court costs. James lost a leg after reaching adulthood, but in spite of this handicap he filled seventeen missions for the Mormon Church and published an interesting autobiography.

President Brown remembers his maternal grandfather as being a stern disciplinarian also. He punished his children severely and they were afraid of him. Despite this background, his mother was gentle, loving, and considerate — perhaps reflecting the character of her own mother, Lydia Jane Tanner Brown, who died when her namesake daughter was only seventeen. It is an interesting reflection on James S. Brown that in his long autobiography he was so caught up in his missionary experiences that he mentioned the names of none of his plural wives and only four of his numerous children. He failed to record any of the vital statistics and other important factors of his family life.

Of such patriarchal pioneer stock came Hugh B. Brown. His father and grandfathers are remembered as so ironhanded as to discourage close ties of affection; one grandmother is recalled as a disappointed and bitter woman and the other died too soon to leave Hugh with any impression at all. Only his mother, Lydia, emerges from the record as a strong positive influence on the faith and character of the apostle-to-be. This influence, however, can hardly be overemphasized.

Salt Lake City in 1883, the year of Hugh's birth, was an unusual place. Only thirty-six years old, it was rapidly becoming

James S. Brown (seated) and friend.

a sizable city, the center of the Mormon Church, the capital of Utah Territory, and the economic and commercial "crossroads of the West." The Union Pacific and Central Pacific railroads had bypassed Salt Lake City in 1869, but by 1870 the Mormon leaders had built the Utah Central railroad connecting the city with Ogden, on the transcontinental line, and branch lines soon reached out to the mining camps in the nearby Oquirrh and Wasatch mountains.

Salt Lake City's population was well in excess of twenty thousand, most of whom were Latter-day Saints. However, both railroads and the booming mining industry — gold and silver had not yet given way to coal and copper — had lured a considerable number of non-Mormons into the region. Fortunes were being made and "elegance" was a word used increasingly to describe the buildings and homes that were being erected in the valley. The Salt Lake Theater had been completed in 1862, and the Tabernacle was in use by 1867. The temple itself was nearing completion, having been in the process of building for thirty years.

Brigham Young's old farm had been purchased by the city and opened to the public in 1882 as Liberty Park. An electric light exhibition had been held in front of the Intermountain West's first department store, Z.C.M.I., in September 1880, but electric lights did not come into general use in town until 1888; Hugh Brown's childhood evenings were illuminated by kerosene lamps. The telephone had come into use in Utah in 1879, and just two months before Hugh Brown's birth the city had ordered a house numbering system with a view to inaugurating a free mail delivery. Street railways appeared in 1872 on several of the still-unpaved streets, the horsedrawn vehicles being replaced by trolley cars in 1888.

Brigham Young had been dead only six years when Hugh Brown was born. The Young estate on East South Temple was enclosed by a wall, with public access to City Creek Canyon on the north through Eagle Gate. West of the two Young residences, the Beehive House and the Lion House, stood the adobe General Tithing Office, also enclosed within a stone and adobe wall. The Hotel Utah would rise on this site a generation later.

Although there was a considerable degree of prosperity in Salt Lake City, the Church hierarchy was in serious trouble in 1883. Four years earlier the United States Supreme Court had unanimously ruled in the case of Reynolds v. U.S. that the federal anti-polygamy statute of 1862 was constitutional, thus stripping the Mormons of their First Amendment defense of the plural marriage system. The Edmunds Act of 1882 then strengthened the law enforcement machinery and declared polygamous cohabitation to be a misdemeanor, opening the way for successful prosecution of many Mormons. The Church leaders decided to defy the decision and go "underground" rather than submit to the legislative regulation of marriage practices which they held sacred, and before Hugh was four years old over a thousand Mormon men, including George Q. Cannon of the First Presidency, and other prominent civic and ecclesiastical leaders, had served terms in the Utah Penitentiary for their plural marriage ties.

Hugh B. Brown's immediate family was not directly affected, since it was monogamous, but his grandfathers were involved as well as many friends of the family and local Church leaders. This problem was put on the road to solution by the Woodruff Manifesto of 1890, which officially ended the Church sanction of plural marriages. The manifesto made it possible for Utah to achieve statehood in January, 1896, and twelve-year-old Hugh witnessed some of the celebrations which attended that happy event.

All this political and social turmoil seems to have made little impression on young Hugh, for his principal memories are of the long hours of hard work on the various farms his father acquired during the first sixteen years of Hugh's life. The family was living on the old Crismon Ranch on Redwood Road near Forty-eighth South when Hugh was born. About 1887 they moved to the Lawrence Ranch, which was about ten miles west of Salt Lake City, beyond the old Brighton Ward, where Hugh first went to school. His father managed this ranch for about two years and then acquired the Lake Breeze Farm on Redwood Road (present-day Seventeenth West) between North Temple and Second South.

President Brown's earliest recollections of family activities

Hugh's parents, Homer Manley Brown and Lydia Jane Brown Brown, and their first seven children l. to r. (back row) Sarah Edna, Minnie, (front row) Lydia Jane (Lillie), Scott, Hugh B., Lawrence, and Homer (Bud).

begin at Lake Breeze, although he does remember events that occurred earlier, including the goring of his Uncle James T. Brown by a large Holstein bull. He also remembers the prancing thoroughbred stallion that the owner of the Lawrence Ranch kept there. Perhaps this was the beginning of that love of horses that has persisted throughout his life.

By the time the Brown family began to develop the Lake Breeze farm there were seven children: Minnie, who died at sixteen; Sarah Edna, who became the mother of Nathan Eldon Tanner; Homer James; Lydia Jane (Lillie); then Hugh, followed by Scot B. and Lawrence M. After moving to Lake Breeze Hugh's mother gave birth to six more children: Owen S., Gerald S., Roumelia, twins Winona and Verona, and Zola. A fourteenth child, Harvey B., was born in Spring Coulee, Alberta, in 1901, three years after the Browns moved to Canada.

Much of Hugh's adolescent life was devoted to such chores as taking care of the livestock and helping his father and older brother develop their fourteen-acre orchard. He remembers that there was a commodious red-brick home on the Lake Breeze Ranch, adequate for the growing family, but he does not remember whether his father built it or bought it along with the ranch. His father installed a hydraulic ram at the bottom of a small hill which pumped water into a large wooden tank purchased from the railroad; this made it possible for the Browns to have running water in the house. The pipes running back and forth in the cellar made shelves on which pans of milk were set for cooling and skimming when the cream rose. The children retained vivid memories of that big cellar, which in the fall was stored with apples, potatoes, carrots, turnips, beets, cabbages, a barrel of sauerkraut — in fact, practically a year's supply of food. Hugh helped his father and brothers plant many of the trees in the Lake Breeze orchard and also milked cows, fed pigs, cared for horses, and cultivated the garden and orchard.

Free tax-supported schools had only recently been established in Utah, and many classes continued to be held in Mormon meetinghouses. Hugh attended school first in the old Brighton Ward, and he was close to graduating from the eighth grade at the Franklin School when the family move to Canada ended his formal childhood education. President Brown

Outside Lake Breeze home: In buggy, Hugh's sister Sarah Edna, husband Nathan Tanner, and baby N. Eldon Tanner (future counselor in First Presidency). Hugh's mother stands by buggy; his father, in front of porch. Hugh (with dog) is seated in grass with brother Scott.

remembers that spelling and math were his best subjects, but the misspellings scattered through his earliest letters and journal suggest that his skill was sharpened by later reading and writing. The children, of course, had to walk to school. Hugh was so pressed by morning and evening chores that he had little time to play ball or marbles, and he apparently did not have many close friends.

The boy was especially close to his sister Lillie. She took a loving interest in him, helped him with many of his tasks, listened to his troubles, and reinforced the good counsel which he was receiving from his mother.

He was also fond of his older brother Homer, whom he called Bud. Bud called him Dutch because when Hugh first began to talk he could not pronounce his "r's" and had trouble with his "g's"; he said "bed" for "bread" and "dull" for "girl" and generally distorted the English language. Hugh remembers his brother for his active sense of humor, with a flair for practical jokes which sometimes got Hugh into trouble. One day at Lake Breeze, Bud said of the little donkey which had just been added to the ranch's four-legged inventory, "Dutch, you know you don't ride a donkey like you ride a horse; you always get on backwards, and when you get on you lean forward and take hold of the donkey's flank and he will know what to do." Hugh took it literally and Homer helped him on. He evidently neglected to instruct the donkey, who went into a bucking spree and dumped Hugh on his back on the ground.

A similar experience happened when the two boys saw a weasel as it ran into its burrow. They fetched spades to dig him out. After they had invested some time and energy in this enterprise, Bud said, "Dutch, I think I can hear him down there. We're getting pretty close to him. Maybe you had better reach in and see what he is doing." The younger brother obediently rolled up his sleeve and reached into the hole and the weasel got him by the finger. Bud had a hearty laugh, and Hugh still has the scar on his finger as a memento of the incident.

There were other practical jokes, including a rather dangerous one which might have taken Hugh's life, but the close relationship between the two boys was not marred by any sustained ill will. Hugh took the pranks as part of his education, and with the passing years Homer's inclination to push his brother into leadership responsibilities among the Brown children helped to reinforce that sense of responsibility — that awareness of mission — which his mother and Lillie were also cultivating in the youth.

There were good times, of course, and Hugh remembers with pleasure participating in Halloween pranks as well as family celebrations of Thanksgiving, Christmas, and the Fourth of July. He also remembers such special events as the dedication of the Salt Lake Temple. Since he was by then a baptized Latter-day Saint and so not required to attend the special sessions for children, he was present with his mother at at least one of the more than fifty repetitions of the dedicatory ceremony which were held in April and May 1893.

But the fleeting joys of youth ended abruptly for Hugh when his father decided to go to western Canada in 1898 to seek a new life for his family. Taking his eldest son with him and leaving Hugh to be "the man of the house," Homer Brown told the youth that he was expected to take care of the farm just as his father had done. Although Hugh was only fourteen years old, he took this charge very seriously. For more than a year it was his job to milk several cows night and morning, feed the pigs, care for the horses, till the garden and orchard, and in general supervise the operations of the farm. Small wonder that he had to miss the fall and spring terms of school, for which he compensated by reading at home and in the process cultivated a great love for books. It is also small wonder that he looked forward to leaving the farm and joining his father, brother, and eldest sister (now married) in Alberta.

2. Canadian Cowboy

Homer Manley Brown's decision to pull up stakes in Salt Lake Valley and move to Canada had a profound impact on the life of his son Hugh as well as the other members of the large family. Although the first Alberta residence lasted only twenty-eight years, President Brown still thinks of himself as a Canadian. It was during this time (1899-1927) that he grew into manhood, represented his ward as a missionary in England, met and married his wife, fathered seven of his eight children, served his country in World War I, gained a legal education and began his career at the bar, and served the Church as a bishop's counselor, high councilor, and finally as the first president of the Lethbridge Stake. Many years later he lived in Edmonton for three years as an oil company lawyer and executive, but it was his formative years that made him a Canadian. (Under Canadian law he still retains dual citizenship; he satisfied the repatriation requirements of U.S. law after his return to Utah in 1927.)

Two explanations appear in President Brown's recollections of his father's decision to go to Alberta. One relates to the ambitions which Homer cherished, albeit without sentimental display, for his six sons. On the low-priced land between Lethbridge and the international border they might become prosperous farmers rather than wage earners — an optimistic but not unreasonable expectation since the completion of the Canadian Pacific Railroad in 1885 had opened the region to commercial farming and stock raising, and a decade of Mormon colonizing had demonstrated that agricultural settlement was feasible in spite of the rigorous winters.

The second explanation relates to an aspect of that Mormon colonization, a Church-sponsored canal building project to which Homer and his family were called as work missionaries. In a sense, then, Hugh's long career of missionary service began when he was sixteen. His father's ambitions were also fulfilled in that Hugh found in Canada the path to a successful career, not as a farmer — prosperity consistently eluded him in that direction — but as a barrister and businessman.

Cardston, the center of Mormon activity in southern Alberta, was founded in 1887, barely a decade before Homer Brown bade temporary farewell to his family in Utah and entrained for Canada. The town bore the name of its founder, Charles O. Card, one of whose daughters would one day marry Homer's son, Hugh. In time the faith and dreams of Cardston's pioneers would find expression in the first LDS temple built outside the United States.

Political conditions arising out of the campaign against plural marriage prompted the first LDS colonizing in Canada. Under the same peril of imprisonment which led other polygamists to establish settlements in Mexico, President Card of the Cache Valley (Utah) Stake and a group of associates sought and obtained Church approval to found a colony beyond the northern boundary of the United States. At a cost of $900 (of which the Church provided one-third), President Card and two companions made an exploratory trip in 1886 which took them by rail and stage through the Pacific Northwest to Calgary, Alberta, then overland a hundred and twenty-five miles to the south. (Until the linking of the Union Pacific, Great Northern, and Canadian Pacific Railroads through Montana late in the 1890s, most of the traffic between Utah and Alberta followed this circuitous route.)

"On October 24," says Card in his diary, "we decided that at Standoff, between the Belly and Kootenay rivers, was an excellent place for settlement." Leaving John W. Hendricks to guard the camp, he and Bishop Isaac E. D. Zundell "went out into the prairie . . . and bowed before the Lord and dedicated and invoked the blessings of God upon the land and water and asked His preservation of the same for the benefit of Israel, both white and red." The tract thus dedicated is about twenty miles north of the present site of Cardston, and was known as the Cochrane Ranch.

The explorers returned to Utah for the winter, and in the following spring Card led a party of eight families, forty-one people in all, together with teams, cattle, farm implements, and household goods, back to Alberta. Finding to their disappointment that the Cochrane Ranch was not for sale (the Church purchased it later), the colonizers were forced to go a few miles to the south where, on April 26, 1887, they planted their settlement on Lee's Creek, a tributary of St. Mary's River, and adjacent to the Blood Indian Reserve.

Economic survival was made possible during Cardston's first years by the growth of some crops, employment on the adjacent Cochrane Ranch, and a high degree of self-help. Following the pattern of Mormon colonization in the Great Basin, the first community building was a "meetinghouse" that also served as a school, and a social and recreational center. A cooperative store also was organized, which was to employ Hugh Brown as manager some years later. Undergirding all was a religious homogeneity which made for effective cooperation and social control. In the words of one analyst, "Cardston was a colony with a purpose which was extra-economic, or super-economic. It was dedicated to a cause." (Lowry Nelson, *The Mormon Village* [Salt Lake City: University of Utah Press, 1952], p. 231.)

The colony grew slowly, only sixty-eight people "wintering on Lee's Creek" the first year. There was almost immediate reaction against polygamy by the older settlers and provincial officials, and despite Card's promise that the Mormons would not actually practice plural marriage in Canada, the Dominion Parliament passed the Thompson Bill in 1890 which defined polygamy as a crime punishable by fine and/or imprisonment. A few months later the Woodruff Manifesto satisfied the

Canadian critics and ended the first phase of LDS migration to Alberta.

By this time, however, the economic prospects of southern Alberta seemed so promising that Cardston was no longer seen as a place of refuge but as the center of an expanding colonizing enterprise. The possibility of purchasing thousands of acres of arid land from the railroad companies at low prices and using the Mormon knowledge of irrigation to bring the land into productivity was exciting. President Card undertook the purchase of 116,000 acres and Elder John W. Taylor bargained for more than a half-million acres in December 1891, payment to be spread over twelve years. Though Elder Taylor's contracts were cancelled in 1895, Card continued to promote settlement and was a leader in persuading the Canadian Pacific to extend branches into the region and in forming the Canadian Northwest Irrigation Company. He also won Church support for his proposal to build a fifty-mile canal eastward from Cardston and to establish Sterling as a Mormon settlement on the railway between Lethbridge and Great Falls, Montana.

This is the undertaking which, according to President Brown, caught the interest of his father. Under a contract with the irrigation company in 1898, the Church leadership agreed to furnish all the labor for the building of the canal, paying the workmen half in cash and half in land at the price of three dollars per acre. Two towns were to be established along the canal. Charles O. Card was charged with the responsibility of carrying out the Church contract. He flooded Utah with newspaper articles and circulars extolling the opportunities in Alberta, and when work on the canal was delayed he visited many of the towns of Utah recruiting colonists.

At least a few faithful Latter-day Saints were formally called to assist the enterprise. A letter from President Lorenzo Snow to one prospective work missionary mentions the canal contract and colonization, but adds:

> . . . it has been reported to us that some of the immigrants who have gone into that country are not, in every respect, the class of people best adapted to build up a new country, and it therefore becomes necessary, in order that the contract might be satisfactorily

filled, to call a certain number of more desirable men to settle on the lands selected by us, and to work on the canal.

It has been reported to us that your circumstances are such that you can go and settle in this country, and that you are willing to do so. We therefore take pleasure in selecting you and your family to go and help colonize . . . , subject to the direction of Pres. C. O. Card. (Lorenzo Snow to William Pierson, May 25, 1899, cited in Melvin S. Tagg, *A History of the Mormon Church in Canada* [Lethbridge, Canada: Lethbridge Herald Co., Ltd., 1968], p. 66.

It cannot be documented that Homer Manley Brown received one of these personal calls, but it seems certain that he was influenced by the publicity concerning the religious and economic opportunities in Alberta and responded. Hence the departure of the advance party of the Brown family in 1898 — father, eldest son Homer, daughter Edna and her husband, Nathan W. Tanner — leaving Lydia Brown in charge of her large family and the Lake Breeze farm, with fourteen-year-old Hugh assigned to do most of the farm work. An interesting sidelight is that, while the three men remained in Canada, Edna returned long enough to have her baby born in the United States. The boy, Nathan Eldon Tanner, would one day become first counselor in the First Presidency of the Church.

Having worked for a year on the canal, Homer sent for his family to join him in the fall of 1899. Family and belongings went by rail to Lethbridge by way of Great Falls in October. After a tedious four-day trip, Hugh was delighted to see his father and Bud waiting at the station with teams and wagons to transport the family to their new life. Homer had acquired a thousand-acre farm at Spring Coulee, forty-seven miles southwest of Lethbridge and fifteen miles northeast of Cardston, at the Church contract price of three dollars per acre. A two-room log house, erected on the edge of a spring (which the children believed to be bottomless), greeted the travel-weary family when they looked down upon their future home.

Living conditions were primitive and crowded that first Canadian winter and were made more so when Homer's brother, Walter, his wife Emmerette, a son, and two daughters moved into one of the rooms of the cabin. Hugh and the other boys were required to sleep in a tent, unforgettably uncomfortable, with the temperature often reaching 45° below zero. Imagine the feelings of the mother who had left a large, comfortable home in Salt Lake Valley and now had to adjust to such living conditions. But Lydia was a woman of character and she encouraged her brood — the eleven children at home ranged from nineteen down to almost three years in age — to make the best of a bad situation.

To make matters worse, Homer became ill and was forced to spend the entire winter in bed. Prior to this misfortune he had purchased a hundred "dogie" cattle, intending to fatten them during the winter. But an early storm crushed and flattened the bunch grass so that it could not be reclaimed. There was nothing left to do but to brand the animals and turn them loose to forage for themselves. It became Hugh's job to ride herd on these pitiful animals in an attempt to help them survive the winter. It meant days in the saddle in the bitter cold, with the roughest of men for companions. Let him tell this part of the story in his own words:

> Often I got lost in blizzards and had to depend upon my horse to take me home. . . . My older brother rode with me part of the time, but mostly he took care of affairs around the ranch. . . . On the advice of the older settlers and through experience we learned how to dress for this heavy winter. I remember having silk underwear next to my skin, covered with heavy woolen underwear and trousers, a leather jacket and a fur coonskin overcoat. Our feet and legs were protected by two pairs of socks, heavily lined boots and chaps. We were so heavily laden with clothes that it was often difficult to get onto the horse. We had a fur cape with a headpiece with coverings to protect nose and face from freezing. However, in spite of all this precaution, I often froze my nose, cheeks and chin, and sometimes my fingers and toes. This was an experience that I shall not forget while I live.

The young lad rode for many days with two very rugged cowboys — hard-working, hard-swearing, hard-riding, and hard-drinking types of whom he had had no previous experience. Bill Short and Bob Wallace worked for a big ranch near Spring Coulee, and Hugh formed some very strong opinions as he saw how tobacco and liquor dominated their activities. He particularly remembers an episode in which he and these companions had gone from Spring Coulee to Lethbridge for loads of lumber. On their way homeward, they stopped for a drink at a spot appropriately called Pothole. As the bottles were un-limbered, one was carelessly dropped on the frozen ground, shattering. Nothing would do but that the men cast lots to see who would ride one of the wagon horses back to Lethbridge for a new supply. The rest loitered by their wagons in discom-fort while their thirsty companion made his twenty-mile round trip for a bottle of whiskey. "I thought then and have often reflected since," writes President Brown, "on the sad propensity of mankind for strong liquor. These experiences, even more than the teachings of my parents and Church, I feel, saved me from the habit of smoking and drinking."

With the coming of spring, Homer's health improved, and he began the construction of a large frame house which the family was able to occupy in time to welcome the fourteenth and last Brown child — and the beginning of the twentieth century. Hugh spent his second winter in Alberta driving horse-drawn scrapers on the great canal with Bud, under the super-vision of his mother's half-brother, Van Brown. This, too, was remembered as a rugged experience, with rough weather, rough companions, and a straw boss whose life style did not reflect his Mormon ties. After Van had met the defiant challenge of one of the canal workers by knocking him over the dump, "the Finlander said God himself could not lick a man like Van."

Homer Brown stayed in Spring Coulee about two years, but shortly after moving into the large house, he decided to move again — to Cardston — so that the children would be able to attend school. He traded his holdings for some farms near Cardston and a town lot on which Elder John W. Taylor, the apostle, had originally built a house foundation. In the trade he acquired a section (640 acres) of land south of Cardston and two quarter-sections east of town.

The boys were kept very busy with the farms, often leaving home on Monday mornings and staying until Saturday night, returning only to attend Sunday services. The father, an ex-cellent craftsman, remained in Cardston erecting a spacious home on the Taylor foundation. Remembered by Hugh as the

finest home in Cardston at the time, the house had several bedrooms, a large basement, and a large living room. This was
the living room in which Hugh first saw his future wife, Zina
Card, who came to a wedding reception there. But more of
that in another chapter.

These years of young manhood were brightened by Hugh's
expanding interest in girls and books. Of the first, he remembers
"having ridden from Spring Coulee on horseback to Cardston
to see my girl and take her on a date on many occasions." There
was no going steady, and "never did I do anything that now,
as an old man, I look back upon and regret. This is due to
my mother."

Of books, the LDS scriptures received serious study from
his sixteenth year, and "a little book called *Reminiscences of
a Mormon Missionary* whetted his appetite for the call which
would shortly come. Two self-improvement books by Orison
Swett Marden, *Architects of Fate* and *The Secret of Achievement,* were read in the tent by lamplight, and other books from
the little Cardston library were read "as often as I could." From
books and from perceptive contacts with well-schooled people,
Hugh began to acquire that poise, breadth of awareness, and
facility with language which would characterize his adult life.

Since Spring Coulee was on the road traveled by most
visitors to the Alberta Stake, many Church leaders visited in
the Homer Brown home, sometimes staying overnight. Here
young Hugh met Francis M. Lyman, Heber J. Grant, Orson
F. Whitney (whose poetry and speaking style he much admired),
and President Joseph F. Smith — whose prophet-like counten-
ance and stories of faith-promoting experiences profoundly
moved the lad. "I looked upon him as a man who truly was
a servant of the Lord, and he became an ideal of my life."
Reminiscing more than sixty years later, President Brown observed:

> President Smith was, in a way, a very rugged man who had
> been raised in the school of hard knocks. . . . In some ways Joseph
> F. Smith seemed to me to be a man that I would like to have for my
> father, but I know if I had that, his severe discipline would have been
> hard on me. . . . I think the thing that impressed me the most was

his prophetic calling. He seemed to carry with him an aura of deep
devotion, and when we heard him pray at night, as he did, we
knew that he was talking with God. And I then thought in my soul,
I hope someday I can talk with God as does this man.

Within a year of the move to Cardston, Homer Brown's
family was well situated and the younger children were able
to attend school. This opportunity was denied Hugh, however,
because there was so much farm work to do. Only after another
year brought Hugh to the eve of his twentieth birthday did he
have a chance to return to the classroom, not in Cardston, but
in Logan, Utah.

Brigham Young College, the Church-sponsored academy
which offered a high school and limited collegiate curriculum
to Mormon youth from 1877 to 1926, opened up new vistas
to the Canadian cowboy who enrolled for the winter of 1903-
1904. The liberal arts curriculum emphasized languages and
literature, and debating and drama vied with sports in the
extracurricular program. Daily devotionals required attendance
by all students, and a missionary class taught the scriptures,
gospel doctrine, and techniques of proselyting to forty or fifty
young men who came in anticipation of mission calls. Hugh
was an energetic but not yet polished participant in this group.

Interestingly enough, Hugh Brown stayed in Logan with
his future mother-in-law, Zina Presendia Young Card, who
was a daughter of Brigham Young and a plural wife of Charles
O. Card. She had accompanied her husband to Canada in
1887, and there her namesake daughter was born a year later.
Two years after the Homer Brown clan moved into Cardston
and the two families became acquainted, the Cards moved
back to Logan, and now "Aunt Zina" was very kind to the
tall and handsome young man who came into her home. As for
the fifteen-year-old daughter, she saw the boarder from Canada
more as a brother than a beau.

While at Brigham Young College, Hugh became friendly
with Franklin S. Harris, later president of both Utah State
University and Brigham Young University. They went together
to seek advice from Dr. John A. Widtsoe concerning their
futures. Already a scholar but not yet an apostle, Dr. Widtsoe

Group picture taken in Logan, probably in 1904: Hugh Brown is in back row, Zina Card in front row, both extreme left. Zina's mother, Zina Young Card, is in center of middle row between her sons Joseph (left) and Rega.

advised the young men to pursue programs in agriculture. Harris did this and became an internationally famous agronomist and educator.   Hugh Brown accepted a mission call to England in the summer of 1904, and except for a few months as a University of Utah student and occasional church-related courses, he never returned to the classroom until, years later and largely self-taught, he briefly joined the faculty at BYU.

3. Mormon Missionary
in England

It is not certain when Hugh Brown first decided he would
like to become a Mormon missionary. His memoirs note that he
began studying the standard works because he "knew that I
had to go on a mission someday and I wanted to be prepared
so I studied all I could. . . ." Family and community expectations
doubtless contributed to this anticipation, but the young man's
absorbed study of the Bible, Book of Mormon, and other Mormon scriptures suggests a strong personal interest in the prospect
of a mission call.

Other books and family lore added to this interest. Missionary reminiscences were staple fare at Church gatherings and
figured prominently in Hugh's adolescent reading. Stories of the
seventeen missions of his maternal grandfather, James S. Brown,
were first heard at his mother's knee and then probably read
in the autobiographical *Life of a Pioneer* when it appeared in
1900. Hugh grew to share his father's admiration for Wilford
Woodruff, and he took particular comfort from the fact that
the fourth Mormon president was a farmer with little formal
education who became a very successful missionary primarily
because of his deep spirituality and great faith. John W. Taylor,
son of President John Taylor, was frequently in Cardston during

those years prior to his excommunication for continuing advocacy of plural marriage, and his powerful personality and confident prophecies strongly impressed Hugh. Hugh was also influenced by the experiences of Joseph F. Smith, the current Church President, whose visit in the Brown home has already been mentioned.

It seems apparent that Hugh Brown, like many Mormon boys, assumed that a two-year mission for the Church would be part of his life. He was happy to accept the call when it came and was unusually well prepared in terms of doctrinal knowledge and personal commitment. Both would be tested — and some of the outcomes would be remarkable.

In the middle of 1904 he was called to England, a rich area for Mormon proselyting ever since Heber C. Kimball, Orson Hyde, Willard Richards, and Joseph Fielding had launched the work there in 1837. Nevertheless, emigration to America had kept the resident LDS population small — the annual report of the British Mission for 1903 listed sixty-four branches and 4,883 members — and the popular image of Mormonism during this last stage of the controversy over plural marriage was no better on the east side of the Atlantic than on the west. Elder Reed Smoot of the Council of the Twelve had just been temporarily denied his seat as United States Senator from Utah for alleged complicity in an illegal marriage system. In April, 1904, the Church had issued a second manifesto which clarified the Woodruff Manifesto of 1890 by declaring that plural marriage must cease throughout the world and that excommunication could be the penalty for advocacy and performance of such marriages. Many whom the young missionary from Canada would encounter in England had absorbed the stereotypes developed during a half century in which the "Mormon menace" had drawn the attention of writers, evangelists, and social reformers from Los Angeles to London and from Boston to Berlin.

When Hugh Brown left Cardston he was nearing his twenty-first birthday. He was a tall, handsome, well-built young man who would stand out in almost any crowd. He felt inadequate, however, and described his feelings during that somewhat lonesome period "when as a raw ranch boy, I found myself in a large city with educated young men going on missions, and I knew little of what lay ahead." His parents were unable to accompany him to Salt Lake City, but a bit of farewell advice from his mother was a precious parting gift. More than sixty years later he described it to a Brigham Young University audience:

> "My boy, you are going a long way away from me now. Do you remember," she continued, "that when you were a little lad you used to have bad dreams and get frightened? Your bedroom was just off mine, and frequently you would cry out in the night and say, 'Mother, are you there?' And I would answer, 'Yes, my boy, I'm here — everything is all right. Turn over and go to sleep.' You always did. Knowing that I was there gave you courage.
>
> "Now," she went on, "you will be about six thousand miles away, and though you may cry out for me I cannot answer you." She added this: "There is one who can, and if you call to him, He'll hear you when you call. He will respond to your appeal. You just say, 'Father, are you there?' and there will come into your heart the comfort and solace such as you knew as a boy when I answered you."
>
> I want to say to you young people that many times since then, in many and varying conditions, I have cried, "Father, are you there?" I made that plea when in the mission field. . . . And though I didn't hear a voice and I didn't see his person, I want to tell you young people he replied to me with the comfort and assurance and testimony of his presence. It made me unafraid; and with that presence, I am grateful to say, we did not suffer much. (Hugh B. Brown, *Vision and Valor* [Salt Lake City: Bookcraft, Inc., 1971], pp. 236-237.)

Hugh was thankful for his mother's sister, Zina May Gerstner, who was kind to him during that brief period in Utah in which he and other prospective missionaries received the orientation which was provided by the Church at that time. When he left on the train, Aunt May packed a lunch that would help to sustain him for the three days and nights it took to reach New York. En route he visited the Pan-American Exposition in St. Louis, and he observed his birthday in Chicago.

The crossing from New York to Liverpool by cattleboat is remembered as uneventful but hardly luxurious. The British seaport, from which thousands of European converts had sailed for the American Zion, was alive with fireworks, bonfires, and overturned carriages when Hugh and his companions disembarked; it was November 5, Guy Fawkes Day. These were the boasted years in which "the sun never set on the British Empire." The heirs of Guy Fawkes were Irish nationalists and Labor radicals, but the dominant mood of Edwardian England was optimistic pride. This, too, had something to do with the declining response to the Mormon message in the pre-war decade within which Hugh Brown's first mission to England fell.

At the Church headquarters in Liverpool, Hugh met Heber J. Grant, apostle, president of the European and British Missions — the beginning of a long and important friendship for the young missionary. Assigned to labor in the east of England, Elder Brown arrived in time to attend the sessions of the Norwich Conference, November 12-13. The *Millennial Star* did not list him among the speakers but noted that Elder Grant presided.

The new missionary was then sent to Cambridge, accompanied by a senior companion, Samuel S. Downs. Although the missionaries who labored in the historic university town the previous spring had reported to the *Star* that their initial reception was favorable, trouble must have followed because President Brown remembers Conference President Darwin R. Harris telling him that there had been threats on the lives of the next Mormon missionaries who dared to set foot in the city. "As you are the missionary that is going to set foot in that city I thought you might be interested," said Harris. Hugh Brown was very interested, indeed.

Upon arriving in Cambridge the two elders found that word of their coming had preceded them. Near the station platform there were posters with such legends as "Beware of the vile deceivers; the Mormons are returning. Drive them out." Despite their apprehensions, the missionaries encountered no immediate violence, and Elder Brown's uneasiness was soon augmented by loneliness. After they had found a place to stay, his companion showed him how to make the tracting approach and then left the next morning. To Latter-day Saints accustomed to the rigorous insistence that today's missionaries must always work in pairs, it seems rather strange that the conference president would have sent a new missionary into such a difficult situation and left him there alone, even for a few days. But the era of standardized missionary plans, reports, and policies was yet future, and so in November, 1904, Hugh Brown found himself in the storied city of Cambridge, facing an apparently hostile public, with no Church members within many miles.

Over the years many thousands have heard President Brown tell the remarkable story which is associated with this circumstance. "I felt very lonely," he recalls, "but I decided to go tracting, which of course is simply going from house to house knocking on doors, trying to hand out missionary tracts and engage people in conversation." He was unsuccessful all that first day, a Friday, finding neither invitations into homes nor responsive conversations. After a downcast night, he returned to his tracting on Saturday, again without positive results. By evening he was sick at heart and convinced that a mistake had been made in sending him as a missionary when he was unable to reach the people.

Then an unusual event happened, remembered in these words:

> As I was sitting in that room alone on Saturday evening, I heard a knock on the door. The landlady answered and I heard a man's voice say, "Is there an Elder Brown lives here?" I of course thought it was the advance guard of the mob and I was terribly agitated. The landlady said, "Yes, come in," and he came into my room. He was holding a tract in his hand and as he looked at me, a raw cowboy type of lad, he asked, "Are *you* Elder Brown?" I could understand his amazement at finding so young and apparently incapable a man representing the Church, but when I told him I was, he said, "Did you leave this tract at my door this afternoon?" My name was on it and I couldn't deny it, so I said, "Yes."
>
> He said, "Elder Brown, last Sunday a group of us in the Church of England left the Church because we could not agree with our minister. He was not teaching what we believed to be the Gospel." And then he said, "Will you come by tomorrow night and be our pastor?" He told me of having prayed through the week that before the next Saturday, the Lord would send them a new pastor. "There are seventeen of us in all, and we believe the Lord has sent you to us."

"Of course I said what any missionary would say, that I would come," writes Elder Brown. But the visitor had barely left when Hugh began to wonder what he was up against. He had been in the mission field only a few days, he had never attended a proselyting meeting or spoken to an audience of this type. He worried about it all evening and went to bed without supper. His narrative continues:

> I went up to my room, prepared for bed and knelt at the side of the bed and for the first time in my life I actually talked with God. I told him of my predicament and of the challenge that lay ahead, told him of my inadequacies, lack of training and knowledge and asked for his help. I seemed to get no reply and I got back into bed and lay there for some time; then I got out and renewed my prayer for help and this went on for most of the night.

The next morning he advised the landlady that he wanted no breakfast and went for a walk among the beautiful old buildings of Cambridge University, feeling terribly lonely and forlorn. He returned at noon to tell the puzzled landlady that he would not want any lunch and went back and walked all that Sunday afternoon. "I seemed to have a short-circuited mind," Hugh remembered. "I did not seem to prepare or try to prepare what I might say, but simply going through my mind was the thought, 'You are to be the pastor of these people who are seeking the truth. How are you going to do it?'" The question remained unanswered as he sat by the fire in his quarters until finally the time came when he had to go. The rest of the story must be told in President Brown's own words:

> At a quarter to seven I arose and put on my Prince Albert coat and my tall stiff hat, which was foreign to me, and I suppose I looked rather peculiar, as I had so recently come from the ranch. I took my walking cane, put my Bible under my arm and started out for the house. I had to drag myself there; in fact, I think I only made one track all the way. Before I entered the gate, the man of the house came out on the porch, bowed politely and said, "Welcome, Reverend Sir. Come in." I had never been called a Reverend before and that frightened me and made me feel very much out of place. But we went into the house and found a large room completely filled with people. They stood out of respect for the new pastor, and that scared me.
>
> Not until that moment did I realize that the whole of the session would depend on me, that I had to do the praying, the preaching and, as it turned out, the singing. Not knowing anything else to do, I said, "Let's sing, 'O My Father.'" They looked at

me with a blank stare, but we sang it. It was a terrible cowboy solo and I was much embarrassed. Thinking that I would be less ill at ease if they would kneel and take their eyes off me, I suggested to them that they turn around and kneel at their chairs while we offered the opening prayer. I knelt with them and at that time every bit of worry and concern and doubt and question left my mind. I dispensed with the second hymn and started to talk to these people and was able to talk for forty-five minutes. More accurately, the Lord spoke to these people. While I was praying, I said, "These people are seeking for the truth. We have the truth, but I am not able to give it to them without Thy help. Wilt Thou take over and speak to these people through the Holy Spirit and let them know the message of truth." I spoke, as I said, for forty-five minutes, at the end of which time, after closing the meeting, the people came around me with outstretched hands, many of them with tears in their eyes, and said, "This is the Gospel we have been asking for. This is the message we wanted our minister to give us, but he would not." They were so delighted that they indicated a desire for us to meet again.

I mentioned that I dragged myself to that house. On my return to my lodging that night it seemed to me that I only touched the ground once, so elated was I that the Lord had come to my assistance. . . . Before many months every man, woman and child in that room was baptized. . . . Many of them later emigrated to America and it was my pleasure to know some of them after returning from my mission. It was a marvelous demonstration of the power of God. . . .

Overt hostilities did not, it appears, manifest themselves thereafter, and Elder Brown and the companion who shortly joined him, Wilford West, wrote to the *Millennial Star* in March 1905 that "prospects are very encouraging at present in this part of the vineyard." A local minister had been sufficiently impressed to offer the use of a hall for their meetings, and several baptisms were reported.

Although President Brown recalls his mission as being filled with exciting experiences, many of the days were uneventful and some activities were routine, like attending meetings and cleaning rented halls so that meetings could be held. The Norwich Conference was one of the smallest in the British Mission, with twelve to fifteen missionaries and thirty to thirty-five baptisms per year during the period of Hugh's service. There were only four branches until a fifth was organized in Cambridge in

December 1905 — with seventeen members. The impulse to "gather to Zion" was strong among the British Mormons, with the result that the resident LDS population of the conference hovered around 275 from 1904 through 1906.

Hugh was transferred to Ipswich in the spring of 1905, where his companion was Martin J. Bushman. "We feel very much encouraged with the prospects," he wrote to the *Star* in September, "for although we are not permitted to hold street meetings, our hall is so situated that by raising the windows the public can hear our hymns, and often we have a large audience on the street who can hear every word uttered by the speaker. . . . One by one they are venturing inside, and our attendance is constantly increasing as well as our membership. 'Truth shall prevail!' "

Shortly thereafter he was assigned to Norwich, with Elder George F. Webb, but the pattern of activity was much the same. One street meeting produced a "novel experience." "At one moment," says a journal entry, "I had a very attentive audience and in ten seconds I stood talking to the air. A horse had fallen in the street . . . . and the people ran to see the excitement." The Sunday School in Norwich was more faithful; Hugh taught the "theological class" there for more than a year and the members gave him "a lovely photograph album" when he left them for home. (Hugh's missionary journal begins when he was in Norwich.)

A Church conference in London in April, 1906, gave the elder from Cardston opportunity to tour the metropolis, and several pages of journal notes reflect that enthusiasm for sightseeing which would remain keen for a lifetime. Shortly afterward a reorganization of the Norwich Conference made Henry A. Grover president and Hugh Brown conference clerk. Responsibility for the sale and distribution of the *Millennial Star* was now added to his tasks; years later he would do two stints as editor of that longest-lived of Church publications.

A second oft-recalled proselyting episode is associated with this latter phase of Hugh's mission. It attests that the years in England gave the Canadian cowboy both experience and self-confidence. A local preacher in one of the other conferences,

No. 4 Valentine St., Norwich, where
Hugh lived during part of his mission.

Missionaries in England,
Elder Hugh B. Brown on right.

it appears, was giving the elders much opposition and challenging them to debate with him. He sent his challenge finally to President Grant, demanding that the best man in the mission be assigned to meet him on the platform. The mission president forwarded the letter to Elder Brown, adding a comment which must have flattered the young missionary: "You are the man who should go and meet this man and represent the Church." What follows is remembered in this way:

> I was elated with the prospect of such an encounter as I had considerable faith in my ability to meet such a man. On my way down I thought, "I can lick that fellow with the scriptures that I now have at my command," and I did just that. This man spoke first and I spoke afterwards, occupying almost an hour in teaching the first principles of the Gospel and the Restoration. At the close of the meeting the man said, "I have been opposing you Mormons right along, but I want you to know that what I have heard tonight has convinced me that I am wrong and you are right. I want to join the Church." He did join, and I was very proud of what I had accomplished. But I came to feel later that I had been unduly proud and had not given proper credit to the Holy Spirit who had worked through me to bring this incident to a successful conclusion.

Several incidents during his British Mission strengthened Hugh Brown's personal testimony and the sense of destiny which his mother and sister had already begun to cultivate in him.

One experience involved a seemingly miraculous recovery from a severe illness. Shortly after a special conference in London in August, 1906, occasioned by a tour of the European missions by Church President Joseph F. Smith, the young Canadian was stricken with a stone in his kidney. A doctor advised immediate surgery as his life was in jeopardy. When President Grant was informed of the situation, he hurried to Norwich and offered Elder Brown an early release from his mission so that he could return home for the necessary medical care. The suffering man's reply was that he wanted to fulfill his mission and that he had faith that if the president would give him a blessing, he would be able to remain in the work. President Grant asked him if he really believed that and Hugh said, "I know it is true." Whereupon the mission leader gave him a blessing and Hugh reports that he was instantly relieved of pain. Although there were some recurrences of the ailment, Hugh was able to complete his mission, reinforced in the feeling that the Lord had a special work for him to do.

Other remembered events also involved President Grant in one way or another. The conference in London was vividly recalled, at which President Smith and President Grant invited all the missionaries to meet with them. Hugh Brown was elated with the thought that he would be able to come again in contact with the President of the Church. Years later he said, "I have never, I think, before or since felt the feeling that came over me as I sat and listened to those two men speak. I was young and untrained, but somehow I knew in my heart that what they said was true. I thought at that time how wonderful it would be if by righteous living I could come to a point where I would be in companionship with such men, little knowing what lay ahead for me. It was the highlight of my mission. . . ."

Another missionary conference held in Bradford had a profound influence on the Canadian elder. In his mission journal he remarked, "We had the best and most spirited meeting I have ever attended. President Grant spoke with great power and gave me some very good instructions. Most every elder wept with joy." In his memoirs President Brown recalls that the apostle paused before closing and said, "Brethren, there is sitting in this audience someone who will someday be a member of the Council of the Twelve and I predict this in the name of Jesus Christ." Like the others, Elder Brown wondered who that might be and thought little of his own chances.

Despite these highlights, Hugh Brown's mission was filled with the routine activities known to almost every Mormon missionary since the days of Joseph Smith. Day after day the pages of his journal are filled with comments on the weather and such excerpts as these: "Tracted all morning — studied in the afternoon — visited friends in the evening." Occasionally there are statements like, "We were blessed of God in our street meeting," or "We were greatly blessed of the spirit, even unto prophesying." In his own modest words, "I labored with no more than the average success that attended the other missionaries."

When he received notice that he would be released from his mission to sail for home on October 25, 1906, he did not record any sense of regret.

The voyage homeward on the S. S. *Canada* began at Liverpool in company with eleven other elders and about a hundred Church members who were emigrating to America. Hugh remembered "feeding the fish" for several days, but the ocean eventually became calm, and he enjoyed the remainder of the trip despite more high seas as they approached Newfoundland. The group landed at Montreal on Sunday, November 4, the trip up the St. Lawrence River being especially scenic and pleasant. The Canadian Pacific Railroad carried Elder Brown to Lethbridge and the stage brought him home safely on November 9. All of the family were in Cardston for the homecoming except his older brother Homer, who was in California.

The British Mission was an important part of Hugh's life to that point, and he had every reason to feel satisfied with his performance as well as his personal growth and development. He little dreamed, however, just how much of his later life was to be spent in England and under how vastly different circumstances.

4. Hugh and Zina—
The First Years

A penny postcard left Cardston on June 4, 1908, addressed to Miss Zina Y. Card in Salt Lake City and bearing the message, "We are having another flood and things look very swampy. I hope it will not affect the R.R. or I will have to walk to S.L." Signed, "Your anxious Hugh," the card bore a sweetly sentimental picture of a small boy looking devotedly at a small girl with blond curls. The caption was "Little Sweetheart," and the salutation which Hugh Brown had written was "gnilraD" — which modern sophisticates may not immediately recognize as "Darling" spelled backward.

So it has been through the long years that have elapsed since Hugh and Zina, in spite of floods, took their wedding vows in the Salt Lake Temple two weeks later, on June 17. Flowers, love poetry, presents, and other tokens of endearment have characterized their true-love story. Surely it must be one of the most affectionate, enduring marriage unions of all time.

It all began in Cardston not long after the Homer Brown family moved into their newly completed home, which young Hugh claimed was "the finest home in town." A wedding and reception were held here, and the eighteen-year-old cowboy was very much impressed with a petite, thirteen-year-old girl

ZINA Y. CARD LINE

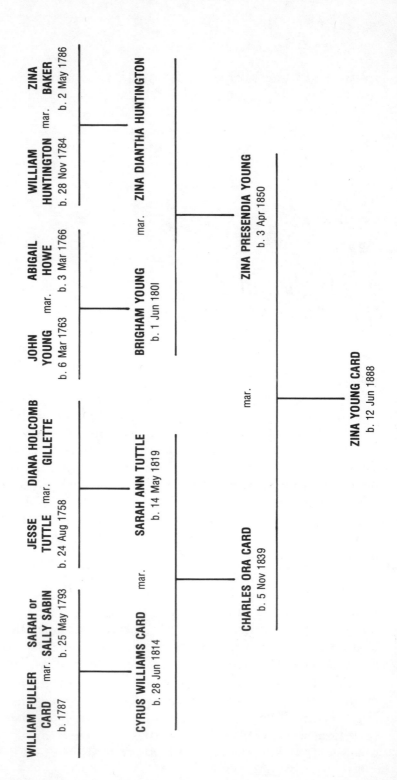

WILLIAM FULLER CARD b. 1787 mar. SARAH or SALLY SABIN b. 25 May 1793

CYRUS WILLIAMS CARD b. 28 Jun 1814 mar.

JESSE TUTTLE b. 24 Aug 1758 mar. DIANA HOLCOMB GILLETTE

SARAH ANN TUTTLE b. 14 May 1819

CHARLES ORA CARD b. 5 Nov 1839

JOHN YOUNG b. 6 Mar 1763 mar. ABIGAIL HOWE b. 3 Mar 1766

BRIGHAM YOUNG b. 1 Jun 1801

WILLIAM HUNTINGTON b. 28 Nov 1784 mar. ZINA BAKER b. 2 May 1786

ZINA DIANTHA HUNTINGTON

ZINA PRESENDIA YOUNG b. 3 Apr 1850

mar.

ZINA YOUNG CARD b. 12 Jun 1888

with golden curls hanging down to her shoulders, who gave a recitation. She was Zina Y. Card, daughter of Charles O. Card, the stake president and founder of Cardston, and Zina Young Card, one of President Card's plural wives (and a daughter of Brigham Young). When Zina finished her part on the program, Hugh turned to his mother and said, "Some day I am going to marry that girl." His mother replied, "I hope you will."

She was, no doubt, sincere in her reply, for "Aunt Zina," as she was affectionately known, was one of Lydia Brown's dearest friends, and photographs of the period show that little Zina was a very attractive girl. Hugh did not immediately communicate his intention, according to the cherished family remembrance of the courtship; in fact, he did not have any dates with her until after his return from England five years later. By the time he was in a position to act, she was already planning to marry someone else.

He must have seen Zina often during the months after that first meeting. The Card's new brick home was a Cardston social center, and their old log house—remembered as "Mother's Canton Flannel Palace" because of the colorful and original way Aunt Zina had covered its interior walls—was still a showplace. Young Zina's brothers, Joseph and Rega, were Hugh's contemporaries; she was still in her early teens when the Cards moved to Utah in 1903.

It is likely that Hugh's decision to go to Brigham Young College was influenced by the fact that the Cards were in Logan. During the winter prior to his mission, he lived in their home, and he saw the daughter almost daily. President Card was now broken in health, and one of Zina Brown's memoirs records that Hugh "helped care for father so tenderly. He won our hearts." However, there was no commitment when Hugh left for England. Zina attended the B.Y.C. and the correspondence which passed between them is described in President Brown's reminiscences as "just a 'dear Sister Zina' type of letter ending with 'your brother Hugh.' "

Hugh Brown claimed that he never told anyone about his love for Zina until he mentioned it to one of his missionary companions, Elder George Webb. When Webb returned home

first, he went to see Zina, then studying dramatic reading at the
LDS University in Salt Lake City. He told her that he had
come to see "the girl that Hugh Brown is going to marry." She,
of course, was startled and said she didn't know anything about
it. The surprise was undoubtedly genuine, for she was engaged.
President Brown later described his rival as "a fine young man
from Logan."

When Hugh called upon President E. J. Wood for a post-
mission interview, the head of the Alberta Stake asked whether he
was planning to get married. Hugh said, "I had hoped to marry
the girl I love, but she is engaged to another man." Told that she
was Zina Card, Wood said, "I promise you that if you will go
down to Salt Lake and make known your intentions, she will
break her engagement with the other man and marry you."
"I believed him implicitly as I had seen previous evidence of his
prophetic gifts," President Brown recalls, "and of course I was
glad to believe!"

The opportunity came at the time of the 1907 April general
conference of the Church. Hugh went directly to the Lion House,
where Aunt Zina was working. (President Card died in 1906
and Zina's family moved shortly thereafter to Salt Lake City.)
On hearing that Hugh had come to get her daughter, she replied, "You can't have her. I won't let her go back to Canada.
I've had enough heartache and heartbreak in that country myself." Unabashed, the young suitor pressed on. "All I ask of
you, Aunt Zina, is to be neutral in the case and let me fight
my own battles." This she promised to do. Hugh then went up
to the Card home on Fourth Avenue and told a surprised young
lady the purpose of his visit. On her seventy-seventh birthday,
Zina confessed to a reporter, "It was quite a shock, as I had
always looked upon Hugh as my big brother." "I told her,"
President Brown recalls, "that I thought the Lord wanted us
to become man and wife. She asked me to postpone the matter
for some months, and I went back to Canada full of high hopes."

During the weeks of waiting, Hugh's case received invaluable assistance from his former mission president. Not quite
content to let nature take its course, Aunt Zina went to ask
Elder Heber J. Grant for his opinion of her daughter's Canadian
friend. He replied: "I have seven daughters. Hugh Brown can

choose any one of them. That's what I think of Hugh Brown."
What Hugh may have done in his own behalf is not recorded,
but at the next April conference, according to the summary
journal which he kept during these years, "I became engaged to
Miss Zina Y. Card, who promised to become my wife in June."

When the bridegroom left Cardston in early June, 1908,
he did not have to walk, but he was forced to go by way of
Spokane because the rains had washed out all the railroad
bridges between Lethbridge and Butte, Montana. The marriage
was performed in the Salt Lake Temple, Church President
Joseph F. Smith, one of Hugh's favorite people, uniting the
twenty-four-year-old groom and his twenty-year-old bride "for
time and all eternity." A number of friends called at Aunt
Zina's home in the afternoon and evening and the young couple
received "some nice gifts."

The newlyweds' return trip to Canada was preceded by a
ten-day round of visiting with friends in Salt Lake and receiving
congratulations. Of the journey itself, the bridegroom later
recalled that "Zina's mother accompanied us as did John
Talmage, a younger son of Dr. James E. Talmage . . . , so our
honeymoon was not the kind that is usually anticipated by an
enthusiastic young couple." But it ended with a happy surprise.
The long and frequently delayed train trip through Montana to
Alberta left them ill-prepared to be met at Raley, the train
stop east of Cardston, by Hugh's brothers and a rattle-trap
buggy with an old broken-down horse. "They looked like the
tail-end of nothing," Hugh remembers, as they rode into
Cardston in a rig held together with baling wire and rope.
But at their journey's end they found a new rubber-tired buggy
and a fine span of black mares — the gifts of Homer, Scott,
Lawrence, Owen and Gerald. Sixty years later Elder Brown
wrote, "I have never felt so proud of any automobile I have
had since, as I was of that pair of black mares and that little
buggy."

The couple stayed with Hugh's family for a few days and
then moved into a house they had rented from Charles Burt.
Purchasing some second-hand furniture, a fold-down bed, and
necessary things for housekeeping, they settled down and "were
very happy."

For Hugh Brown it was the beginning of a career as husband and father, businessman and lawyer, civic and church leader, a central motivation for which was to be Zina's confident expectations. For Zina, it was the assumption of a responsibility previously borne by his mother and his sister — helping Hugh to achieve the greatness which they never doubted was his destiny.

The first steps were humble enough. On the first of August Hugh was promoted to manager of the Cardston Mercantile Company, where he had been employed as a clerk for a year. Within a few months his salary rose from $75 to $100 per month, and according to one of the eight employees, Ida Archibald, he was an easy man to work with. (Ida married Hugh's brother Owen two years later.) The Cardston firm had been founded in 1888 by Zina's father; later it had become a cooperative of the late nineteenth-century Mormon pattern. The cheese factory, pig farm, sawmill, planing mill, butcher shop, farm implement store, coal mine, ice business, and glove, boot, and shoe factory which were parts of the co-op in the 1890s were soon discontinued or converted into separate private enterprises, but the co-op carried on as a general merchandise store. Charles Card remained the leading stockholder, and it was he who asked Hugh to take the managership when the position became vacant. As President Brown remembers, the store then sold everything "from toothpicks to threshing machines."

In October the couple moved back into Hugh's parents' home, and two months later Zina, now pregnant, went to Utah to spend the Christmas holidays with her mother. Hugh was lonely, but this first of many separations served only to strengthen the ties of affection. He and Zina were living in Telitha Carlson's home in Cardston when their first child Zina Lydia (who would quickly become known in the family as Zina Lou) was born on July 21, 1909, at 2:30 A.M. His journal entry bespeaks pride, affection, and a notable spirituality:

> Zina gave birth to a beautiful girl and now I am the proud father. The Lord has blessed me with one of the best women on earth and these 13 months of married life have been a foretaste of heaven in which my joy is now crowned by the arrival of an im-

*Three generations of Zinas: Zina Young Card, daughter
Zina Card Brown, and granddaughter Zina Lou.*

portant spirit clothed in a beautiful tabernacle of flesh of our own
offering. All honor be to the Father of Spirits and may he aid us
to so live that we may be worthy guardians of others and in faith
fully discharge the sacred duty of parenthood.

Happy father was soon parading Cardston's streets with
pretty daughter in a baby carriage. Eventually there would be
seven other children, but Zina Lou's status as the firstborn was
transformed into a special relationship when polio struck two
years later. Faith, surgery, and loving care limited the permanent damage, but the tie between the father and the third
Zina in his life has remained unique through the years.

The economic fortunes of the Brown family moved through
a series of ups and downs during the first few years. When
Frank Fairbanks met a financial crisis at the Cardston Mercantile Company by investing $10,000, he was given the manager-
ship. Hugh continued to work there until January, 1910, except
for a little time on his father's farm. Ventures in agriculture,
real estate, and grain-marketing followed, with mixed results.
In their midst Hugh established a connection with the Canadian
army which lasted until 1919, but that story will be told in the
next chapter.

In 1910 Hugh joined his brothers in a large-scale farming
venture on that same Cochrane Ranch on which he had worked
as a youth. The LDS Church had finally purchased the property
in 1906. The terms of the negotiation by President Wood permitted the Church to acquire 66,500 acres at six dollars per
acre, to be sold to members on long-term payments in order to
encourage colonization. The Brown brothers acquired a thousand
acres and moved onto the ranch, some twelve miles north of
Cardston. At the outset Hugh was the only married brother,
and Zina did much of the cooking for all in the little granary
building which they converted into living quarters. When Owen
married in 1911, his Ida joined the culinary operation.

It was a trying time for Hugh and Zina. Breaking the
heavy prairie sod required six horses to pull a single plowshare,
and then disc plowing was necessary to make a seed bed. Hugh
later testified that no land in the world is richer than southern
Alberta, and when conditions are favorable the crops are mag-

nificent. However, the Brown brothers experienced one failure after another — early and late frost, snow and hail only beginning the list of adversities. They borrowed from year to year to plant another crop, but they did not have a successful harvest in four years. Homer Brown had brought his boys to Canada with the hope that they would become independent and not have to work for wages, but when the farm failed, all of the brothers left agriculture and entered other pursuits.

In the first blush of optimism about the Cochrane project, Hugh and Zina purchased their first home. It was a five-room house with no inside plumbing; in Hugh's words, "We had a path instead of a bath." The decision to purchase is remembered as rather unusual. "While we were living at the Carlson house, I had a call from Bishop Harris, to whom I was acting at the time as first counselor. He came early in the morning without knocking or ringing, walked over to our bedroom and said, 'I want you to get up and dress and go over and buy a house.' " Somewhat taken aback, Hugh nonetheless accompanied the bishop to see the house for which Nels Nielson was asking $2,200. It was a small house with but a fairly good living room, a dining room and two bedrooms, and an outside pump for water. The large lot from which he later sold strips of land was one feature that made the deal attractive. A mortgage for $1,400 made up the difference between his cash resources and the purchase price.

The little family moved into their new home on September 9, 1909, and began gradually to acquire furnishings, carpets, and and trimmings. Zina, who had been used to a higher standard of housing prior to her marriage, pitched in with skill and spirit and, in the prejudiced judgment of her husband, soon made the place "look like a palace." They moved their folding bed into the front room and purchased a brass bed for their bedroom. Thus they were able to entertain visitors. One of the first was Zina's brother Rega, newly married to Lucena, daughter of George F. Richards of the Quorum of the Twelve. "They came and stayed a few days with us and we had a good time," Hugh recorded.

This humble home was the base of operations for the Hugh Brown family for eight years. In due course the plumbing moved indoors, and during one period of economic reverses the whole

family moved out; between July, 1910 and April, 1911, Hugh
managed the Cahoon Hotel in Cardston; Zina and their one-
year-old lived there with him, and the home was rented to
augment their income. They moved back in time to welcome
Zola Grace into the family. Her father's delight was reflected
in his journal:

> On the twelfth day of April my beloved wife gave birth to
> another lovely daughter to be a companion to Zina. She is another
> fair-haired treasure. . . . Zola Grace is by the grace of God the
> second of his wonderful gifts to us in our happy married life and
> may they both live to fulfill the mission of womanhood as competely
> as their mother is doing.

As the polio attack in the same year drew Hugh and his
older daughter particularly close, so a special bond developed
between little Zola and her mother which would last a lifetime.

During the summers Hugh continued to work with his
brothers on the Cochrane Ranch, but from 1911 onward his
increasing involvement with military and legal training claimed
more time, and he also turned to real estate and to selling insurance to earn what the land was so reluctant to provide. A preparatory course in law drew him to the University of Utah in November, 1912, and he and his family lived with Aunt Zina until the
following April Conference. Thereafter his business activities
expanded. He paid $800 for a half interest in the Cardston
Investment Company, with President Wood and Zina's brother
Joseph as the other partners. The firm marketed about two
hundred thousand bushels of wheat in 1913, purchased, and
subdivided and sold property in a section of Cardston which
they called Grandview, and also handled loans and insurance.
Branches were opened in Regina and Minneapolis, and agents
were appointed to handle operations in the United States. Hugh
recorded, "1913 was a prosperous year for us."

In February, 1914, Hugh took his family to Salt Lake
for surgery on Zina Lou's afflicted leg. She responded well
and in due course was able to walk with a barely perceptible
impediment. It was a testing time for the young parents, with
Zina again expecting and her husband trying to manage an

*Zina Lou,
baby LaJune,
and Zola (standing).*

Proud parents with first baby Zina Lou.

expanding range of activities. Into the busy Cardston menage
came LaJune on June 27. Her father wrote:

> My wife gave birth to another girl, a beautiful body and lovely
> bright spirit. We rather expected a boy, but no disappointment was
> felt as she comes as an additional ray of sunshine into our happy
> home. We thank the Lord for the spirit of love and peace which
> has been with us in our married life and these bright jewels bind
> us together as nothing else could.

It is possible that the parents were more successful in concealing
disappointment from themselves than from their child, for
LaJune played the tomboy role until her metamorphosis into
an adolescent whose style and bearing inspired her father to nick-
name her "Queenie."

Business travel now, in addition to military training and
church engagements, began to take Hugh away from home for
days and weeks at a time. Zina traveled as well, treatments for
her daughter, a strong affection for her mother and her Utah
family, and possibly a nostalgia for the comforts of the home on
Fourth Avenue taking her to Salt Lake City for extended visits.
One might almost suspect that the couple enjoyed separations,
were it not for their letters.

This is Zina, writing from Salt Lake City on June 17, 1912:

> My Dear Husband:
>
> This is our wedding day and it is just such a day as it was
> four years ago, and the roses remind me of it all for I still have some
> left of the many that were given me on my birthday. You are busy
> drilling the boys prior to leaving for Calgary and in spite of it all
> I know that some time during the day you remember this day as the
> anniversary of the one that stands as the most eventful in our whole
> lives.
>
> Your birthday letter with the generous gift for me was my best
> birthday present because it came from the one I love best on earth.
> I hope you will be pleased with what I buy with it for I am going
> to spend it as you said to. Thank you sweetheart; you are so generous
> to me and your love means everything to me.
>
> Zina is sitting on my lap and this at the top of the page is a note
> to Daddie from her. . . .
>
> Remember me to your officers & I hope I can get there before
> camp breaks. I am ever your own for all eternity.

And this is Hugh, writing from Cardston on October 4, 1913:

My Dear Wife:

First you must know that we all love you harder than ever & "mother" is the subject discussed from the time I get home until I leave. Zina wanted to know today if you hadn't been gone three weeks. Zola & Zina both phone several times a day and they are as good as can be. . . .

Hope you find all fine down there & enjoy your trip thoroughly for I doubt if you get another so free-handed as you are now. I intend to keep you employed from now on so make the best of your time. Get yourself fitted out & be as sporty as you like.

Give my love to Lucena & Rega & tell them you are my wedding present as a thirty-day loan of you is equal to a free gift of anything else. . . .

Bushels of love as always.

Hugh

Kiddies just phoned & said to send love to mama XXXOOO H.B.

The outbreak of World War I in August, 1914, changed the world in many ways. It was also the end of an era for Hugh B. Brown and the beginning of an exciting, though ultimately frustrating and bitter experience.

5. Canadian Officer — World War I

Hugh Brown's military career began, curiously enough, as a result of a request by his stake president. Early in 1910, President E. J. Wood asked Hugh and three other men of the community to volunteer to take an officer-training course in order to demonstrate Mormon loyalty to the Canadian government. As with other Church calls through his long career, Hugh responded willingly and effectively — though the final outcome of his career in the Canadian army was a keen disappointment.

The circumstances that prompted this appointment to military service reflected the lingering popular suspicion of the Latter-day Saints. In 1909 the Canadian Parliament passed the Militia Act, which encouraged all men in the country to serve a few weeks each year in military training in preparation for what some government leaders at that time felt was an impending European war. Under the provisions of this law a young man was sent from Ottawa to recruit among the southern Alberta communities. He came into the Cardston district, was entertained by President Wood, and circulated the word that he wanted to enlist as many men as were willing. Unfortunately, the recruiter was, as President Brown remembers, a cocky fellow "with a little turned-up mustache, a swagger in his walk, and a walking cane which he twirled on his arm — in every way the kind of a man our young men would not wish to follow." Completely unsuccessful in his efforts, he returned to Ottawa with the report that the Mormons were disloyal and should be expelled from the country.

Wiser counsel prevailed, however. Southern Alberta's representative in Parliament at the time was W. A. Buchanan, editor of the *Lethbridge Herald*. He knew the Mormon people and was very friendly to them. When he learned of the young recruiter's report, he told the House of Commons, "If you will permit some of their own men to be trained as officers before you try to enlist them, then I promise you, you will get all of the Mormons that are available." On his next trip west Buchanan called on Wood and told him of the flurry that had occurred in Ottawa. The stake leader then called Hugh Brown into his office and said: "I want to call you on a mission to go to Calgary and train as an officer in the Canadian Army. We will have others to go with you at a later date." According to President Brown's dictated memoirs, this action was approved by the First Presidency.

Hugh Brown saw this assignment as a timely opportunity. With a new daughter and a new mortgage, he was somewhat pressed financially, having lost the managership of the co-op and experienced the first of a series of crop failures on the Cochrane Ranch. Here was a chance to secure additional income and at the same time move into a leadership role — something which he had been encouraged to anticipate from childhood but which, at twenty-six, he had not yet achieved.

So it was that Hugh Brown spent February and March, 1910, at the new military school in Calgary. He remembers the awkwardness with which he and his companions participated in the first day's drill and an encounter which resulted. The captain in charge of the camp called one of the Mormon recruits into his office, where the dialogue opened thus:

"I want to get better acquainted with you. Have a cigar."

"I don't smoke."

"Well, have a glass of beer."

"I don't drink."

"The hell you don't!"

Although the new trainee was later chided by some of his associates for rebuffing his commanding officer's sociability, he responded that he didn't want to be in the army at all if these things were required. As President Brown pointed out to many LDS groups in later years, the camp commander actually admired the youth for "standing solid," and their subsequent relationship was good.

Hugh had helped President Wood pick the four men who trained with him for commissions in the Cardston area militia — William G. Ainscough, Benjamin May, Andrew Woolf and Hyrum Taylor — and some of them remained his fellow officers through the war years. He passed the examinations for lieutenant and captain, and then, when the man originally earmarked for command did not complete the course, Hugh was appointed to head C Squadron of the Twenty-third Alberta Rangers. His was now the responsibility to recruit and organize a unit from among the Mormon settlements in time for the two-week summer encampment.

While working with his brothers on the ranch, he made his informal recruiting contacts, and on June 1 the formal enlistment began. In two weeks C Squadron had a complement of sixty-seven mounted men and was off to camp, Captain Brown being in full command in the absence-on-leave of the major who would have had that spot during the training period. The unit performed so well that its members were highly commended by the commanding officer of the district for sobriety and general conduct. On returning to Cardston they paraded before the enthusiastic townspeople and then stored their military equipment in Hugh's parents' home.

In February, 1911, Captain Brown again went to military school in Calgary, this time passing the examination for major and being appointed to that rank in April. The following June he took his squadron again to summer camp; Ainscough, Woolf, Clyde J. Brown, Ben and Frank May, Henry and Carl Tanner are named in the Brown journal as officers and non-commissioned officers who gave particularly good service. The tour of duty was pleasant and successful; the inspector general who reviewed

Hugh B. Brown as young Canadian officer.

C Squadron made special note of the fine-looking men and horses and the neatness of their lines.

After spending the rest of the summer and fall with the farm and his new real estate and insurance business, Hugh went again to Calgary in the winter of 1912. He was then authorized to recruit more men for the Twenty-third Alberta Rangers, and within a few days more men enlisted than could be accommodated. All were uniformed, equipped, and supplied with horses by the time of the summer encampment. Misfortune befell C Squadron in November, 1912, when fire destroyed the Homer Brown residence, which was still performing the storage functions of an armory. All equipment was lost except for the uniforms of the officers, tailor-made apparel which each man kept in his own wardrobe. Hugh Brown was beginning a preparatory law course at the University of Utah at the time, but the written accounting which he submitted as unit commander led to all concerned being absolved from blame. New uniforms were issued before the next summer camp.

As war clouds gathered over Europe, C Squadron continued to shape up as a very smart, well-equipped unit of cavalry, with a commander who was understandably proud of his troops. A lover of horses since his youth, Major Brown had hand-picked all of the mounts, matching them for size and color, and when they went into the summer camp at Calgary in 1914 they made a very fine impression. There were 120 horses in the squadron, one complete troop of bays, one of grays, one of blacks, and one of sorrel. Captains and lieutenants were outfitted with suitable horses to ride in front, and Hugh Brown had a sorrel horse much larger than those usually chosen for military work. This was what he wanted, however, and he felt that Steamboat was the best horse in the whole outfit.

The loss of this horse a year later was one of the keen disappointments of Hugh's military career. In the summer of 1915, when the Cardston militia had been taken into the regular army and were training at Calgary, he was visited by a Colonel Walker, who had come from Winnipeg, as Hugh later learned, to purchase "the best horse in Canada" for a newly commissioned general. Walker came to Major Brown's tent and said, "I under-

On favorite horse "Steamboat."

Outside his army tent with wife, mother, and mother-in-law.

stand you have a good horse. May I ride him?" Not suspecting
his purpose, Hugh acquiesced, pleased at the interest. After a
short ride Walker asked, "What will you take for it?" Major
Brown immediately answered, "Five hundred dollars," an out-
landish price, since he had bought Steamboat for less than
seventy-five dollars a year previously. He thought he had set the
price high enough to dissuade any buyer, but without hesitation
Colonel Walker said: "The horse is sold. I want you to deliver
him next week." Remembering the incident after many years,
President Brown said:

> This broke my heart, as I had become very much attached to
> this horse. At the time I had bought the horse I designated one of
> the men who I had been told was a horse trainer to take charge of
> him . . . , put him in good shape and have him ready for service
> in the summer. This he did in an expert manner and I was very
> proud of my mount. I could ride him on the reservation, put the
> rein across his neck and he would lie down. I could lie down beside
> him and fire my rifle and he would not move until I commanded.
> I could walk away from him and blow a whistle and he would jump
> and come to my bidding. In other ways he was a well-trained horse
> which I learned to love very much. Two years later when I was in
> England . . . I learned the whereabouts of the general to whom
> my horse had been sold and went over to his camp and found the
> horse in the stable. I went in and shouted his name and the horse
> jumped as though he had been shot. I put my arms around his
> neck and wept like a booby, and I think the horse wept also. The
> general would not sell him, and I never saw him again.

World War I broke out in August, 1914, and what had
been a paid avocation, long on parades and amiable fellowship,
became very soon a full-time and very serious vocation for Major
Hugh B. Brown. The Canadian government pledged full support to the cause of Great Britain and her allies, and steps were
quickly taken to augment the tiny regular army of three thousand
men with volunteers from the seventy-five thousand members of
the active militia. (A military draft was not instituted in Canada
until 1917.) While many of the militia units were not so well
trained or well led as C Squadron of the Twenty-third Alberta
Rifles, their officers and men figured prominently in a war effort
which ultimately put more than six hundred thousand of Canada's total population of eight million into uniform, four hundred

Major Brown (nearest camera) and officers and men of C Squadron.

thousand of them sent to Europe. The Canadian death toll in the long struggle from 1914 to 1918 was almost equal to the losses experienced by the United States, which had a population twelve times as large. This grim fact must be remembered to understand the outcome of Hugh Brown's military career.

The offer of an appointment in the regular army came two weeks after Major Brown's thirty-first birthday. Lt. Col. A. C. Kemmis, charged with organizing and commanding an Alberta regiment to be known as the Thirteenth Canadian Mounted Rifles, asked him if he would assist in the effort. In accord with his LDS sense of obligation to his adopted country, Hugh responded favorably, and in December, 1914, he received provisional appointment as a major and orders to raise a cavalry squadron of 158 officers and men.

Major Brown spent the month of January, 1915, traveling through southern Alberta, holding patriotic meetings to encourage enlistments. His experience as missionary, law student, and bishop's counselor stood him in good stead; within six weeks more than two hundred men were recruited for Col. Kemmis's command, and arrangements were made to station one squadron in Cardston. Space in commercial buildings was pressed into service for billets and mess, and by mid-February C Squadron — almost all Mormons and mostly militia veterans — was responding well to training and regular army discipline.

One of the Cardston enlistees was a non-LDS Englishman, Arthur Perry, older than most of the men and a servant in a fine home before his migration to Canada. These being the days when military officers had personal servants assigned, Perry asked to be Major Brown's "batman." The offer was accepted, and it is recorded: "He was the best batman, I am sure, in the Canadian army, and he stayed with me through to the end." Perry also kept a diary which throws interesting light on Major Brown's war years.

Like the militia-based armies of many nations, the Canadian Army in World War I had its share of untrained and incompetent officers, some of whom complicated — and one of whom almost ruined — Hugh Brown's army career. The tedium of training and the temptations of off-duty diversions were also hard on morale; the young men of Lethbridge, Cardston, Magrath, and the nearby communities were by no means immune. The challenges presented would test his abilities and — at times — depress his spirits.

Some of the men of the new C Squadron organized a military band and recruited Hugh's brother Lawrence as leader. The town instruments were borrowed and the band rehearsed diligently for its first concert in Calgary, where it was given a great ovation. The sequel was disappointing, however. Some months after they had moved to Calgary and shown what could be done by a group of enthusiastic men, Col. Kemmis, whose alcoholism eventually led to his forced resignation, ordered Major Brown to transfer the band and all the instruments to another squadron. Hugh explained that this could not be done because the instruments belonged to the town of Cardston. The colonel was very determined, however, and although the instruments went back to Cardston, he put a new man in charge of the band, ruining the spirit of the whole project. Lawrence Brown returned to Cardston after such shabby treatment, so Hugh lost the comfort of having his brother's companionship as well as the good will of his commanding officer.

After four months of drill in Cardston — without horses — C Squadron was transferred to Calgary, the departure enlivened by "a nice farewell supper." Major Brown wrote in his journal that a quarterly conference of the Church was held about this time, with Elders George Albert Smith and Joseph W. McMurrin in attendance. The diary records: "George A. Smith gave me a blessing and promised me that I should not have to shed blood or have my blood shed and that I would return to my home in safety." This blessing had a remarkable, albeit soul-testing, fulfillment, as will be seen later.

The five months of training in Calgary were marred by wet and disagreeable weather on the Sarcee Reserve, where Sarcee Camp housed the newly rechristened Thirteenth Overseas Mounted Rifles. Harvest furloughs took most of the men away in the late summer, while Hugh earned high marks in army courses in signaling and musketry. Since Zina and the girls spent considerable time in Calgary, home visits were only occasional.

In preparation for an anticipated move overseas, Hugh sold his interest in the Cardston Investment Company to his brother-in-law, Joseph Y. Card, and took town property in return. He also paid off the mortgage on his home and cleared up other debts so as to leave his wife with as few problems as possible. A highlight of this autumn was his attendance at the laying of the cornerstone of the Cardston Temple on October 19, 1915.

In November the Thirteenth O.M.R. moved to Medicine Hat, about two hundred miles southeast of Calgary, where it remained until ordered overseas eight months later. There it was enlarged from regimental to battalion size, and, as a junior major in the new organization, Hugh Brown was assigned again to recruiting duty. In two months he was successful in enlisting about sixty men from the predominantly Mormon towns in Alberta, in spite of the fact that mounting casualties in the stalemated war in France had long since taken the glamor away from the prospect of military service. Zina and her daughters were in Medicine Hat for the Christmas holidays, and their husband and father spent the spring "seeding furlough" in Cardston, remodeling their home and making other preparations for the long separation which was now expected.

The boredom of protracted training and waiting, plus the ineptness of some of the officers, contributed to significant morale problems in the fairgrounds encampment at Medicine Hat. Col. Kemmis's involuntary resignation occurred here, but according to Hugh Brown's journal, the new commander of the battalion was not much of an improvement; he "had been a street car conductor in Regina, with no military experience, and he proved to be totally inefficient." As senior battalion major now, Hugh had to exercise command on several occasions when discipline threatened to break down. Since the war was rapidly making cavalry obsolete, the Thirteenth was required to take infantry drill, and insubordinate behavior by some of the cowboy soldiers was the not surprising result. On at least one occasion the troops "were addressed by Major Brown on rioting and drunkenness." He also initiated a sports program, with considerable success, when spring weather made it feasible.

At long last the Thirteenth O.M.R. Battalion was ordered to England. An affecting family tradition recalls Zina's bravery as she buckled on Major Brown's sword and bade him farewell; among the preserved mementoes of the war years is a calendar-type picture showing an unidentified couple in a comparable parting scene. On June 22, 1916, the 34 officers, 55 non-commissioned officers, and 882 enlisted men marched to the Medicine Hat station to the cheers and tears of wives, children, sweethearts, and friends. The rail trip across Canada was punctuated by a parade before the Parliament Building in Ottawa, with the Duke of Connaught, Governor General of Canada, in the reviewing stand. Hugh noted that the flags and cheering civilians were less evident as the troop trains passed through Quebec, but there were no incidents.

The S. S. *Olympic,* "the largest vessel afloat," was waiting at Halifax for Major Brown and some six thousand other Canadian soldiers who went aboard on June 28. The luxurious flagship of the White Star Line had been converted into an armed troopship, but the combination of plush surroundings, good weather, and the absence of submarine sightings made the week-long Atlantic crossing a very pleasant experience for most of those involved.

On July 5 the northern coast of Ireland came into view and that evening the *Olympic* docked at Liverpool. The next day the men of the Thirteenth made the rail journey to their assigned station in Kent, not far from the white cliffs of Dover. Here they began active preparations for combat duty in France.

When the Thirteenth O.M.R. battalion arrived in England in July, 1916, the Canadians in France had already established themselves as formidable fighting men, despite their peace-loving background and lack of military training and experience. The first division to reach the battlefront early in 1915 had been thrust into the Ypres salient, where on April 22 the German army attempted a breakthrough by the use of poison chlorine gas. The French line broke in panic, but the Canadians held and were credited by Prime Minister David Lloyd George with "saving the British Army." In so doing, the Canadians lost seven hundred men killed and two thousand wounded. Lloyd George added: "For the remainder of the war, they were brought to head the assault in one great battle after another. Whenever the Germans found the Canadian Corps coming into the line they prepared for the worst." (Edgar McInnis, *Canada: A Political and Social History* [New York: Holt, Rinehart and Winston, 1960], p. 406.)

Major Hugh Brown and the men of C Squadron moved into Caesar's Camp, near Folkestone, just at the time the British were getting involved in the Battle of the Somme. This action along the Somme River was a phase of that long, indecisive war of attrition which would leave the region north and east of Paris dotted with military monuments and cemeteries. The Allied purpose was to wear down the German resistance rather than to gain ground; for six months both sides engaged in tremendous artillery bombardments, with fearful slaughter. Canadian units were not committed until September, and soon their losses were so severe that there was constant demand for replacements. The Mounted Rifles were consequently sent to France in small drafts rather than being committed as combat units.

Major Brown's nine months in England were marked by exciting and uplifting experiences, frustrations, and finally bitter disappointment. While the conduct of training and other military tasks required much of his time, there were opportunities to visit Canterbury Cathedral, London, Glasgow, Edinburgh, Dublin and the scenes of his missionary service in Norfolk. The enthusiasm for travel and the remarkable powers of observation and description which would produce fascinating sightseeing reports to his family for more than five decades are reflected in the journal entries of this period. The tour of an English submarine and the flight in a Royal Air Force trainer were obviously more memorable than the drilling and waiting in the camps.

The Norwich visit witnessed the fulfillment of a promise which Hugh Brown had made as a missionary. Years later it was described to an LDS general conference in these words:

> [As a missionary] I had gone to a certain house several times and had been rejected. . . . And then as I was attempting to walk past that house, I was prompted to go in and try again to make contact. I used the big brass knocker on the English door without any response. I could see a lady in the front room knitting, and I made considerable noise with that knocker. She did not come out, and I went around to the back door. There was no knocker

on that door so I used my walking stick, and I knocked with considerable vigor. . . .

Very soon the lady came out, and her coming out reminded me of my early days on the farm when I teased a setting hen off the nest. . . .

I apologized and said, "I am sorry to have interrupted you and have insisted upon an interview, but, my dear sister, I have come over six thousand miles to bring you a message which the Lord wants you to have. . . ."

She said, "You mean the Lord sent a message to me?"

I said, "That is right; he did." I told her of the restoration of the gospel, the organization of the Church, and the message of the restoration. She was quite impressed by what I told her. And I said when I left, "I am sorry to have disturbed you, but I could not refuse to carry out the message and the mission that was given to me when I came here. When we meet again, and we will meet again, you are going to say, 'Thank you for coming to my back door. Thank you for loving me enough to carry the message of the Lord to me. . . .' "

Ten years later I was in England again, this time as a soldier, and at the end of the meeting a lady came up with two grown daughters. She said, "I do thank God and thank you that you came to my door with that message many years ago. I and my daughters joined the Church and we are going to Utah in a short time, and we thank God that you had the courage, the fortitude, and the faith to come to me with that divine message and to leave it with me in the name of the Lord." (*Ensign,* July 1972, p. 86.)

A friendly encounter with the Northwest Mounted Police was another highlight of Major Brown's first weeks in England. He had had some contact with the "Mounties" in his earlier years of riding as a young cowboy, and while they had made fun of him because he wouldn't smoke or drink, he had great admiration for them and at one time considered joining their ranks. One of their off-duty pastimes was horseback wrestling, a sport in which two teams of ten men each, mounted bareback, faced each other at one hundred yards and then came together at a gallop and grappled. The highly practiced police unit stationed at the camp had been able to defeat all opponents. When the commander came to Brown one day and challenged the Mormons to a public contest in this sport against the Redcoats, Hugh quickly accepted and expressed confidence that his team would win. What followed is remembered in these words:

The time for the contest came. The police said on many occasions they would teach those milkhead Mormons how to wrestle.
We happened to have in our squadron a number of experienced
wrestlers, not horseback wrestling, but wrestlers who developed their
strength in their legs, arms and shoulders. They were all good
horsemen who could ride anything that wore hair. When we met
for the contest, there were more than twenty thousand men to
witness it. The gun was fired, the two teams came together with a
clash, and when the struggle was over there was not one Mounted
Police on his horse and not one Mormon dismounted. The leader
of our group took one policeman under each arm and carried them
through. It was a startling thing. It gave us a lot of fine publicity and made it easier for them to accept us as associates in the
army.

Other humorous episodes with which Hugh later regaled his
children include a parade competition in which some of the
Canadians put burrs under the saddles of their British rivals and
another parade in which, the chemist's shop (drugstore) having
apparently provided the wrong mixture, Major Brown rode at
the head of his troops with his mustache dyed green.

Before the end of July, 1916, Major Brown and almost all
of the men in C Squadron were transferred from the Thirteenth
O.M.R. to the Canadian Army's cavalry depot at Shorncliffe
Camp, on the English Channel. They were attached to the
reserve regiment of the Fort Gary Horse, and Hugh was given
command of B Squadron, 7 officers and 350 non-commissioned
officers and men, including most of those who had joined the
old Alberta Rifles from the Cardston district. Soon "drafts" of
men were being sent to France to replace losses at the front;
by October, B Squadron had lost almost all of its men who were
fit for action and the prospects for its commanding officer were
becoming uncertain. Still Hugh performed his training responsibilities with good spirits and looked forward to an assignment
in France.

A cable from home brought the good news that Zina had
given birth to another daughter, Mary Myrtice, on August 8.
Hugh noted in his journal that "she was just as welcome as the
others were. Children are a heritage from the Lord." Apparently
he did not confine his reaction to such sober sentiments, for he
later wrote: "I think Zina never did quite appreciate my com-

ment when I replied to her notification of the birth by saying,
'Don't have any more until I get home.' This, I guess, was
characteristic of my foolishness."

A few days later he wrote: "The Great War is progressing
favorably for the allies, but it looks like peace is still a long way
off. I hear from home where all is well, but I fear I shall not
see my dear ones again for some time." News that some of his
friends from the old Thirteenth were now casualties was also
noted with sadness.

Efforts to maintain the morale and testimonies of the young
Latter-day Saints in his command produced memorable experiences. On one occasion a Canadian general looked into Major
Brown's tent. Seeing the officer sitting on the floor with several
enlisted men, he roared, "Brown, you'll never maintain the respect
of your men if you get down with them like that!" Major Brown
was holding an MIA meeting.

A request to visit a serviceman in a London hospital provided the basis for one of President Brown's most frequently retold
stories. Expecting to be asked for some military favor, and being
received by the hospital personnel with the deference due to his
rank, he was momentarily taken aback when the young man on
the cot looked up and said: "Brother Brown, I sent for you to
ask that you intercede with God in my behalf. . . . Will you
administer to me?" The ordinance was performed and the promised blessing of recovery was in due course fulfilled. As for the
priesthood officiator, the lesson was clear. "I went into that
hospital a proud British officer. I came out a humble Mormon
elder."

On Sunday, November 12, 1916, Hugh Brown was sent to
France on escort duty, which meant leading replacement troops
across the English Channel, delivering them to the front lines,
and then returning. On this occasion he spent a few days at
the front. His batman recorded on November 24 that the major
had received orders to conduct another group to France but
was not well enough to go. The illness dragged on past Christmas. On January 2, 1917, a Major Bradbrook was named acting
commander of B Company, possibly because of this illness and
possibly as the first step in a plan by Lt. Col. Carman to replace

Major Brown. When Hugh returned from a brief escort mission to France, January 5-9, to find that Bradbrook's appointment had been made permanent, he was convinced that the latter was the case.

Reassigned to Company C, without command responsibility, Major Brown soon discovered the reason for the change. The army had required each unit to declare a certain number of senior grade officers as surplus to be sent back to Canada, and Major Brown was notified that Col. Carman had mentioned him as one who could best be spared. It is apparent that his batman felt that Hugh Brown was the victim of favoritism, for he wrote, "Comments are unnecessary and unwise." The next day, January 17, Perry wrote, "The Major has to report to the adjutant in London today, and before going to town he wished to have an interview with the Brigadier but was refused." In brackets again he wrote, "Comments are unnecessary." The trip to London to seek reconsideration produced only a promise of a few weeks in France before the trip home. Even his expressed willingness to accept a lower rank if he could be assigned to combat did not change the outcome.

This keenly disappointing experience was apparently the occasion of the incident which would be many times retold, with varying details, as part of the story of the currant bush. At the time of Elder Brown's appointment as an apostle in 1958, Elder Harold B. Lee referred to this turning point in these words:

> He had been led to believe that upon arrival in England in command of one of those Canadian contingents, he would be promoted to a higher rank, possibly a Brigadier General, and placed at the head of the troops going into combat. . . . To his bitter disappointment he was not promoted but was returned to Canada as a recruiting officer. (*Relief Society Magazine,* June 1958, p. 354.)

Six tedious and then anxious weeks followed, waiting for orders. Finally, on March 9, the faithful batman wrote: "Major Brown left for France about noon today. End of record."

The two weeks in France were in a way anticlimactic, but they brought Hugh into direct contact with the fighting and undoubtedly contributed to that empathy for the fighting man which was a valuable asset to the servicemen's coordinator during the Second World War. Attached to a Canadian unit at Bruay, near the northern end of the long and bloody battleground which extended from the English Channel across northeastern France to the German frontier, he "spent several days in the front line trenches, saw the effect of shell fire, bombs, grenades, etc., and on several occasions narrowly escaped being blown to pieces by exploding shells." His journal adds:

> . . . we spent considerable time in observation posts where we were within 40 yards of the enemy. We lived in dugouts and did most of our work at night. Spent some time among the bones of French soldiers who had not been buried after having been killed between there and the enemy lines almost a year before. Our trenches were facing the Vimy Ridge. . . .

The oft-recounted story of "the unsentimental cuss" — a rough officer who risked his life to establish the identity of a fallen Canadian soldier — is probably to be associated with this frightening but exciting experience. Years later President Brown would point the moral in these words: "Help me, oh God, never to judge another man. However he may appear, there is something in him better than I."

On returning to England, Major Brown was ordered to be prepared to sail for Canada. Accompanied by Captain Ainscough, he bade farewell to London on April 2, and two days later he boarded the *Olympic* at Glasgow, along with about fifteen hundred others, eight hundred of them wives and children of Canadian soldiers. After ten days aboard ship waiting for sailing orders, Hugh found the six-day Atlantic crossing uneventful. Every caution against submarine attack was taken; the ship moved in a zigzag course, and the passengers were required to wear life belts and to participate in lifeboat drill regularly. The train trip from Halifax to Cardston took another ten days, with stopovers in Quebec, Montreal and Ottawa. Here Captain Ainscough and Major Brown met W. A. Buchanan, the member of Parliament who had been indirectly responsible for starting Hugh's military career some seven years earlier, and Hugh protested having to return home.

The reunion with wives and children at Calgary on April

30 was a joyous one for the two weary travelers, but the return to Cardston the next day was bitter, because a number of people were ready to cry "cold feet," thinking that the officers had come home at their own request. Some old friends even refused to shake hands with Hugh. He was also distressed to learn that, while he had been fretting aboard ship in Glasgow harbor, some of his men had been killed or wounded in the Battle of Vimy Ridge. This was the major action of the war as far as the Canadians were concerned, and Hugh felt that he should have been there with the men whom he had led and learned to love during the years of training together. His journal records:

> I spent most of the month of May at home visiting family and friends and learned by bitter experience of being misjudged, for some who had appeared to be my friends were most harsh in their criticism of my returning home, thinking I came on account of my fear of the battle line. But God knows I did not have any choosing and that I tried to do my duty and play the game.

An interesting sidelight on this painful period is provided by a letter which came all the way from the battlefield in France to some of the citizens of Cardston. Signed by Archibald F. Bennett and four other soldiers from Alberta, it said in part:

> It is with extreme regret that we have learned from our recent letters from home of the hostile attitude adopted toward Major Brown on his return to Canada. . . . I believe one must have been a soldier to appreciate in full the work of Major Brown. One must have seen the glaring incompetence of other officers to appreciate his efficiency, have come in contact with the prevalent vices of army life to appreciate his exemplary conduct, have felt the spirit of petty superiority adopted by many officers to have welcomed his well-known comradeship, and have known the conditions under which he labored to appreciate and realize the true cause of his return. . . . We have no hesitancy in saying that Major Brown was the best officer we ever had either in Canada, England or in France. His efficiency and generous, kindly attitude toward his men gained him popularity wherever he went. There was one exception to this. There were a few who appeared to our eyes to be jealous of him and his methods; his ways were not their ways and his ideals could not help but clash with theirs. And these few, happening to be his superiors in rank, thwarted his efforts and opportunities

to come to France as he should have done. In the blunt common parlance of the soldier, those who know of his treatment say, "He got a dirty deal."

Still there was joy for him in being with Zina and the girls — and in holding little Mary for the first time. Church duties and law training quickly claimed his attention and helped to revive his spirits, as did a trip with Zina to Waterton Lakes for a few days' outing. Much of the summer was spent cutting and baling hay on a newly purchased farm. Early in August he received a discharge from the Canadian Expeditionary Force and was given the assignment as a reserve officer to take over local stores and equipment of the Twenty-third Alberta Rifles. He continued his political interests, supporting the Union Party and helping to reelect Buchanan to the Dominion Parliament. When the Canadian draft law went into effect in October, he served for several weeks as a military representative on the local exemption tribunal. At this time he wrote in his journal:

> The war looks black at this writing for the Allies. Russia is treating with Germany for peace and Italy is practically out of the fight, having been defeated by Germany. Still the entrance of the United States more than offsets this, only it will take more time for the Allies to subdue the enemy.

Throughout the winter the legal studies were pursued diligently, and in April, 1918, the first examination was passed at Calgary, a big step along the road to admission to the Alberta bar.

This progress was temporarily halted when, on June 7, Hugh received orders recalling him to active duty and placing him in charge of a draft of fifteen hundred men who were going to England. Pleased to be again in command, Major Brown left Calgary on June 22 with fifteen other officers sharing the responsibility for three troop trains. A highlight of the sweltering journey across the Canadian plains came when the major ordered the trains to stop where the tracks paralleled the river. A bugle call sounded to detrain and all fifteen hundred men lined up facing the water. They were ordered to disrobe, the bugle sounded a charge and the whole group went into the river for a refreshing frolic and swim. One reluctant soldier was immersed against his will, fully clothed, but he was quickly rescued when it became obvious that he really couldn't swim.

A six-week quarantine at Camp Petawawa, Ontario, for measles, mumps, pneumonia and influenza gave the troops a severe morale problem and Major Brown a chance to show the stuff of leadership. Denied leave or passes, and with a number of ruffians and ex-convicts among them, the conscript soldiers finally rioted. One morning at 2:00 A.M. the major was awakened by the sergeant major and advised that the men were tearing down the tents and destroying equipment. What followed was later recalled by President Brown in these words:

> I told him to summon all the officers. . . . Upon their arrival I noticed that all of them were wearing their equipment, side arms and short sword. I ordered the officers to disarm and leave all their military equipment in my tent. This they reluctantly did and we marched down to the scene of the riot. I got up on a table and started to talk to the men despite their vociferous and rebellious attitude. I talked to them from 2:00 in the morning until 5:00 A.M. I feel now as I felt then that I was inspired in what I said and I felt to thank God for the experience I'd had on the street corners of London and other British cities back when I was a missionary. . . . At the end of the period the men agreed after some grumbling to go to their tents and go to bed. . . . The next morning I had to hold military court to handle the leaders of the rebellion. . . . I talked rather sternly to them and told them that if they would co-operate from then on there would be nothing more said about it. I reported the event to the commanding general of the area next morning and he complimented me on the way I had handled a very difficult situation. I felt very grateful for that experience. . . .

A small New Zealand freighter, the *Kia Ora*, carried Hugh Brown on this, his third trip to Europe. Part of a fifteen-vessel convoy which sailed from Halifax on August 10, its crossing was unmarred except by the Spanish flu — by then epidemic in North America — which made Hugh and several of his companions quite sick for several days. On approaching the coast of England the convoy was met by "eight torpedo boats and destroyers, three dirigible airships and some bombing planes," and so was well escorted through the submarine danger zone. Hugh accompanied his troops to Aldershot Camp and then, his responsibilities discharged, returned to London, where he stayed at the Royal Auto Club, a favorite spot for officers on leave, until departing for home on September 19.

The S. S. *Aquitania* provided comfortable and speedy passage to New York, where Hugh heard President Woodrow Wilson address a Liberty Loan rally and visited the LDS branch in Brooklyn. By the time he reached Cardston on October 7 the War was rapidly drawing to a close and the reception was much less traumatic than the year before. Zina and the four girls had all recovered from the flu, and a few weeks later Hugh could happily record the Armistice. "And so the great war has ended with victory on the side of the right."

The military experience of Hugh B. Brown, in retrospect, was a mixture of heights and depths — of satisfactions and sorrow. Certainly it was a gratifying experience in many ways, especially during the years when he was organizing his squadron, picking the horses, parading in the uniforms, and training the men. He had great skill in this and was a natural leader, handsome and proud of bearing, as the pictures in uniform show. A major from the time of his entry into the regular army late in 1914, he was very successful as a commanding officer, impressing senior officers wherever he went. He had every reason to expect a successful military career, and there is evidence that he considered making the army a lifetime vocation.

Yet the picture began to change almost as soon as he got to England in 1916. First came the disbandment of his unit and the sadness of parting from men he had recruited, trained and grown to love. Then came the shocking realization that he was to be denied that role of combat leadership for which he had been preparing for seven years, and apparently for reasons which had nothing to do with his fitness for command. Finally came the bitter homecoming, mandated by a high command which could find no better disposition for qualified officers made surplus by the slaughter of the troops they were equipped to lead, but thoughtlessly construed by former friends and associates as a cowardly desertion of comrades in arms. The convoy assignment in 1918, by its nature and its timing, was merely an epilogue to his military story, and when he laid aside the uniform a few months later he had no desire ever to don it again.

An interesting sequel occurred a few years later when Hugh Brown, by then a Mormon stake president, was asked to speak at the dedication of a monument to Cardston's war dead. The incident was recorded in his journal on July 1, 1925:

> Dominion Day at Cardston, where a monument was unveiled in memory of the noble men who gave their lives for their country. I gave an address at the unveiling ceremonies, which was somewhat difficult on account of the feelings of some of the people occasioned by my own untimely return from overseas. Many who had criticized me and who had believed me to be a coward were present. But more than this did I feel the influence of those whom we had met to honor. To them I owe no apology. They, if they could speak, could only testify that my conduct towards the men under my command was fair and just and that I would have gladly accompanied them to the front lines if it could have been. . . . I often felt inclined to retaliate and heap coals of fire on the heads of those who were responsible for my seeming ignominy. To restrain such impulses. . . . Surely Victor Hugo must have suffered to be able to say so well what I have so often thought, viz.: "Unjust criticism and burning blushes of shame, that terrible and admirable crucible into which nature casts a man when she would make a demon or a demi-God, from it the weak come forth infamous, the strong sublime." Thank God for our adversities.

In time Hugh Brown realized that the strange twist of his military fortunes may have saved his life for another mission. If the message of the currant bush did not make him entirely impervious to the barbs of his critics, it did in time — in another great war — assist him in rendering a far greater service to men in uniform, and to the cause of peace on earth, than that which was dreamed of in 1916-1918 by young Major Hugh Brown.

6. Law Clerk and Lawyer

Hugh B. Brown's legal career covers a considerable period of his life — from the time he began preparing for the profession in 1911 until he was called to be a General Authority of the Church in 1953. However, the principal years of his law study and practice began with his first release from active military service in 1917 and ended with his acceptance of the chairmanship of Utah's first liquor commission in 1935. During this period he was able to gain admittance into Alberta's legal apprenticeship program and to pass the bar exams in spite of the fact that his formal schooling had been confined to eight grades plus the few months at Brigham Young College before his mission and a short preparatory course at the University of Utah. After a successful private practice in Alberta and then Utah, his legal pursuits led him into politics and public service and finally into a remunerative position as general counsel and chief administrative officer in a Canadian oil company.

Although he states in his memoirs that it had been one of his lifelong ambitions to become a lawyer, the first indication of Hugh Brown's active interest in the profession is a journal entry for August 27, 1911, which records the release of Bishop D. E. Harris from his calling in the Cardston Ward and adds, "As I intended to begin the study of law I was also released after serving as a counselor for about three years." Hugh, then almost twenty-eight years old, took his wife and daughter to Salt Lake City in November, and they all lived with his wife's mother while he participated in a short pre-law program at the state university until the following April. Returning to Cardston after the general conference, he sought next to gain admittance to the Law Society of Alberta, a prerequisite to enrolling as a student of law in the office of a licensed barrister. (Although law schools then existed in a number of American and Canadian universities, and Harvard's case method of instruction was replacing the traditional European system of academic training in the law, the apprenticeship system which had produced such great lawyers as Thomas Jefferson and Abraham Lincoln was still widely used in both countries. By 1900 some preparatory college work was generally required to qualify for such "on the job" training.)

Hugh wrote to the president of the University of Alberta about his varied experience, including his missionary work, and asked if an exception to the normal academic requirements for admission might be made. The reply was that he would need at least two more years of formal schooling to qualify. This was very discouraging to Hugh, who had limited means and could not afford to leave income-producing work again. For a time his career plans were derailed.

Then a remarkable incident put his hopes back on the track. The Alberta Stake conference was being held in Cardston when the head of the University of Alberta happened to be in the little Mormon community en route to Waterton Lakes. He came to the meeting and was invited to sit on the stand. Recognizing the pulpit talent for which Hugh already had a local reputation, President Wood announced at the beginning of the meeting, "We're going to ask Elder Hugh B. Brown to be the speaker today as we have a number of distinguished visitors. Elder Brown has recently been on a mission to England and can represent the Church well." Hugh, who had been home from his mission for six years, later recalled that he spoke on "the first principles of the Gospel and the restoration thereof." He then sat down by the university president, who turned to him and asked, "Are you the Mr. Brown who wrote to me about joining the Law Society?" Hugh said, "Yes, sir." The educator continued, "And I turned you down, didn't I?" "You did," was the answer. The president then said, "If you will write me tomorrow morning, I'll change the verdict. No man can talk like you have done today and not be entitled to be a law student."

"This," President Brown observed more than a half-century later, "was the most profitable sermon I ever preached." It made it possible for him immediately to sign an agreement with David Elton, a Lethbridge barrister and solicitor, to clerk and study law in his office. There arc discrepancies in the documents as to the precise time that this apprenticeship training began, but it appears that Hugh worked with Elton for less than a year before World War I began. In any case the employment was less than full-time, for Hugh was active with his family, his Church assignments, his business, and more especially with his military career.

When the war came, Elton suggested that the Law Society might give him some credit for the time he spent in the service, provided that he did certain reading. This was no problem for Hugh Brown, to whom books were tonic, not bitter medicine. Elton provided some regular textbooks which were carefully read by Captain/Major Brown. When he came back from England in 1917, Hugh first worked around the farm and community and then on October 1 transferred his articles of clerkship from Elton in Lethbridge to Z. W. Jacobs in Cardston. Convenience and economic considerations probably prompted this change. Jacobs paid Hugh thirty-five dollars a month, and the thirty-four-year-old clerk took care of the office — sweeping and cleaning, making the morning fires, and "as it turned out, delivering much of his mail by hand to save stamps." He worked here during almost three years, except for the interval in 1918 when he was called back into the army to lead the large contingent of draftees to England.

It must have been particularly difficult for such a man as Hugh B. Brown to perform menial tasks after his experience as a field grade officer in the Canadian Army. He had been used to a good salary, tailored uniforms and the power of command. But because this was the only way he could achieve his professional goal, he gritted his teeth and carried on. It appears that his clerkship allowed some leeway for other activities, and by working early and late he eked out his income, dabbling in real estate, insurance and bookselling. The days began particularly early when farming was added, and the years from 1918 to 1921 are remembered as a time of struggle for the growing family.

During the winter of 1918-1919 an epidemic of influenza swept over the United States and Canada. The six Browns were all sick at once, but both parents felt very fortunate that all recovered, since many people in Cardston were severely ill and some died.

However, there were also cheering developments. On October 22, 1919, Hugh wrote:

> My wife gave birth to a beautiful son, fair hair, blue eyes and white skin like his sisters. He is a joy to the household and the cause of continuing thanksgiving to his parents. May we have wisdom to care for, train and direct the footsteps of these precious jewels so that our old age may be made glorious by the knowledge of their worthy achievements and faithfulness to the truth.

Hugh Card was their first son and a very welcome addition to the family of four daughters.

Shortly after beginning his clerkship with Z. W. Jacobs, Hugh Brown decided to provide better accommodations for his family and purchased the Cazier home, one of the largest in town, for $4,600; and according to the new owner, it had a good location and some rather striking architectural features. The Browns paid for it by selling their other home and the farm purchased from James T. Brown some years earlier, and making arrangements to handle the balance on installments. This was their home for about three years. (During the first fifty years of her marriage, Zina Card Brown lived in only one house for as long as a decade.)

In April, 1919, Hugh also purchased the Anderson farm, about two miles south of Cardston, for $7,500, with the idea that he could make some money on milk, eggs, cheese, butter and other produce. A very hot summer produced very little while Hugh and his family lived on the place, and the bitterly cold winter of 1919-1920 produced a similar failure when the Browns returned to town and Hugh's brother Scott moved onto the farm to run it on shares. He was still there in April, 1920, but the venture netted little for either brother.

Reading was such a part of Hugh Brown's life in these years that he later credited Zina with complaining that "she only saw the part of my face which she could see above a book or newspaper." Mary remembers her father standing before the kitchen stove, reading a book, when something impelled him to move an instant before the stove exploded and a piece of iron flew out with a force sufficient to have decapitated him.

A salesman for the *Harvard Classics* for a time, Hugh added a set to his library and explored much of this popular collection. Literature, philosophy, and religion he particularly relished, and Will Durant, Harry Emerson Fosdick, and Henry Nelson Wieman were among his favorite contemporary writers. His enthusiasm for biography ranged from Plutarch's *Lives* to Beveridge's *John Marshall* and Cowley's *Wilford Woodruff*. An aging notebook now in daughter Mary's possession lists 276 books which apparently were owned by the Browns during this financially Spartan period.

Attorney Jacobs gave Hugh an outline to study on such subjects as torts, contracts, and constitutional and international law, and recommended certain books. Hugh purchased many volumes which interested him and developed a modest law library even before he passed the bar. His Church duties as a high councilor necessitated traveling many weekends, and secular as well as sacred literature traveled with him. The sermons which would move audiences for two generations would be marked by breadth of allusion as well as experience, and one of these sermons would affirm that "he who loves and becomes acquainted with great books is the richest and happiest of men."

President Brown later suggested that he was not as good a husband or father in these years as he wanted to be because he spent so much time working and studying that he had little left for his wife and children. Zina Lou, Zola and LaJune were by now in school. To his second daughter on her tenth birthday he wrote an affectionate note from Calgary, where he was cramming for the last bar exam: "Daddie will be home on the 26th if all goes well and then we can have some good rides together in the car as I hope I will not have to study so much after I return." He also voiced the hope that Zola might be worthy of her mother, "for no girl ever had a better mother than you have."

Zina was a great support. "She believed in me," he remembers. "At times when I lost faith in myself she would say, 'You must stay with it. We must see it through. It will be the greatest boon in our lives if you become a lawyer, for that will introduce you to many things that you would otherwise not get.' " This proved prophetic; the legal career opened many doors to Hugh B. Brown.

Hugh went to Calgary in April, 1920, and wrote his intermediate exams, some of which, unhappily, he failed. A second effort in September was successful, and he entered the ordeal of preparing for the finals. Recognizing the need for the fullest concentration, he went to Lethbridge and took rooms with a fellow student, Chauncey E. Snow. This was a fortunate circumstance, for Snow was a brilliant young student with much more regular schooling and better study skills than his older colleague. Both men successfully wrote the first half of the final exams in Calgary in December.

It is evident that Hugh Brown's enterprising spirit was not totally immersed in the law books, for he decided in January, 1921, to move his family permanently from Cardston to Lethbridge. He felt that if he passed the final parts of his examination he would have a much greater potential clientele in the larger town. (Cardston had sixteen hundred inhabitants and Lethbridge eleven thousand at this time.) He sold his farm and cattle earlier, and now he bought a home in Lethbridge from F. S. Swanson for $12,600. He paid $7,500 cash and traded another farm, whose acquisition is not recorded in his journal, for the balance. It was, as Hugh described the Swanson place, a fully modern bungalow and the best home that the Brown family had yet owned.

Transferring his articles of clerkship to Hjalmar Ostlund at Lethbridge, Hugh continued to collaborate with Snow in pre-

Brown family home at Cardston, bought by Zina's brother Joseph (seated in picture) at time of move to Lethbridge.

paring for the coming exams. In April they went to Calgary again — and they passed!

So it came to pass that on Wednesday, July 20, 1921, in his thirty-eighth year, Hugh B. Brown was "called to the bar by Mr. Justice Stuart, being introduced by Mr. McKay of Calgary." Wrote the editor of the *Lethbridge Herald* in an article which was accompanied by a picture of the young officer in uniform: "Major Brown is one of the best-known men in the south, having been identified with municipal movements in Cardston for some years." As for the fledging lawyer, he gave thanks in his journal:

> I am at last a barrister with authority to practice in the Supreme Court of Alberta. We had some little difficulties during the time I was a student but were blessed of the Lord and are better off financially than when we started to study. My wife has been a very faithful support and help in all of the course, and I hope to make good in this profession.

Hugh Brown opened a little office of his own in September, and he described business as being "quite satisfactory." He was happy to respond, however, when Ostlund asked him to manage his office for a share of the fees while the former mentor went to California to convalesce after an illness. This was a fortunate opportunity, for Ostlund had a large clientele. The neophyte lawyer tried all of the cases which were on the docket, and when Ostlund returned after six months he was so pleased that he offered Hugh a partnership and 40 percent of the total income of the office. After a year the income division at Ostlund and Brown became fifty-fifty, and by the end of the third year Hugh was doing so much of the work that Ostlund agreed that the junior partner would receive 60 percent of the fees. As early as May, 1923, Hugh could note in his journal, "Business keeps good at the office and prospects look good for the future."

It is recorded in the journal for 1921 that "on the 19th of November . . . my wife gave birth to our sixth child, a fine 8 lb. boy for which we thank the Lord. We have decided to name him for his two grandfathers, viz., Charles Manley Brown, and will call him Manley." Two-year-old Hugh, his baby brother, and his four sisters — now five, seven, ten and twelve — received somewhat more attention from their father than they had en-

Hugh B. Brown family in 1923.

joyed during the scrambling and cramming years just past. But both law practice and Church duties — Hugh B. Brown became a stake president nine days before Charles Manley's arrival — took him away from home often and left most of the burden of home management still on Zina's shoulders.

Hugh B. Brown handled a wide variety of cases and had some unusual experiences while serving as a lawyer in southern Alberta. One which he vividly remembers involved a woman from a mountain village near Cardston called Crow's Nest Pass. Having killed a man who had attempted to assault her, she came to Hugh's office and said, "I killed this man and I want you to know that I expect to pay for it with my life, but I am told that I have to employ a lawyer, so will you come?" Investigation clearly showed that this was a case of self-defense and her attorney was quite disturbed when the woman repeated again and again that she intended to pay for her murder by sacrificing her own life. He had a hard time convincing her that she was legally innocent but thought that he had finally succeeded.

When the case came before a trial division of the Supreme Court of Alberta — Hugh Brown's first such appearance — and the clerk asked the defendant, "Are you guilty or not guilty?" she paused for a moment, turned to the judge, and said, "I am guilty, my Lord; I don't care what my lawyer says." Whereupon the judge said, "What are you going to do about that, Mr. Brown?" He replied, "I am pleading for her, as she does not understand the law, and I am pleading not guilty." He won the case, and the next morning the local newspaper headlined, "Woman Says She Is Guilty But Judge Says She Lies." A few days after the trial, Hugh received word that his client had hanged herself in an orchard near her home. His fee for the case was never paid.

Experiences with people similarly oppressed by excessive guilt feelings led Hugh B. Brown many years later to give this counsel:

> Keep your eye on the Savior of the world. . . . He is with you and if you have made mistakes and have truly repented, he will forgive you. . . . This gospel is primarily the gospel of second chance, the gospel of repentance. Don't forget that, young folks. Do not insist

upon remembering what God is willing to forget. Every one of us have made mistakes, but though we must pay the full price, our mistakes should be remembered only as guides to better lives in the future. (Hugh Brown, *The Abundant Life* [Salt Lake City: Bookcraft, Inc., 1965], pp. 270-271.)

Another oft-retold case attracted considerable local attention because of a dramatic courtroom incident and a successful gamble in the appeal hearing. At issue was a suit against a wealthy North Dakotan by the nephew he had hired to handle an Alberta farm on shares and then tried to dismiss. Representing the nephew, Hugh Brown challenged the contradictory testimony of the defendant so vigorously that the American became excited, exhausted, and fainted and fell out of the witness box. Attorney Brown caught him, carried him from the courtroom into the judge's chambers and finally won the case. When the appeal was taken to the Alberta Supreme Court, Hugh was at first happy for the opportunity to prepare the briefs and to have this new courtroom experience. So ably did the opposition counsel present his case for a reversal, however, that Hugh began to lose some confidence in his own brief as he had filed it. Risking everything in a flamboyant gesture, he addressed the bench: "I don't believe it is worth the Court's time for me to take an hour to restate my case when the defendant has made such a fatuous appeal." The Chief Justice is remembered as saying, "Thank you very much, Mr. Brown. We appreciate your thoughtfulness and consideration. The appeal is dismissed."

It is interesting to note that most of the entries in Hugh Brown's journal from 1921 to 1927 relate to his activities as stake president rather than his legal business. From scattered items it is clear that Ostlund and Brown handled many kinds of cases in many locations. Medicine Hat, Calgary, Cardston, and Lethbridge are among the trial sites mentioned, and cattle stealing, murder, and relatively minor police court cases competed for the partners' time with duties as counsel for a labor union and for the Canadian operations of the Utah-Idaho Sugar Company. Hugh Brown authored and was primarily responsible for the passage of the Alberta small debts law, which saved much time and expense for lawyers and clients. He was employed by the

Church to push a bill through the Dominion Parliament incorpor-
ating the Lethbridge stake president for the purpose of holding
title to Church properties in Canada, and also was employed by
the government of Alberta to prosecute all liquor cases in Lethbridge. This latter work may have been one reason why he felt
that he could accept the invitation to head Utah's first liquor
commission a decade later.

Expanding business justified bringing P. Drew Clarke into
the firm, but the partnership name remained Ostlund and Brown
when branch offices were opened in Cardston, Magrath and
Raymond in the fall of 1925. When Hugh decided to move to
Salt Lake City a few months later he was earning in excess of
twenty thousand dollars a year — an impressive income in those
days when twenty-five cents an hour was considered a fair wage.

Now at last there were resources and occasions for the cul-
tivation of hobbies and the enjoyment of vacations. Horses remained a passion, to which good cars were now added. In 1923
Hugh "bought a new Overland Sedan car" and did "considerable travelling in it"; replacement with a later model was an
almost annual ritual thereafter, red being the preferred color.
Fishing and hiking took him to the Canadian Rockies with his
brother Gerald and younger companions such as Chauncey Snow
and Eldon Tanner. On July 4, 1923, he witnessed the Dempsey-
Gibbons heavyweight match in Shelby, Montana. A vacation
with Zina in British Columbia was a particular delight, and frequent trips to Utah at general conference time probably contributed to the decision to relocate there. The lifelong custom
of taking some, but rarely all, of the children on trips with educational or entertainment potential began during this period;
eventually it would take all of them to exotic and exciting places.

In the midst of all this promise came the fortieth birthday.
The journal entry for October 25, 1923, tells quite a bit about
the feelings and character of Hugh B. Brown:

> I have passed another milestone in life. Yesterday the 24th was
> my birthday, being my 40th. I had thought that I would have made
> more of a mark in life than I have done and no doubt could have
> done if I had taken advantage of all of my opportunities. I find now
> that my plans, hopes, and aspirations are centered in my family.

The Lord has blessed me with a most devoted and capable wife. In all of my travels I have never seen one who could so fill the place of wife and mother. Our six children are well and happy and we feel greatly blessed in them. I give considerable time to the Church and public work but I am more than compensated in the joy that comes from service.

This is an interesting reaction in view of the fact that Hugh B. Brown at forty had served his country faithfully in a world war, was the youngest stake president in the Church, had completed a law degree despite a lack of formal education, had a good business and a fine income, and was surrounded by a wide circle of friends, six lovely children, and a wife who adored him and whom he adored in return. Surely he had come a long way back from the disappointment which attended his finale as a military officer. Perhaps recent experiences at the Cardston Temple dedication and the October conference in the Salt Lake Tabernacle had called to mind those high presentiments which his mother had expressed before the move to Canada. Did he sense that he had yet far to go to fulfill his destiny?

Three years later, while attending another October conference, Hugh Brown visited with his long-time friend, President Heber J. Grant, and told him that he desired to move to Utah. He had initially thought of Logan but had been advised to go on to Salt Lake City by Albert E. Bowen, who pointed out that the opportunities to build a successful practice were better in the Utah capital. Leaving Alberta was quite a sacrifice, but Hugh and Zina felt that their children deserved a better education and more LDS association than were available in Lethbridge. None of the officials in the city or the schools at the time were members of the Church, and sometimes the Browns felt that their four daughters and two sons were being rebuffed and mistreated because of their religious convictions.

After returning to Alberta, Hugh was released from the stake presidency and made arrangements to dispose of his law practice. He then went back to Salt Lake City in November 1926 to make arrangements to move his family.

While in Utah he suffered a severe attack of trigeminal neuralgia, commonly called tic douloureux, an affliction which was to plague him for nearly twenty years with excruciating pain in the affected side of the head. Attacks were intermittent but almost unbearable.* Hugh had had some pain before leaving Lethbridge and had gone first to a dentist. After pulling some teeth and not finding anything wrong, the dentist had recommended medical treatment and suggested Salt Lake City as a place where it might be found. This doubtless reinforced Albert E. Bowen's recommendation of the place the Browns should resettle. The medical treatment ultimately prescribed was periodic alcohol injections into the afflicted area to reduce pain. This procedure was carried on until diminishing response required more radical measures during World War II.

Hugh Brown arranged to purchase a lovely house which had been built by Claude Richards at 1354 Stratford Avenue, in southeastern Salt Lake City. When he brought Zina and the children to Utah in February, 1927, they were delighted. This became the center of family activities for ten years and most of the children still look on it as home. Margaret Alberta was born on January 9, six weeks before the move, and the youngest, Carol Rae, joined the group on December 15, 1928. (The entries in Hugh Brown's journal are synoptic and increasingly widely spaced from 1925 to 1937. To this fact the unembroidered notations of the births of the last two children should probably be attributed.)

Although the move to Utah was not primarily for occupational reasons, Hugh Brown's first employment there reflected his ingrained disposition to accept what looked like a good opportunity, even if it took him in new directions. If any of these optimistic ventures which salt and pepper his eventful life had fulfilled initial hopes, he would have realized that ambition for wealth which was a powerful motivator during his first seventy years.

Radio was becoming a major industry in the United States, and in February, 1927, Hugh Brown took a position as manager

---

*The attack may be brought on by the mere touch of the lip or nose or tongue. Speech is rendered difficult because as the lip moves, the trigger zone can set off the reflex neuralgic attack. Eating is also interfered with because any contact with the lip or tongue may trigger the attack. Even washing the face becomes a problem because touching the nose may set off an attack. The resultant pain is said to be the most severe known to man.

of the Eddington-Cope Radio Company of Salt Lake City. Fifteen thousand dollars was quickly raised and the production of speakers began in a rented building on East Second South. Trips to Chicago, Los Angeles, and other capital and marketing centers punctuated the year and a half he was in this business. Problems with some of the speakers led to a reorganization of the company in January, 1928, but Hugh continued as manager and a member of the board of directors of the rechristened Great Western Radio Corporation of Utah. His connection as a director continued after his resignation as manager to return to his first love among the professions — the law.

The office of the law firm of Brown and Stewart opened on September 1, 1928, Hugh's partner being Robert Murray Stewart, the son-in-law of the apostle and later President George Albert Smith. This quickly became a successful practice; a journal note in April, 1929, mentions "a very good business." Hugh was also busy filling speaking engagements in churches, clubs, schools, and other organizations, and he was elected to the board of trustees of the LDS Business College and to directorships in the Utah Woolen Mills and the Old Mill Club.

Again the "big chance" beckoned, and this time the outcome was a financial disaster. In June Hugh sold his home in Lethbridge, using the proceeds and funds borrowed on his Salt Lake home to join David and Samuel Neff in purchasing the Ogden Hotel for $75,000. Then they traded the hotel in September for a sheep ranch in Wyoming for which they paid $325,000, the hotel's value of $125,000 being applied on the purchase price. The ranch comprised winter and summer range and lambing grounds, plus sixteen thousand sheep, two hundred head of cattle, and one hundred horses. Within weeks the stock market crash marked the beginning of the Great Depression; and according to President Brown's recollection, this last involvement in agriculture ended in a total loss.

The firm of Brown and Stewart was dissolved on January 1, 1930, and Hugh Brown moved into the Boston Building to join the prestigious firm of J. Reuben Clark, Jr., Preston Richards, and Albert E. Bowen. It is interesting to note that all of the partners became General Authorities of the Church except

Richards, and he was later a stake president in California. Corporation law was the firm's specialty, and Hugh was chosen as general counsel by the Merrill Mortuary Company for a retainer of $10,000 a year. This association continued intermittently for a long time and proved to be a real blessing during the war years. Merrill's vigorous program of expansion involved their attorney in litigation and work with legislatures and government agencies in several western states, and Hugh spent considerable time on the road. On one business trip in 1930 he accompanied his eldest daughter to Portland, where Zina Lou (he had nicknamed her "Birdie") had been called as a missionary to the Northwestern States Mission. On another trip he successfully argued a case before the Supreme Court of Montana. A reminiscent note mentions that his "horse trading" abilities were regarded as a valuable asset by the firm of Clark, Bowen, Richards, and Brown.

The Pullman rides and lonely hotel nights produced some superb letters to his family, as is shown by the following excerpts from one written to his wife on a train near Omaha, Nebraska, on New Year's Eve, 1931:

> We are now in Nebraska, a country which looks much like Alberta with its rolling, snow-covered plains — dotted with farm houses and a few trees. We have been in a real blizzard all day with a very high wind and . . . I feel a little lonely this eve with memories of other days when blizzards were raging and I was not experiencing them through Pullman windows in comfort and disdain.
>
> These big silent trees along the way bending to the wind, leafless but fairy-like in the clinging snow — the desolate-looking cornfields — the striped stocks standing like markers in a graveyard — the mules and cattle along the fences, heads down and backs to the wind, patiently enduring for a short season what cannot last for long — the occasional flock of wild birds seeking shelter where there is none, too cold to take wing as the train rushes by — nature in fact in the grip of winter reminds one of death and depression and other cycles of life which are not an end but only an incident in the adventure of a soul — "The falling leaf which tells of autumn's death is in a subtler sense but a prophecy of spring."
>
> It will be great some time when we can enjoy leisure together and give expression to our thoughts — or attempt to. We cannot express all we think — and we feel some things which are deeper than thought. Each one lives in a world of his own — his friends

and even his nearest relatives only see the margin of his life with an occasional glimpse of the "inland."

I often wish I had the power to portray to my audiences what I feel — that the best of both thought and feeling were not lost on the threshing floor of speech. Only now and then do we get a gold kernel — most of the best is too subtle to be caught in the mortal burlap which we hang over the spout.

Well, it is New Year's Eve, and tonight many will sit up to see the old year pass away as the new one crowds it off the stage. With what hopes and fears the world hails 1932 — what does it hold of fortune and of disaster, of life and of death. Luckily it is only given to us one day at a time — most of our trouble comes from doubt and fear and anticipating trouble. Let us as a family in 1932 make sunshine in the winter rather than blizzards in summer by entertaining only cheerful and hopeful thoughts and thus store up courage to meet what comes to us, remembering that reverses may rob us of what we have but cannot take from us what we are. . . .

An anecdote recorded by his daughter Mary relates to these depression years and reveals the compassionate side of Hugh B. Brown. During a restless night there came to him an impression that a medical student in Chicago, the younger brother of one of his good friends, needed help. What followed appears thus in the *Instructor*:

That morning the first letter that Elder Brown opened upon reaching his office contained a check for $100. It was a legal fee he had long since despaired of collecting. . . . Without a moment's hesitation, he . . . endorsed it and sent it to the young student along with a note which read: "Thought perhaps you could find some use for this."

March had really come in like a lion. A young medical student and his wife had talked most of the night, trying to figure some way for him to continue his schooling. Finally, they both agreed that there was nothing left to do but leave school and go to work full-time. So now, he was on his way to tell the dean. He paused outside the dean's door. Somehow he just could not do it. Perhaps he would wait until tomorrow.

As he opened the door of the small furnished room, he saw that his wife held a letter in her hand. She was crying. He . . . took the letter which she held out to him. "Thought perhaps you could find some use for this," he read.

Years passed. In the fall of 1937, Elder Brown was called to preside over the British Mission. The morning mail brought many letters from well-wishers; and among them was one from his friend's

brother, who had recently completed his schooling. Pinned to the
top of the letter was a check, and at the bottom . . . were the words:
"Thought perhaps you could find some use for this." (Mary Brown
Firmage, "Cast Your Bread," June, 1958, pp. 176, 180.)

President Brown remembers that the family came through
the depression years "without too much difficulty." His children
remember that there were pressures for household economy,
especially during the transitional interludes in their father's di-
versified career — the loss of the Wyoming ranch, the political
defeat in 1934, the wind-up of the liquor commission appointment in 1937, and the period following the return from the
British Mission, 1940-1942. The evidence is clear that Hugh
Brown provided a comfortable middle-class life style for his
family almost continuously after the first lean years in Cardston,
but his openly avowed ambition to be financially able to provide
a few luxuries for his large family was always eluding fulfillment. The flirtation with affluence which came nearest to
a marriage was late in life (Alberta, 1950-1953) and it, too,
was brief. The "currant bush" which did not produce a general's
stars would not produce a millionaire's bank account either.

A Democrat by political affiliation since his arrival in Utah,
Hugh Brown became a strong supporter of Franklin D. Roosevelt's New Deal. Early in 1934 he left the law partnership to
open up his own office and represent the new Home Owners
Loan Corporation as counsel. This new direction of his work
promised to be remunerative and also satisfying from the stand-
point of service. Within a few months, however, he made a
fateful decision to oppose incumbent William H. King for the
Democratic nomination for the United States Senate. This unsuccessful bid, and its aftermath, took him away from his legal
career, and he returned to it only briefly during the next sixteen
years. Neither his work for Merrill Mortuary in the early 1940s
nor brief associations with P. Drew Clarke and Emmett Brown
during the same decade represented a primary commitment to
the bar. In 1950 he was employed by the Richland Oil Company
to work in Edmonton, Alberta, as their legal representative in
an oil and gas exploration. From this activity he was called three
years later to be a General Authority, and his professional practice of law came to an end.

7. Local Church Leader

Next to his association with his family, the activity which brought Hugh B. Brown the greatest joy during his first fifty years was fulfilling various callings as a leader in the church. Following his mission he served almost continuously in bishoprics and high councils in the Alberta Stake, then as president of the Lethbridge Stake and of the Granite Stake in Salt Lake City. His willingness to give his time, money, talents, and energy in promoting and serving the Church is revealed from first to last, and his journals and memoirs are filled with memorable meetings, prayer circles, difficult journeys, valuable lessons, and spiritual growth. It was a labor of love.

Young Hugh Brown had been home from England barely long enough to win a bout with typhoid fever when he was called to be a home missionary, which meant devoting part of his time to the same kinds of efforts among the inactive and insufficiently active Latter-day Saints in the Cardston area as he had performed on a full-time basis in Norfolk. Then as president of the Cardston Ward Young Men's Mutual Improvement Association he had opportunity to apply his musical, dramatic, and forensic talents and to provide leadership for youth. On May 2, 1908, on the eve of his marriage, he was ordained to the office of high priest and set apart as second counselor to Bishop Dennison E. Harris. Within a year, first counselor James Rampton moved to Utah, Hugh Brown replaced him, and Walter Low became the new second counselor.

The ecclesiastical partnership with Bishop Harris lasted more than three years. It was one of the most influential relationships in his life, President Brown recalls. Bishop Harris was an educated man in his middle forties whose maturity and wisdom profoundly affected his young and zealous counselors. A favorite anecdote illustrates that influence:

> A young woman was brought before the bishopric accused of sexual sin. She confessed . . . and tearfully asked for forgiveness. The bishop asked her to retire to another room while they considered the verdict. Then he said, "Brethren, what do you think we ought to do?" As first counselor, Hugh Brown said, "I move that we cut her off from the Church." And the second counselor said, "I second the motion." The bishop took a long breath and then said, "Brethren, there is one thing for which I am profoundly grateful and that is that God is an older man. I would hate to be judged by you fellows. . . . I am going out and . . . bring her back. The worth of souls is great in the sight of the Lord."

Hugh did not agree with him at the time but he later changed his mind, a reversal which was reinforced a long time afterward when he returned to Canada as one of the General Authorities and discovered that one of the real stalwarts in a certain ward was the woman he had once voted to excommunicate. According to the local leader, "She is stake president of the Relief Society after having been ward president, has sent four sons on missions since her husband's death, and has been faithful and true all the days of her life." President Brown states that "it confirmed in his mind that God is no respecter of persons and in this sense he wants us to have charity and love and tolerance for our fellowman. He said that if we forgive, He will forgive us."

Hugh Brown continued in the bishopric until Bishop Harris and his counselors were released on August 27, 1911. Following his months at the University of Utah, Hugh returned to Cardston to be sustained as superintendent of the ward Sunday School. When the ward was divided early in 1914 and James Brown was retained as bishop of the Cardston First Ward, Hugh B. Brown was chosen to be one of his counselors. However, the war and the call to full-time military service came in a few months and Hugh had to be released.

Although he held no formal church appointment during his four years as an army officer, Major Brown performed many of the functions of an LDS chaplain, as has been noted earlier, in the camps in Canada and England. When he returned to Cardston in the spring of 1917 he was active in the Church despite the criticism he received from some of his friends. In July he accompanied President Wood on a mission to the northern wards, having a very pleasant time, according to his journal. While still working on his law degree, he was called in June, 1920, to attend a five-week teachers' institute at Brigham Young University in Provo, Utah, where such teachers as Guy C. Wilson and Adam S. Bennion provided "an enjoyable and profitable time." His wife met him in Salt Lake City for a visit with relatives and friends. Later in the same year Hugh Brown became a member of the Alberta Stake high council. The visits to wards and branches usually took him from his young family, but he used the free time to read books that would help in his law career.

While the paint was still wet on the sign outside his first law office, Hugh B. Brown (on November 10, 1921) was named the first president of the newly created Lethbridge Stake. Set apart by the President of the Council of Twelve, Elder Rudger Clawson, he became at thirty-seven the youngest stake president in the Church at that time. His counselors were George W. Green and Asael E. Palmer, and the high council included his law partner, Hjalmar Ostlund, and his former bishop, Dennison Harris. To his journal Hugh Brown confided, "I feel very weak in undertaking this great responsibility but I will do the best I can with the help of the Lord."

Comprised of nine wards, two branches and 2,534 members, the Lethbridge Stake "included everything north of the international boundary as far as the north pole," President Brown likes to tell his grandchildren. Actually its wards were distributed about 75 miles east and 140 miles northwest of Lethbridge, through area traversed by the Canadian Pacific Railroad. By

*First presidency of Lethbridge Stake: President Hugh B.
Brown and counselors George W. Green (left) and
Asael E. Palmer.*

train and then by car over primitive roads, and sometimes accompanied by family members, President Brown and his associates rode circuit over the Alberta prairies and mountains, organizing new branches wherever a few Mormons could be found.
Five months later, in a talk in the Assembly Hall on Temple
Square, in connection with the April 1922 general conference, he
reported eleven branches, the northernmost six hundred miles
from Lethbridge. He added, "If we were able to discover all
of our people there, we would have the largest stake in the
Church . . . because I believe we have in our stake the Ten
Tribes. . . . "

In that address Hugh B. Brown showed the same platform
poise, the same blend of anecdote, wit, admonition and testimony, which would eventually win worldwide audience. Time
would sharpen his skills and deepen his spiritual insight, but he
was already at that point where, as he enjoyed recalling to his
family, a woman could say after a later extemporaneous speech
in the Tabernacle, "Oh, President Brown, you are the only man
in the Church who can talk without thinking."

It is probable that Hugh Brown's call to the Lethbridge Stake leadership, as well as his invitations to speak in general conference, should be attributed in part to the favorable regard in which he was held by President Heber J. Grant. He took nothing for granted, however, but set out to establish that he was not merely the youngest but one of the most effective stake presidents in the Church. Charismatic, adequately self-confident, an admirer of the pulpit power of such men as Melvin J. Ballard and Brigham H. Roberts, Hugh Brown blended his natural and cultivated gifts with the leaven of the Spirit and achieved his stake objectives to a remarkable degree.

It is recorded that in 1922 there were no non-tithepayers in the Lethbridge Stake, evidence of a high degree of commitment on the part of the people and a major effort by the entire leadership group. The journal for 1921-1926 is full of Church activities — the organization of a monthly prayer circle, the first performance of a marriage, the visits to wards and branches, the quarterly conferences, the talk at Brigham Young University in April, 1925, the special fast meeting in Lethbridge for the purpose of praying for rain, after which "a fine rain came in all parts of the stake." Hugh B. Brown has always loved such experiences; the prayer groups, testimony meetings, miracles, and times of deep religious feelings have been counterweights to those secular ambitions which have competed for his allegiance.

"I tried to put into practice what Bishop Harris taught me in the matter of tolerance and understanding," he remembers. To illustrate, he recalls the following experience:

> We had been some time looking for a bishop for the Taber Ward and . . . we could not find a man on the record. We were acquainted with practically all of them, so the three of us, my two counselors and I, got in my car and started for Taber. As we were driving along we beheld a car approaching us in the opposite direction and I immediately recognized the driver and hailed him to stop. He . . . got out of the car. He was smoking a cigar. After exchanging pleasant greetings and talking for a time, I said, "Burt, we want you to be bishop of the Taber Ward." He held up his cigar and said, "Hell, with this?" And I said, "Hell, no, without it!" He threw it down on the ground and stepped on it and said, "By hell, I'll try it." He never smoked again and became one of the best bishops that we had.

Another incident took place at a stake conference in which President Brown was giving the principal address. A well-educated non-Mormon woman from eastern Canada happened to be present. At the close of the meeting she asked, "Are you available, sir, to transfer to some other part of the country?" Hugh Brown asked, "Under what circumstances?" She responded, "We'll pay up to $12,500 to get the man we want because our minister is leaving us. I can recommend you to them for that amount and perhaps it can be arranged for more if you desire." President Brown explained that he could not accept. Asked then, "Does your church pay you more than that?" he laughingly answered, "Well, hardly, but I cannot take up your offer." (He had come a long way from the somewhat tongue-tied little boy whose brother called him "Dutch" because he could not pronounce some words properly.)

An unforgettable occurrence at one of the meetings of the Lethbridge Stake presidency and high council is described in these words:

> We had made our reports, had borne our testimonies and were about to dismiss when suddenly I said to them, "Brethren, I have an impression that I know what each of you will come to." And then, starting with the senior member, I went round the circle and told each one of his weaknesses, his shortcomings, his strengths, his aptitudes, and his ability, and pleaded for them to measure up to their potential. I think I have never been more inspired in any effort and never has a group responded more wholeheartedly than they did. Many of them told me afterwards that I told them things that no one knew but themselves. I reminded them of some of their weaknesses and some of their failings and then told them what the future would hold for them if they would be true to what they knew was right. . . .

One major event for the Mormons in Canada happened on August 26-29, 1923, when the Alberta Temple was dedicated. Many of the Church leaders were present in Cardston, including President Grant and his second counselor, Anthony W. Ivins, and members of the Quorum of the Twelve—Elders Rudger Clawson, George A. Smith, George F. Richards, Joseph Fielding Smith, James E. Talmage, Stephen L Richards, Richard R.

Lyman, Melvin J. Ballard, and John A. Widtsoe. President Brown reported that some very spiritual services were held each day.

Such associations with the General Authorities were a great delight to Hugh and Zina Brown. Entertaining Elder Widtsoe during a 1924 stake conference brought occasion for "becoming better acquainted" with the noted educator whose significance for one generation of Latter-day Saints would be matched by his host in the next generation. The opportunity to speak in the Sunday afternoon session of the 1924 October general conference was Hugh Brown's first before such a large audience, and it was a thrilling experience.

Counseling was a particularly challenging part of this stake president's work. Hugh Brown wrote, "To be in a position where we must urge others to carry on is of itself a blessing as the words of cheer offered to others are a constant source of encouragement to the leader and he dare not give up."

In the same journal entry for January 2, 1925, he wrote reflectively: "Another year has passed and much has happened and much has been learned." It may be that even then he was thinking of his future in Canada. He was a prosperous and respected member of his community, but Mormons were a minority and his children may have been objects of some discrimination. Could they take it? If they remained in Lethbridge, would they receive a good education and have the opportunity to marry within the Church? Within a year he had made up his mind. With Zina's approval, he would ask for release as stake president and move his growing family back to Utah, from whence as an unpolished teen-ager he had come almost thirty years before.

When Hugh B. Brown moved to Salt Lake City early in 1927, he had several advantages as far as Church service was concerned. Having been a stake president in Canada, he was well known among the General Authorities, and he had an especially close relationship with President Grant. The house on Stratford Avenue was located in the Highland Park Ward of the Granite Stake, and almost immediately Hugh Brown was appointed to be a member of the high council. After approximately a year, he was chosen to be second counselor to Stake President F. Y. Taylor, being set apart by President Grant on February 26, 1928.

Less than two years after his release as a stake president in Lethbridge, Hugh Brown was called to a similar position in the Granite Stake. With the release of President Taylor on September 9, 1928, Hugh was sustained as his successor and set apart by Elder Rudger Clawson. He chose Marvin O. Ashton and Stayner Richards as his counselors and kept the existing high council. (Both Elders Ashton and Richards later became General Authorities.)

Reflecting on his experiences in this position, which he held until 1935, President Brown later wrote:

> I think while I was President of Granite Stake we had some of the most interesting and impressive experiences of my lifetime. We organized a prayer circle and met each month in the Temple with the High Council, Stake Presidency and Patriarch. . . . Some very unusual experiences were had during that time in our High Council meetings, in our ward conferences, in our stake conferences. We were among the leaders of the whole Church practically in every activity on which reports were made and it was a rich spiritual time of our lives.

Documentation on this period is meager, since professional, religious, civic, and family activities reduced Hugh Brown's journal-keeping to a few scattered summaries of several months' highlights. He was away from his family often, attending meetings and fulfilling speaking engagements, but until the older children began to go away on missions and to college, the occasions for personal correspondence were infrequent. Both Hugh and Zina Brown were inveterate letter-writers, but as long as 1354 Stratford was the center of the family's universe and the orbits of the members rarely extended beyond the Wasatch Front, the production of the kinds of letters which are grist for the biographer's mill was small. Happily, several choice items were preserved.

With approximately thirteen thousand members at the time of Hugh Brown's appointment to its head, the Granite Stake was the largest in the Church. He knew only a small fraction of the people, but by energetic application of his capabilities as speaker, promoter and counselor, he quickly established himself as a popular and respected Church figure. Many who knew him during this period would later assert that they expected Hugh B. Brown to become an apostle sooner or later.

The records of the Granite Stake show the busy round of meetings and conferences in which President Brown was involved. One of the activities in which Hugh was most interested was the building of a new stake center, estimated to cost two hundred thousand dollars. On May 1, 1930, he wrote: "We have finished our new tabernacle and it is a credit to the people. It is the best stake house in the Church." A fellowship activity in which Hugh and Zina Brown took delight was a newly formed Church history study group whose membership at one time or another included the J. Reuben Clarks, the Albert E. Bowens, the Harold B. Lees, the Marion G. Romneys and other prominent Latter-day Saints; its monthly meetings have continued to the present.

As hard times enveloped Utah and the world, President Brown spoke in the Salt Lake Tabernacle in January, 1931, on the theme, "Adversity, Too, Has Its Proper Place." Cautioning against "the false impression that reverses, disappointments, tragedies come only as the result of sin and disobedience," he cited Robert Louis Stevenson, Samuel Johnson, Aristotle, Alexander the Great, Ecclesiastes, and the Gospels in his admonition to take courage. He concluded:

> I bear testimony that in the hour of trial, in the hour of test, in the hour of disappointment and disillusionment, one can turn always with hope and confidence to the Father of the race, to our Father, who is our Friend. I trust that we may go forward today with renewed courage to face life, believing that after life is over all that has come to us in a disciplinary way has been for our good, believing in the words of the Lord to the Prophet Joseph Smith, recorded in the Doctrine and Covenants, wherein the Prophet, while in Liberty Jail, raised his voice to God and said: "How long must these things be?" The Lord said: "My son, peace be to thy soul. . . . All these things shall be . . . for thy good. The Son of Man has descended below the mall. Art thou greater than he?" (Hugh B. Brown, *Eternal Quest* [Salt Lake City: Bookcraft, Inc., 1956], p. 257.)

Despite the onset of the Great Depression, these were generally happy times for the Browns. Carol Rae was still a toddler when her sister Zina left for her mission, and the whole family shared in what they felt to be a "spiritual blessing." The house — enlarged in 1930 by the addition of five bedrooms and another bathroom — was full of human traffic of all ages, including President Brown's legal, political, and ecclesiastical associates, and the widening circle of friends which he, Zina and the children enjoyed. Business was good and the prospects were bright.

That these circumstances did not last should probably be attributed primarily to the fact that in the mid-1930s Hugh Brown's several interests and ambitions came to be at cross-purposes. The details of his ventures into professional politics and government service are for other chapters, but the impact on his career as a Church leader was profound.

Following his unsuccessful bid for the Senate in 1934, Hugh Brown was offered the chairmanship of the state liquor commission. He accepted after consultation with President Grant, both men apparently sharing the belief that Utah would benefit from having a strong person with LDS moral commitments in the position. Six months later, in October, 1935, the Granite Stake was divided and Hugh Brown was released as president. President Brown was disappointed, and later described it as "a time of heartbreak for both Zina and me." The circumstances are detailed in a later chapter.

When advised of the intention of the First Presidency to divide and reorganize the Granite Stake, Hugh Brown, by his own account, sought to change the decision and offered to leave the liquor commission if necessary, though Granite Stake was certainly oversized by prevailing Church criteria. The members of the First Presidency — Heber J. Grant, J. Reuben Clark, Jr., and David O. McKay — attended the conference and assured the people that the change reflected no lack of confidence in President Brown, an assurance which was confirmed two years later when he was called to be head of the British Mission at a time when his career was at its lowest ebb.

Two full-time appointments as mission president, 1937-1940 and 1944-1946, and two modestly compensated Church-related jobs, as servicemen's coordinator, 1941-1944, and BYU professor, 1946-1950, occupied most of the years from 1935 to 1953. In between and coincident with these positions he taught Sunday School classes, served as a home teacher, and fulfilled other tasks which are a part of the way of life of most Church members. His popularity as a speaker remained high and his voice was heard in chapels and halls wherever he went. That he would one day become a General Authority was the expectation of many who heard him.

8. Politician and Political Philosopher

Hugh B. Brown's enthusiasm for politics seems natural, given his early interest in oratory, his admiration for such men as B. H. Roberts and Reed Smoot, his legal training, his active participation in civic affairs both in Alberta and in Utah, and his driving ambition to make "a mark in the world." This interest led him into an ill-advised campaign to gain nomination for the United States Senate in 1934 and into acceptance of positions with the Home Owners Loan Corporation and the Utah State Liquor Commission. It also found expression in an outspoken loyalty to the Democratic Party, a powerful advocacy of patriotism and civic responsibility, and an equally emphatic opposition to political extremism.

It all began in Canada, where Hugh Brown manifested an active concern for politics early in his adult life. His journal first mentions the subject on April 24, 1912, following his return from the University of Utah: "I took part in a political campaign and Martin Woolf was elected M.P.P." (Canadian provincial and dominion elections correspond to state and national elections in the United States.)

Years of military activity followed, but when he returned from England in 1917 and began his legal work with Z. W.

Jacobs, Hugh took "an active part in the election . . . on December 17 and the Union Government was elected by a large majority. W. A. Buchanan was elected in Lethbridge. . . . I supported Buchanan because I felt that the Union Government was best, at least during the war." Press comment at the time of Hugh's admission to the bar in 1921 mentioned that he had been very active in "municipal movements in Cardston" for many years, but his journal does not mention political party roles during the Lethbridge years which followed. As noted in an earlier chapter, he did lobby for legislation in Calgary and Ottawa, and he prosecuted all Lethbridge cases under the 1924 Alberta Liquor Control Act. He had previously participated in the campaign against alcohol, holding "a prohibition meeting" in the Cardston Tabernacle in September, 1923, but this campaign was unsuccessful.

When he moved to Utah in 1927, President Brown recalls, he had the question on his mind whether he should be a Democrat or a Republican. This was the outcome:

> I spoke to several people. . . . President Grant at that time was an ardent Democrat as was his counselor and cousin, Anthony W. Ivins, and also B. H. Roberts of the First Council of Seventy. Each of these men told me at different times and separately that if I wanted to belong to a party that represented the common people, I would be a Democrat, but if I wanted to be popular and be in touch with the wealth of the nation, I would be a Republican.

Hugh Brown took what they said seriously, became a Democrat and remained one, even though President Grant later turned to the Republican Party because of his opposition to Franklin D. Roosevelt and his programs. Some animated discussions between the two good friends followed President Grant's change of political allegiance, especially during the tour of European missions which brought them into daily contact in 1937. By that time both Elders Ivins and Roberts were dead, and the calling of Hugh's former law partner, the brilliant former Undersecretary of State and Ambassador to Mexico, J. Reuben Clark, Jr., to the First Presidency brought a conservative influence into high Church circles at the same time that Roosevelt's New Deal was in the making. Hugh Brown had cast his lot with the Democratic Party and the Roosevelt Administration; he declared himself to be an "out and out New Dealer" when he ran for the Senate in 1934. (Years later he remarked that President Clark was his mentor in law and religion, but not in politics.)

Such was the impact of B. H. Roberts that these reminiscent comments by President Brown should be noted:

> One of the great men that influenced my life was Brigham H. Roberts . . . historian, orator, writer, wonderful man. Incidentally, he was a Democrat. . . . His frequent talks in my presence on political matters had much to do with confirming my faith in the Democratic Party. . . . He and Orson Pratt were the two . . . that could build a case for the Church that could not be gainsaid. B. H. Roberts was perhaps the greatest orator in the Church, a very powerful speaker, a powerful man. . . . He became my ideal so far as public speaking was concerned, and contributed much to my own knowledge of the gospel and my own methods of presenting it. I owe a lot to B. H. Roberts.

Hugh Brown became interested in Utah politics soon after coming to Salt Lake City from Canada. His business activities, and to some extent his Church associations, brought him into contact with many of the leaders of both parties; his law partner, J. Reuben Clark, Jr., had a long record of service in Republican administrations and GOP Senator Reed Smoot was an occasional golf partner. But Hugh's sympathies were Democratic, and he came in time to believe that he had a political future in that party. In 1932 he made the nominating speech for Henry H. Blood, who was elected governor in the Democratic landslide in November. The Roosevelt response to the worldwide depression increased Hugh's enthusiasm for a role in public affairs. Finding that his interests and political opinions were moving him away from his legal associates, he withdrew from the firm of Clark, Bowen, Richards, and Brown early in 1934 and plunged actively into organizational politics and government service.

Opening his own law office, Hugh enlisted the aid of Senator William H. King, through President Ivins, to obtain appointment as general counsel for the Home Owners Loan Corporation, a new federal agency. The position helped Hugh to gain favorable statewide exposure, because the HOLC aided people who were in danger of losing their homes. It was also intrinsically satisfying work, quite compatible with the Church responsibilities which hard times had magnified.

In April, 1934, Hugh Brown was elected state chairman of the Democratic Party, which increased his statewide contacts and also brought acquaintance with some national party figures. The association with the Democratic National Chairman, Postmaster General James Farley, ripened into a friendship which has lasted through the years. It also opened the White House doors, and an amiable acquaintance with President Franklin D. Roosevelt resulted.

Such contacts and activities, together with his personal qualities and Church position, produced a public image which made Hugh Brown attractive to some of the Democratic leaders of the state, despite the fact that he was a relative newcomer. With a congressional election approaching, he seemed a potentially successful standard-bearer for the growing New Deal wing of the party. Nevertheless, Hugh B. Brown's entry into the race against incumbent Senator King is puzzling.

In 1934 Senator King was coming to the end of his third six-year term. He had been only lukewarm in his support of Roosevelt's policies, and quite a few influential Utah Democrats thought it was time for him to retire. One of these was Herbert B. Maw, University of Utah political science professor and active "New Dealer," who announced his candidacy on June 16, 1934. By the end of the month King had let it be known that he was planning to seek re-election, and soon both he and Maw were campaigning up and down the state.

Hugh Brown was still state chairman of the Democratic Party. After a trip to southern Utah he predicted on July 17 that the Democrats would make "great gains over the 1932 elections."

The following day the race was complicated further by the announcement by William B. Wallace, Utah Water Storage Commission Chairman, that he would be a candidate for the Democratic senatorial race. The *Salt Lake Tribune* suggested that with three men in the contest, a deadlock could develop that would open the door to new candidates before the September convention. This may have been the thinking that led Hugh Brown to believe he had a chance to benefit from such an impasse.

During this time Hugh's name was in the news for a different reason. On July 21 the *Tribune* reported that a rule adopted by the federal Home Loan Board would require him to drop either his position with the HOLC or his party chairmanship. The rule stated that no HOLC employee could hold a political office. Hugh protested the rule, but apparently to no avail. By August 14 there were rumors in the press that he would ask for a two-month leave of absence from his government post because he felt it his duty to "serve his party through the pre-election days." There were also rumors that he was seriously considering resigning both positions and running for the Senate himself.

Hugh Brown had declared on August 1 that he would not be a candidate, no matter what the outcome of the ruling on his dual positions. However, four days later some of his associates met to organize a canvass of the state to test Democratic sentiment, and on August 9 he was visited by party members from twenty-five of the twenty-nine counties asking him to become a candidate. As a result of this request, and seeing himself as possible leader of the FDR New Deal wing of the party, Hugh B. Brown announced that he was "offering himself to the people of his state in an honest effort to see to it that the 'New Deal' is a 'square deal'." At the same time he resigned from his positions as legal counsel for the HOLC and Democratic state chairman in order to devote his full time to the campaign for the nomination.

The key people behind the Brown campaign included Delbert Draper, Leonard A. Brennan, Roy A. Mollener, Delbert Brinton, Henry D. Moyle, and Calvin W. Rawlings. They saw in Hugh a handsome, intelligent, attractive person in the prime of life, an excellent speaker and fine churchman who would certainly make a good race against King. The New Deal was gaining support among the people, and perhaps the spirit of the times led them to be overconfident of their ability to defeat the incumbent. In any case, according to Rawlings, they all told Hugh Brown that they thought he had a better than fifty-fifty chance to win the nomination.

A campaign folder listed several reasons for supporting the candidate. "He represents thousands of forward-looking citizens of all parties and classes who believe in the *new deal and the new day under new men.*" Convinced that states' rights doctrines cannot cope with depression-born problems, he "believes that national problems must be solved by national leadership and that we must . . . give unwavering support to the present Democratic national administration." The choice is clear: "The times call for . . . men whom the world has not passed by. Hugh B. Brown is such a man. . . ."

King had a strong political organization and was a very good campaigner, and it seems apparent that Hugh's decision to make the race at this time was a mistake. The brief campaign was vigorously pressed. (Because Zina had little enthusiasm for politics, LaJune often accompanied her father on the trips out into the state, and she remembers being mistaken on one occasion for his wife.) Audiences were not unresponsive, but it soon became apparent that Hugh Brown was not lining up the delegates.

When the Democratic state convention met in Provo on September 1, William H. King won renomination easily with 445 votes. Herbert Maw had 112 and Hugh Brown came third with 98 votes. It was a crushing defeat. Remembering the race years later, President Brown wrote, "I entered, in fact, against the advice of my wife, which I have regretted ever since."

Out of employment, and also out of pocket for some of the expenses of his campaign, Hugh Brown found himself in a situation in which Governor Blood's offer of the chairmanship of the new state liquor commission was very timely. The details are for another chapter. The two years in this controversial position kept him in touch with the political scene and closely involved with the governor and many state legislators, but he was not a candidate for elective office. The outcome of the commission work was a second disillusionment with practical politics and he was never again a party officer, public official or political candidate.

The years 1937-1946 were spent largely outside Utah and produced no political activity, though the responsibilities of citizenship were strongly urged both in England and in the United States. During the four post-war years at BYU, Hugh Brown participated in local political affairs to some extent but was not involved in any campaign. From 1950 to 1953 he was tied up in Canadian business. Only then, at the age of seventy, did he enter the phase of his life in which his political convictions would be most strongly and effectively urged.

As a General Authority, Hugh B. Brown appealed for active participation by all citizens in the political processes of the nations to which they gave allegiance. Because most of his audiences were American Mormons, he addressed himself most frequently to the civic concerns of that group, but his Canadian background helped him to avoid a narrowly parochial patriotism and his political experience left him sympathetic toward partisanship but impatient with fanaticism. Particularly during his years in the First Presidency, as will be noted in a later chapter, he was prominently involved with some of the political events and issues which affected the Latter-day Saints as a group.

"You may ignore politics," Hugh Brown told the 1958 Utah Democratic State Convention, "but politics will not ignore you." His acceptance of the invitation to be the keynote speaker only a few months after his appointment to the Quorum of the Twelve Apostles was frankly calculated to underscore the importance of Mormon participation in both major parties. "I am here," he observed wryly, "with the approval of close associates, some of whom are mildly Republican." As reported in the *Salt Lake Tribune,* July 13, he congratulated the delegates on representing a "party of uncommon leaders dedicated to the common man; a party which had contributed to the nation most of its great and near great presidents and had enacted the greatest legislation of the 20th century."

Contacts with national Democratic leaders expanded during his years as apostle and a counselor to President David O. McKay. Having represented the Church at the inauguration of John F. Kennedy in 1961, Hugh Brown found himself again cast in that role at the memorial services for the assassinated president less than three years later. While in Washington he called upon a congregation of LDS mourners to "weed out all hatred and contention," and at a special exercise at Utah State University honoring "the most promising young man of this generation," he sounded this sober challenge:

> Let us seek rather the historian's perspective and see this con-
> flict with Communism, not as a holy war, but as a difficult and
> perilous struggle with an implacable foe. We live in a world in
> which there is a diversity of economic systems, political creeds and
> philosophic faiths. We know, in part at least, what a nuclear war
> would mean. To avoid it is the common interest of all mankind and
> this interest must transcend all conflicts of ideology and national
> ambition. We need cool heads, strong hearts, dauntless courage, and
> mutual confidence if we are to bridge the dark abyss. (*The Abundant
> Life*, p. 14.)

Another prominent Democrat, W. Averill Harriman, was welcomed to Palmyra in the summer of 1958 when he came as governor of New York to open the Hill Cumorah Pageant. On Hugh Brown's eightieth birthday, five years later, he accompanied Harriman to Provo and introduced the then-ambassador at large at a BYU United Nations Day meeting for a talk on the recently negotiated nuclear test ban treaty. Several times Hugh Brown met with groups of congressmen during visits to the nation's capital, and through his grandson Edwin Firmage, who held a White House Fellowship and served on the staff of Vice President Hubert Humphrey, a warm friendship developed between him and the vice president. On Tuesday, May 20, 1969, President Brown was invited by the chaplain of the United States Senate, at the suggestion of Edward Kennedy, to deliver the opening prayer at the Senate session. Invoking divine blessings upon the country, its flag, constitution and national leaders, he prayed finally for "peace, O Lord, both at home and abroad" — a petition very timely in that distraught year.

There was something of a sense of mission in President Brown's public identification with the Democratic Party during the mid-1960s, when some Latter-day Saints were striving to establish an institutional identification with right-wing politics. In 1964 he gave the invocation at the Democratic state convention and made some informal remarks. During that campaign year one of the party leaders told Charles Manley Brown in Dallas that his father had "single-handedly saved the Democratic Party in Utah." This surely exaggerates Hugh B. Brown's influence, but it is indicative of the role he was able to play because of his speaking ability and his stature in the Church.

President Brown seemed to feel that he should demonstrate that it was possible for one to be a Democrat and also a good Mormon. In commenting on this later, he said:

> It has been definitely established that . . . membership in either party should not affect a person's standing. . . . For the Church to take a position and announce it on a political issue [would be] a dangerous and unwarranted thing. . . . There must come a time when there will be no more reflections on the man who belongs to one party or the other.

He also expressed in the same memoir his view on the proper Church relationship to politics in other countries:

> . . . in view of the fact that this is a worldwide Church. . . . if [in] a foreign country . . . the majority vote for a socialist, we should not do anything as a Church that would reflect adversely on that country's political system. . . .

Although he has expressed the opinion that "it would be best if all the General Authorities would take a position where their loyalties to one party or another would not be known," Hugh B. Brown clearly does not intend to lead out in that direction. In his nineties he is still vitally interested in the political process. Despite the disappointment of his own political ambitions and the unhappy ending of his government service, he is one of the Church's most powerful advocates of civic participation. Not least among his contributions has been to confirm the legitimacy of liberal political opinions and party affiliations and to exert the influence of his character and personality in exemplifying the principle that, whatever a person's calling may be, all members of the Church are free to make and express their political choices.

9. Liquor Control Commission Chairman

While Hugh Brown was a young missionary in England he had a spiritual experience which profoundly impressed him. He remembered it not as a vision or a revelation, but probably as a dream:

> I saw or dreamed that I was near the top of a circular stair and that for some reason I had dropped a vessel that was valuable. It fell down the stairwell and crashed at the bottom and I had to go back down and pick it up. As I made my way down past the others who were ascending, I was made aware of . . . some of their expressions of delight that the fall had come. I went down and picked up the pieces, and I started my climb back up and passed many of my friends and got nearer to the top than I had ever been before. . . .

Hugh related this dream to his mother when he returned home, and he often had cause to think about it when, as in England in 1917, his life took a sudden setback after a series of promising developments. In the mid-1930s he received three such shocks in rather rapid succession. First was the defeat in the bid for the Senate. Then came the release from the Granite Stake presidency. Finally, after two difficult years as interim head of the Utah Liquor Control Commission, his appointment as permanent chairman was not sustained by the Utah Senate, and he left the commission a disappointed and disillusioned man. At this time he felt that his dream had been literally fulfilled; he was indeed at the bottom of the staircase after having climbed so near to the top.

Hugh B. Brown's appointment as chairman of the control commission came as a result of the adoption of the Twenty-first Amendment to the United States Constitution. Ironically, Utah's ratification on December 5, 1933, accomplished the repeal of the Prohibition Amendment, and almost as ironically a teetotaling churchman who had fought for prohibition in Canada was called upon to help perfect and then enforce the liquor control laws of the state. The story is complex and depressing; only the broad outlines need be reviewed here.

The vote for repeal meant that alcoholic beverages would be available in Utah, but the question of how they should be dispensed was still open. This was the situation that brought Hugh Brown to the fore and finally led to his appointment as chairman of the first liquor control agency. He began as a member of the Committee of Forty-Nine, which was created by the governor in January, 1934, to investigate and make recommendations for legislation. By virtue of his work with Canadian liquor laws, his standing as Democratic state chairman, and his strong views on the subject, Hugh Brown soon came to be one of the committee leaders. As to the options of a licensing system (sale in private establishments) or a state authority system (sale in government package stores), his recommendation was categorical:

> We must find a solution that will be of benefit to society. . . .
> We must find a condition that will not be ideal for the bootleggers.
> . . . I had a lot of experience with this in Alberta . . . and with that
> background and experience and observation, I am unalterably op-
> posed to the licensing system and in favor of state control. (Report
> of Second Meeting of the State Advisory Committee on Liquor Con-
> trol.)

The law ultimately adopted by the legislature in March, 1935, was based on the committee's recommendations. It called for a three-man liquor control commission, appointed by the governor with the advice and consent of the Senate. The chairman was to be a full-time employee and the other members were to serve on a part-time basis. They had the responsibility to set up the state store system and to oversee the purchase, storage, distribution, labeling, and sale of all wines and hard liquors in Utah. They were also charged with licensing all draft beer establishments according to an allocation system that related the number of licensees to the size and distribution of the population. Finally, the commission was given the task of enforcing all the liquor laws of the state.

Having been defeated as senatorial candidate and having resigned from his position with the Home Owners Loan Corporation, Hugh Brown was at this time looking for remunerative employment. In many ways he seemed a logical candidate for the chairmanship. He had been active in the Democratic Party and was in line for some political preferment; he had been close to Governor Blood since giving the nominating speech at the 1932 convention; and he had been active in the Committee of Forty-Nine and its drafting subcommittee. His work with Alberta liquor prosecutions made him perhaps the most experienced lawyer in the state in liquor-control work, his record as a military officer convinced people that he could take command of a difficult situation, and his association with the Cardston cooperative suggested some competence in business management. Finally, he was president of the largest stake in the Church, and his views on the importance of strict control of the liquor traffic were in harmony with a majority of the people of the state and especially the Mormon leadership. He was felt to be incorruptible and certainly he would give the commission an aura of respectability.

The offer of the chairmanship was made by Governor Blood, himself an active and loyal Mormon. Hugh was pleased at the offer and went to his close friend President Heber J. Grant for counsel. President Grant indicated his concurrence in the appointment and saw no reason why it should have any impact upon his position as stake president. Certainly President Grant felt comfortable with the idea of having a good Church member as head of the commission. According to Charles Manley Brown, his father was also offered the opportunity to head the State Highway Division. But with the encouragement he had received from many quarters and with his previous experience in liquor regulation, he chose to accept the liquor commission chairmanship. There can be no question however that he realized that this would be a tough assignment, and he later recalled that he accepted it with misgivings and certainly against the counsel of his wife, Zina.

The two part-time commissioners were Adam Patterson, an Ogden real estate man, Republican and member of the Church, and George Whitmore, a Nephi banker, Democrat and Presbyterian. They seemed a good team. Shortly before the first liquor stores opened, Chairman Brown announced the commission's program for enforcement, which enlisted all Utah peace officers in the effort, attacked the importation and sale of bootleg liquor, appealed for public support, and flatly asserted that the influence of the commission could not be bought.

On June 1, 1935, Governor Blood officially proclaimed the end of prohibition in Utah, and the new state liquor stores opened for business. As the summer advanced, the commission worked quickly to expand the distribution system and to implement strict law enforcement. Frequent raids were made by the commission's agents; illicit selling was coming under attack. So was the commission, as all who were adversely affected began to come forward with their objections to the new law and its implementation.

This was the context in which Hugh B. Brown experienced the great disappointment which has been mentioned earlier — his release as president of Granite Stake. President Grant stated publicly that President Brown had taken the government post with the First Presidency's approval and encouragement, and that he had "the unqualified love and respect of the Brethren." At the high council meeting that day, President Grant again commented on "the important responsibility of administering the liquor law, and noted that President Brown had the earnest prayers of the Presidency for his success." During the conference, Hugh Brown acknowledged the fact that some thought his position was undesirable, but he felt that the liquor commission was controlling an evil, and he prayed for the support of all in enforcing the law. Finally he expressed his faith and his mood by quoting the hymn, "Lead, Kindly Light." The appeal for guidance "amid th' encircling gloom" seems to reflect his sorrow at being released and the possibility of being misunderstood by some.

In historical perspective the sequence of events is understandable, indeed almost inescapable. Since its inception the liquor commission had come to be the focal point of those competitive interests and pressures, some of them sordid and unscrupulous, which have always been associated with efforts to regulate the liquor business in the United States. As the chairman began to come under criticism, the inherent incompatibility of his state and Church positions — in substance and even more in terms of image — soon appeared. (Years later, when the possible appointment of another Church leader to the liquor commission was discussed in another First Presidency, Hugh B. Brown recommended that the man be discouraged from accepting.)

The storm of problems did not cease with Hugh Brown's release. The rationing of beer licenses among hundreds of firms which had been legally or illegally selling, caught the commission in cross-fire from tavern keepers, revenue-conscious mayors, and local law enforcement officials who lacked either the resources or the enthusiasm to cope with liquor law violators. Allegations of favoritism in the handling of licenses and the purchasing of products for the state stores were heard from those who were disappointed by the commission's decisions. Unfair hiring practices were also charged by those passed over in the recruitment of employees. An investigating committee appointed by the commission made some recommendations for procedural changes but found no substantiation for any of the serious allegations. At the end of its first year, therefore, Hugh Brown felt justified in publicly expressing pride at the commission's accomplishments and a commitment to strict enforcement of the liquor code in the future.

For the balance of 1936 the commission was rarely front-page news, but the nagging problems remained, and it became apparent in time that the critics had not been mollified. Factionalism within the Democratic Party further complicated matters, and when the biennial legislature convened in January, 1937, an investigating committee was appointed to look into complaints about various departments of the state government. The report, which was submitted on March 8, was critical of several agencies, the Liquor Control Commission among them. On reading it, Hugh B. Brown described the report as "formidable."

After a hectic day in which the commissioners denied a charge of disharmony and presented material in refutation of other charges, the Senate met to consider the interim appointments. The governor had decided not to make a fight about the issue, and the vote went against confirmation of seven of his appointees, including the three liquor control commissioners.

Thus Hugh B. Brown moved out of the state government under distressing circumstances. The *Salt Lake Telegram* quoted him as saying, "The nightmare is over." The last meeting of the commission was held on April 30, 1937, and on the following day the First Presidency announced that Hugh B. Brown would be the new president of the British Mission. This appointment marked the end of his short public service career and cast him again in a role of responsible Church leadership.

A special state audit of the records of the Liquor Control Commission showed "nothing whatever that in the remotest way reflected on the integrity or honesty of any member of the commission." And Governor Blood wrote to the former commissioners expressing "appreciation of the integrity and intelligence . . . exercised in the interests of the people. . . ." Still the rumors and innuendoes were painful, and the failure of confirmation was a bitter blow. An undertaking which had started on a high and hopeful note had become the victim of partisan politics and the pitfalls which are apparently endemic to programs of liquor control.

Perhaps the best commentary was made, years later, by a man who in 1937 was a reporter on the highly critical *Salt Lake Telegram*. Speaking of the commissioners, Jennings Phillips said, "They were all decent men but they were naive men. Believe me, the liquor business is worldly, and they weren't worldly men." He remembers Hugh Brown as having said on more than one occasion, "This is no place for a man like me."

Ambition, pride, public-spiritedness, financial need, religious commitment, delight at a new challenge — these and possibly other considerations set Hugh Brown's feet on the spiral staircase of political and governmental advancement. From a point far enough up to inspire envy, he fell to the lowest point in his long career. Twenty years after the first bitter experience in World War I, the "currant bush" was again radically pruned.

10. President of the British Mission

On June 19, 1937, Hugh B. Brown was halfway across the Atlantic on the S. S. *Empress of Australia* bound for England and the first of a series of full-time Church callings which would, with brief interruptions, occupy the remainder of his life. Returning to the practice of journal-keeping, abandoned entirely during the hectic years in politics and government, he noted that there were "some games and dancing aboard, also time for reading and meditation." "One wonders," he wrote, "at the changes of life. There seems to be a guiding hand which shapes our ends. The work into which I go is more to my liking than either law or business, although when one has a family to raise he must do what he can do to ensure his economic security."

When it became likely early in 1937 that the post with the liquor commission was not going to continue, Hugh decided that it would be best for him and his family to change locations and make a new start. With the assistance of his former law partner Preston Richards and his brother Owen Brown arrangements were made to trade the cherished home on Stratford Avenue for a comparably lovely and spacious house at 1830 Verdugo Vista Drive in Glendale, California. Except for Zola and Mary, who by now were married, Zina and the children made the move in April and Hugh planned to join them as soon as the outgoing liquor commission had wound up its business. "To ensure his economic security" by opening a legal practice in California was his apparent intention, but Zina was not enthusiastic about the move.

The call to head the British Mission brought this project to a sudden halt. Hugh was pleased to accept, although he interpreted the appointment as in part an attempt by the Church leadership to "pacify his turbulent feelings" and to give public recognition that he was in good standing despite the earlier release from the Granite Stake and the recent legislative investigation. He had lived in England as missionary and serviceman and in many ways it was like going back home. Certainly the mission presidency was a position of honor and responsibility in the Church.

Hugh Brown hated to leave his family in so unsettled a state in California, but he was happy to accept President Grant's invitation to accompany him and his party on a tour of the European Mission, a highlight of which would be the centennial celebration of the inception of the Church's missionary work in Britain. The group sailed from Montreal to Cherbourg, France, where they would be joined by European Mission President Richard R. Lyman, his wife and others.

So it was that Hugh B. Brown found himself on the high seas, en route to Europe with President Grant and others. He bore a gift and a note of appreciation from eighty-nine employees of the liquor commission and a verbal charge from eighty-four-year-old J. Golden Kimball to "give 'em h - - - over there, Hugh, give 'em h - - -." He also carried thoughts of Zina, busy making arrangements for the Glendale property so that she and the children could join him in England in a few months. On June 17 he wrote in his journal:

> This is the 29th anniversary of our wedding. We've been unusually happy and congenial. I've tried the patience of my loyal and devoted wife many times by my foolish side trips into politics and business, but she has stood by me and never complained. This is another evidence of the existence of God, for only God could have made such wise provisions for man's redemption as to give him a good wife.

It was apparently a beautiful ocean crossing, with much time for "reading and meditation." Perhaps as a result of that period of meditation, shortly after the Browns were reunited in London in September Hugh would confide to his journal some thoughts about the lives of his parents, both of whom had died a year or two before. Feelings about his own recent predicament may possibly be reflected in this tribute to Lydia Jane Brown:

> My beloved mother passed away in June 1935. All of her children were at her bedside when she died — thirteen married sons and daughters. She passed in peace at the ripe age of 79 years and 10 months. No better saint ever lived on earth.
>
> Her life of sacrifice and service, of sorrow and disappointment, and her passing without being rewarded for a life time of devotion to duty proves one of two things — either that there is no God and consequently no justice, or else, and this I believe and know to be the case, there is a life beyond the grave where a just Judge will reward the righteous and where we will be able to understand the why of many of the mysteries of life.
>
> One of the most perplexing of these is — why must the few real saints who come to earth be subjected to so many indignities, be deprived of most of the material blessings which are showered with almost reckless prodigality on the wicked and the ungodly?
>
> Why must God-fearing men suffer contumely and abuse and be deprived of comforts, be lied about and made to suffer what only sensitive souls can suffer? Why does the scoundrel and the libertine go free and grow rich and be hailed by their fellows as great and worthy?
>
> Again I say, there must be another world in which real merit is rewarded and the violation of law followed by the penalty prescribed for sin.
>
> We must overcome impatience and realize that virtue is its own reward and that the law of compensation is exact — that the law of the harvest is inexorable — that what we sow we must also reap; but — and this is important — God is not in a hurry. With a program extending over eternity the events of a lifetime are less than momentary, and timed by his clock each violation is punished and each virtue rewarded in the very moment of its occurrence. That our wrist watches are not proper instruments with which to measure time when considered as a part of eternity.
>
> I believe then that mother's life of loving devotion to duty has earned for her a crown of glory which the richest queen of history

will envy — that there we shall see real justice done, for Truth will leave the scaffold where wicked and shortsighted men have kept her for so long and will occupy the throne where wrong has been so often crowned. The gratifying truth about it all is this — The throne which wrong usurped was temporary, transitory, illusory and vain, while when Truth finally wields the scepter it will be hers forever and forever and all who have loved and served her will have joy and eternal bliss for their reward.

Of Homer Manley Brown, who died in February, 1936, at the age of eighty, his son wrote:

> He too had given his life in service to his family, and while impetuous and hasty he and mother will find comfort in the thought that now, when all is known and understood, their kingdom there will be a great and enduring one and together they will prepare a place for those for whom they gave so much.

The tour through northern France, Beligum, The Netherlands, Switzerland, Germany, and Czechoslovakia was punctuated with inspirational meetings with congregations of missionaries and Church members, but the letters home devoted more space to sightseeing. Of Paris, Hugh wrote, "As we were obliged to go in a group it was not possible to see as much as I should have seen if I had been alone or with one other fellow who could go as fast as I like to go when there is so much to see and do." The battlefields of World War I evoked memories, and an all-day conference in Basel on July 4 stimulated both patriotism and testimony.

An incident which Hugh liked to recall for his family occurred during a brief stop near Frankfurt. All the Mormons in the area were gathered on the station platform, and they sang "We Thank Thee, O God, for a Prophet" while President Grant stood at the train window. As the train pulled away, he turned, tears streaming down into his white beard. Hugh overheard him voicing his private feelings and a prayer: "I am not worthy of that. They used to sing that to Brigham. . . . Help me to be worthy of the office and of the kind of respect which the Saints show." It was an aspect of Heber J. Grant's character which further endeared him to the new president of the British Mission.

From Berlin, Hugh flew to London to help with preparations for the centennial observance and to get acquainted with his predecessor, Joseph J. Cannon. Together they welcomed President Grant's party to England and accompanied it to Preston, near Liverpool, where the anniversary celebration was officially opened. On the banks of the River Ribble, where a plaque had been placed honoring the first convert baptisms in 1837, a memorial service was held on July 30. Speakers included President J. Reuben Clark, Jr., Joseph Anderson, secretary to the First Presidency, President Grant, and President Brown. Meetings were also held with a number of the full-time missionaries in the old Cockpit, so famous in the early history of the mission, and in the chapel in which Elder Heber C. Kimball and others had preached the first LDS sermons in England. A Church history pageant drew large crowds to the Rochdale town hall on July 31 and August 1, and a group of missionary baseball players, representing the town of Rochdale, defeated their opponents handily.

Following a trip to Copenhagen with President Grant's party to attend a mission presidents' conference, Hugh Brown returned to London to assume his new responsibilities. On the steps of 5 Gordon Square, then the mission headquarters, President Cannon handed President Brown the keys to the building and, symbolically, the keys to the British Mission. The Cannons left the next day for America, but the European Mission was headquartered in the same building and the Lymans were helpful in the orientation process. Elder Lyman wrote an editorial for the August 12, 1937, issue of the *Millennial Star* which was very complimentary to the new mission president. Five days later Hugh Card Brown arrived from the worldwide Boy Scout Jamboree in Holland to begin under his father's direction the missionary work to which he had previously been called.

Meanwhile, Zina was busily preparing for the overseas movement of five more Browns. Zola, Mary, and LaJune would not be going. Each of them would later travel abroad with their father on some of his journeys as a General Authority, but now, after intervals as students at BYU, they were pursuing their own careers as wives and mothers. Two grandsons had already come to delight the middle years of Hugh and Zina Brown.

Zina Lou, Manley, Margaret, and Carol, along with Hugh, Junior, would share their parents' European adventure. After her mission, Zina Lou had attended BYU for a year and then gone to Los Angeles to work. Now, after successful corrective surgery on her leg, she was in Glendale and would remain there until October to complete the transfer of the Verdugo Vista Drive home to the people who were to lease it for the period of the Browns' expected absence. Then she would follow the family to England.

Incidentally, the leasing arrangement had an odd and disastrous outcome. Within a month after Zina had joined her family in London, the affluent lessee discovered his wife in the living room with her lover and shot them both. The lease ended with the man's trial, and the best rental arrangement which could be made thereafter was so much less favorable that the house became an expense rather than a source of additional income during the years when the Browns were operating on the modest living allowance provided for mission presidents. In a letter to Zola, her father wryly commented on the bizarre turn of events:

> Things go wrong sometimes for a period and then get worse, but I guess there is only one thing to do and that is to carry on with chins up and keep a sense of humor. I think if he wanted to kill his wife he might have taken her outside instead of mussing up our front room, but we don't all do things in the same way.

On September 15 the two Hugh Browns met Zina, Manley, Margaret and Carol at Southampton as they arrived on the S. S. *Manhattan*. Within a few weeks they were settled at 9 Gordon Mansions, a short distance from the Mission headquarters, while Hugh Card was proselyting in Glasgow and Zina was moving effectively into her role as "mission mother." Wrote her doting husband: "The Saints wherever she has been are in love with her and she is the finest looking and best lady in the British Empire; and I've seen some of their best specimens. How's that for bragging?" As for Zina, on seeing her husband in action in his new calling, she wrote to Zola: "Daddy is magnificent in his work! He speaks like a prophet and looks so royal! He makes friends everywhere."

The British Mission in the summer of 1937 numbered approximately 6,200 members, organized into fourteen districts and seventy-two branches. About 150 full-time missionaries, almost all of them young men from the western United States, were engaged in basically the same kinds of activities as Hugh had pursued in the Norfolk Conference a generation before — tracting, conducting street meetings, teaching investigators, and assisting and often directing the programs of the Church in the local branches. Athletic teams and musical groups among the missionaries were encouraged by President Brown for their public relations value; district and mission conferences served to strengthen the morale of English Mormons as well as to attract potential converts; and prominent LDS visitors from America — General Authorities and others — were often featured in special meetings.

Hugh Brown was delighted with his new challenge but awed by its dimensions. He soon perceived that the England of the depression-ridden thirties was not the Edwardian super-power which he had known in his youth. "I weep for the faded glory of England," he wrote in his journal, and he prayed:

> O for the power to show them what could be done if they would but cut off the supply of drugs and nicotine and rum; if they would establish athletic fields and teach proper diet; . . . above all, if they would return to religion, the integrating force which will hold the tottering world together if it is to be saved from wreck and ruin. How helpless I feel with these one hundred young men to try to bring help to this once-mighty nation. May God help us to find a way to bring the blessings of the gospel to some of them.

The first opportunity to preside as mission leader came at a district conference in Belfast, Ireland, on August 5. Instructional sessions with the elders were followed by a public meeting at which a large congregation heard President Brown speak on the Beatitudes. The journal describes this as "a very spiritual meeting" and notes that within a week fourteen new members were added to the Church.

Conferences in the other thirteen districts followed before the end of the year, and the cycle was repeated approximately every six months until missionary efforts were suspended at the outbreak of World War II. After Zina and the children arrived, she often accompanied her husband on the weekend trips and played an active part in the meetings. She also represented the Young Women's Mutual Improvement Association in Edinburgh at the International Council of Women in company with Amy Brown Lyman, who represented the Relief Society. Occasionally Zina Lou accompanied her father while her mother kept vigil at home, and there were times when the family traveled together. Long before the end of this first mission together, President and Sister Brown won the hearts of the British Saints, and these and other contacts brightened President Brown's perspective on the country and its people.

For the members of the Brown family in England, these were times of closer relationship with their husband-father than they had known during the preceding hectic years. As noted, their flat was near Gordon Square, and when the European Mission was discontinued in mid-1938 the Browns moved into the apartment which the Lymans had occupied in the 5 Gordon Square block. The four flights of stairs were not easy for Zina, whose health was not robust during part of the time in England. But Hugh now often saw her and the children during the day, and they all shared some of the highlight experiences.

Manley, Margaret, and Carol, who were sixteen, ten and eight when they went to England, attended London schools. In September, 1938, Margaret went back to America to live with Zola until her parents' return. Zina Lou was set apart as a missionary during her time in England; she worked primarily in the mission office and in April, 1939, returned to Utah. Hugh Card spent much of his mission in Scotland and Ireland, but the shared experiences strengthened the ties between father and son. Manley anticipated a mission at the completion of his college preparatory work in 1939, but the war sent him home with the rest of his family before the call could be consummated. Only Margaret and Carol were still children when their parents' mission came to an end.

British Mission President Hugh B. Brown with mission-
aries on steps of mission office at 5 Gordon Square.
Behind ten-year-old Carol Brown is her brother Hugh;
next to her is Elder Marvin J. Ashton, who thirty-five
years later would be an apostle.

If one family was growing up and scattering, another kind of family relationship was forming between the Browns and the missionaries. A 1939 journal entry states: "I shall always remember the wonderful friendships formed while in this mission field. . . . The spirit of youth is ever present and acts upon an aging man like rain and sunshine on a tree, helping to keep it alive and green and growing." There is every reason to believe that Zina shared the sentiment. In a letter to Mary she wrote: "It's fun to stuff the elders with cake and be mother to such grand young men. Would like to adopt them all." One was practically adopted; Emmett Brown, Hugh's brother Gerald's son, became virtually a member of the family during his missionary stint in England.

A particular bond developed with the Millennial Chorus, a male choir which reached a high level of musical excellence in 1937-1939 under the direction of A. Burt Keddington and

Lowell M. Durham. Composed entirely of missionaries, it toured the mission singing at conferences and giving public concerts. In the winter its members were assigned to London, where the performance opportunities were most abundant. It is not surprising that some of the missionaries who spent their days in the more mundane tasks of proselyting saw the chorus as an elite group, but it performed an excellent service and built a great deal of good will throughout the British Isles. (Members of the chorus, under Burt Keddington's direction, sang two mission-field numbers at President Brown's ninetieth birthday party in 1973 in the Garden Park Ward in Salt Lake City.)

Another factor that helped to make President Brown's mission very interesting and exciting was the athletic program which he fostered as a public relations activity. Some very fine athletes were among the elders sent to the British Mission and they were permitted to use their skills. In May, 1938, the Catford Saints represented Britain in the European basketball tournament at Lille, France, and defeated a German team for the championship. In October the missionary baseball team from Rochdale became the champions of England. All of this delighted Hugh Brown, who took his enthusiasm for sports to Europe and was jestingly charged with moving the best tennis players into the mission office so that he would always have a strong partner for the doubles matches at Gordon Square.

The *Millennial Star* was another enterprise which gave Hugh Brown an outlet for his ideas and an opportunity to work with some of the outstanding elders. He oversaw its publication for the entire period of his presidency, and he took the editorship in October 1938. One of the associate editors, and an infrequent doubles partner in tennis, was Marvin J. Ashton, who later became a member of the Quorum of the Twelve Apostles. Elder Ashton has stated: "President Hugh B. Brown was a leader who had the love and respect of his missionaries to a man. He had the unique ability to be one with his missionaries while maintaining the dignity and poise he carried so well. In two years of missionary association, some of it on a most intimate basis, I always found him meeting every association with an appropriate blend of courage, friendliness, and firmness. He treated his missionaries like men and they responded accordingly."

As editor of the *Star,* President Brown commented on gospel themes and contemporary world problems with exceptional skill, and some of his favorite anecdotes first saw print in the *Star* — among them the story of the gardener and the currant bush. The "Browsings and Musings" which served as fillers during this and the post-war period of Hugh's editorship combined wit and wisdom, borrowed and original. Illustrative of their range are these:

> God delights in diversity.
>
> The quality of one's intelligence may be related to his sense of humor.
>
> He who obeys with modesty may someday be worthy to command.
>
> Whom God calls he equips.
>
> Does the light of your torch flicker at every breath of doubt or can you make it shine into and make radiant the darkened avenues of uninformed souls?
>
> The man who wants his dreams to come true must wake up.
>
> If your knees knock, kneel on them.
>
> When love and skill work together, expect a masterpiece.
>
> It is best not to tell all you know; you may have to respond to an encore.
>
> Men live best when they neither deny themselves the verdict of the head nor the intimations of the heart, but seek a working harmony of both. (*Eternal Quest,* pp. 429-455.)

The tie which has held the members of the "Gordon Square Club" together through the decades of semi-annual reunions and monthly study groups is made of more than the fun and games of missionary work, of course. Memories of counseling sessions in times of doubt or trouble, of administrations in time of sickness, of shared testimonies in missionary conferences, and of memorable sermons are also involved. Many of the narratives which would become Hugh B. Brown's trademarks as a General Authority were polished in the pulpits of England, and the style and empathy which would keep him a favorite of young people for several more decades were very apparent. The roster of missionaries who served in Great Britain from 1937 to 1940 contains many names which have become notable in civic, educational, business, and Church circles, and President Brown declares that their loyalty, support and friendship have been encouraging and inspiring through the years. He, in turn, has been a continuing inspiration to them.

Highlights of the Church program in England during these years were the summer mission-wide MIA conventions held in 1938 at Bradford and in 1939 at Sheffield. Talent programs, sports, and dances drew both members and investigators from England, Scotland, Wales, and Ireland. The Sunday evening meetings drew more than a thousand persons; in 1938, President Brown was the featured speaker and the next year he shared the spotlight with Elder Joseph Fielding Smith of the Council of the Twelve and his wife, who were touring the European missions. A missionary testimony meeting at Bradford which lasted from eight until noon and from two until five is described in the journal as "a glorious and uplifting time," and a fitting finale to "one of the most successful mission conferences ever held in the British Isles." This was but another evidence of Hugh's great ability for effective listening.

President Brown vigorously sought opportunities to meet non-Mormon groups and was reasonably successful. His Canadian background stood him in good stead when he spoke to the Rotary Club at Wembley in September, 1937, on "Canada and the Rush-Bagot Treaty." This rather obscure phase of early nineteenth-century British-American relations must have been effectively handled, for invitations to make the same presentation to a dozen other Rotary groups followed. Addresses before the Society for the Study of Religions, as well as the Forty-Four Club and several other business groups, are also reported. Of a July, 1939, engagement in "one of the swankiest restaurants in London," President Brown wrote to Mary: "These contacts are worthwhile as it gives one a chance to show them that the Mormons from the West are not a strange species of half-wits as some have thought."

The Forty-Four Club meeting produced an invitation to attend the club's banquet honoring Sir John Simon, the Chancellor of the Exchequer; Hugh and Zina attended this full-dress affair in November, 1938, and "thoroughly enjoyed being introduced to such society."

The one-time Canadian cowboy had already experienced that feeling at least once since coming to England. On November 9, 1937, Hugh was a guest at the Lord Mayor of London's banquet at which Prime Minister Neville Chamberlain was the speaker. By letter he described the evening to his children in America in minutest detail. The following comments are from that letter:

> I was made to feel very much at home; in fact, I think I should not have been surprised if someone had referred to me with the ancient and dignified title of "my lord." I was fortunate in that I spilt nothing on my waistcoat, I had a silencer on the soup, and by observing what others did I believe I used the proper tools at the proper time and I quite enjoyed my dinner even though my attention was constantly attracted by what was going on about me and by the gorgeous splendor of my surroundings. . . .
>
> . . . It was a sight ever to be remembered and as I emerged from the encasing caresses of my stiff shirt, white waistcoat, long tails and patent leather pumps, I came back to earth as a plain Mormon missionary in a foreign land, dazzled by the splendor of earthly things but thankful for the beauty of the inner life of those simple folk who know the language of sympathy for human suffering and are not deaf to the call of duty.

Another encounter with an Englishman of eminence occurred just before the war took Hugh Brown away from England. This member of Parliament, former jurist, prominent lawyer and author was first met on a golf course and then at a Rotary Club where Hugh spoke. At the close of the meeting the man asked President Brown if he would come to his home and tell about Salt Lake City and the Mormons. The upshot was a three-hour discussion which apparently brought the skeptical lawyer to the brink of conversion. Although he died, still unbaptized, before Hugh Brown returned to London in 1944, the distillation of that encounter became one of President Brown's most moving testimonial anecdotes, "The Profile of a Prophet."

But being president of the British Mission entailed much more than speaking to Rotary Clubs, attending formal dinners, listening to the Millennial Chorus, and watching his missionaries win athletic championships. There were numerous tasks to face each day and heavy responsibilities to bear constantly. Weekly missionary reports had to be read and evaluated. Statistical reports had to be made, finances had to be accounted for, correspondence had to be answered; the *Star* publication deadlines had to be met; the office force had to be trained and supervised; sermons had to be written, and interviews with Saints, investigators, and missionaries required hours of mental, physical, and spiritual energy. The lives of 150 young missionaries were "in his hands." President Brown had the responsibility of interviewing incoming missionaries, making judgments as to their abilities and needs, assigning them to fields of labor, inspiring them to do their best, counseling them when they became discouraged or homesick, caring for them when they became ill, and on occasion arranging for their memorial service when they died. His semiannual trips to hold district conferences throughout the mission were exhausting, time-consuming affairs. There is no doubt that he loved the contact with the missionaries, but being a father to "one hundred and fifty adopted sons and daughters" was a heavy burden. It became especially difficult if they became discouraged or unhappy, as they often did, or got into trouble, as young people occasionally do, or became ill or hurt. President and Sister Brown shouldered their triumphs with happiness and their sorrows with heavy hearts. They were abundantly loved by missionaries and local members alike.

Now and again they were able to take a brief diversion, usually in connection with official visits in the mission and occasionally outside of it. Examples were a tour of the Cunard Line's new *Queen Mary* and a motor trip through the English Lake Country and the Scottish Highlands, which included a round of golf in the country where the game was invented.

The 1938 mission presidents' conference at Copenhagen provided Hugh and Zina with an opportunity for sightseeing, with Berlin the focus of this short excursion, and a year later the June mission presidents' conference at Lucerne, Switzerland, provided the occasion for them to take a tour of parts of France, Switzerland, Germany, Hungary, Italy, and The Netherlands. The overhanging threat of war gave an urgency to the sight-

Hugh stands behind Zina (right) at mission presidents' conference. Front row center is European Mission President Richard R. Lyman, apostle, and his wife. Back row, third from left, is Thomas E. McKay, who in 1941 would become one of the first five Assistants to the Twelve.

seeing. More than tourist reporting is in these excerpts from the seventeen-page report which went to all the Brown children at the journey's end:

> After a short and hurried visit, we must move on from Rome, the Eternal City, the cradle of history, the city of irresistible fascination. . . . and as one goes out on the train, he wonders just what history is yet to be written there, for now there is on the throne a modern Caesar with visions of another great Roman empire. Time alone will tell whether he was wise to form an alliance with another dictator; while the interests of both are best served by their travelling together they'll be friends, but the lust for power, the ambition for dominion, the false creed of favored races. . . . will, if followed, prove their undoing. In the meantime, we hope they will not have endangered the civilization of our race.
>
> From Rome we went down to Naples. . . . and from there out to the old Pompeii. As one travels through these ruins, notes the evidences of a high civilization on one hand, and moral degradation on the other, one wonders if civilizations, like other growing things, bud, mature, flower, decline, fall and decay, because they fail to observe the laws which would result in their perpetuation. . . . One must go there to get the vision of the Ghost City upon which Vesuvius spewed the lava to hide her filth from the eyes of God.

Yet the faith and optimism of Hugh B. Brown prevailed over the brooding concern, and a theme which would be often repeated in later sermons concludes the report on an inspirational note:

> And thus concludes another of those trips which we shall long remember. Trips on which one is given to study, thought, meditation, in which one is humbled by the realization that great men have lived and died, great civilizations have flourished and perished, and back of all the Great Creator carries on with a plan so vast that these periods which are ages to us are to Him but passing moments.
>
> We come back after standing before the works of Michelangelo, Raphael, Da Vinci, and instinctively ask ourselves, "If these men created things that were to live longer than themselves, what shall we say of man — the finest work of God — does he live after death or is God's work temporary and unenduring? Unless the soul of man is immortal, unless he lives after death, then man is a greater creator

than the God who made him." Our experience seems to say in all instances, "The Creator is greater than the created." In the presence of these ruins someone whispered, "O why should the spirit of mortal be proud?"

By the time the Browns returned to London the decade of crises which would climax in World War II had almost run its course. The League of Nations and the World Court had become ineffective, disappointing the hopes of many like Hugh Brown who had advocated United States membership in both. Great Power diplomacy had also failed to check the aggressions of Germany, Italy and Japan, and the "peace in our time" proclaimed by Prime Minister Chamberlain after the Sudeten crisis of September 1938 had already been shattered by the Nazi occupation of Czechoslovakia. Among the items on the agenda when the mission presidents met with Elder Joseph Fielding Smith at Lucerne was contingency planning for a possible war.

As early as November 4, 1937, President Brown had written an editorial for the *Millennial Star* on "The Seeds of War." Recalling the signing of the World War I armistice nineteen years before, he condemned subsequent efforts to build national security on revenge, greed, avarice, selfishness, envy and hate. He appealed to religious groups to work for peace, saying, "In the soil of love the seeds of war must die."

When the Czech crisis saw the missionaries temporarily moved out of Germany, President Brown booked passage home for Zina and the children, "just in case." The Munich agreement between Hitler and the British and French heads of state defused the situation temporarily, and Hugh expressed the popular judgment of the time when he wrote reassuringly to his married daughter that Chamberlain was "magnificent in his heroic efforts to maintain peace." He had not yet received instructions from Salt Lake City on what to do in case of war, but he anticipated staying at his post if a conflict came. Six months later the Munich pact collapsed and Zina wrote to Mary: "We think it will not come to war this spring. But I really do feel we may not get to stay all of our last year. For war is surely on its way."

Following the European tour, efforts were made to carry on missionary work in England as usual, but events on the Continent soon changed everything. Hugh accepted an appointment to represent Brigham Young University at an international conference on genetics to be held in Edinburgh, Scotland, in late August, but he had just arrived when the Soviet-German nonaggression pact exploded into headlines. Chamberlain immediately assured Poland that Britain would support her in case of a German attack, and the countdown for war began.

President Brown returned to London on August 23 to find cablegrams from the First Presidency suggesting immediate evacuation of the lady missionaries and of his own family and planning for the possible evacuation of the elders later. Anticipating the need, Hugh had earlier arranged with the United States Lines, the firm which handled most of the Church transportation business, to hold one hundred berths to be called for as needed. Now, with thousands of Americans lining up to try to get out of England, the company agreed to honor its pledge. As seventeen lady missionaries gathered in London, packing went on at a frantic pace at 5 Gordon Square. On August 31, this first contingent of the British Mission's American staff headed for home on the S. S. *Manhattan*, Zina, Hugh C., Manley, and Carol being among them.

Upon the German invasion of Poland and the British and French declarations of war, President Brown implemented the second part of his instructions from Church headquarters. On September 3 the elders were requested to come to London, and by the sixth more than a hundred excited missionaries were in lodgings in southwest London, waiting for embarkation. According to the journal, "Meetings were held each day in the morning and afternoon at the Ravenslea Chapel, testimonies were borne, . . . and the spirit of activity, faith and loyalty was present on every hand." Final arrangements were made with the United States Lines, and 112 of the elders left on September 2 for Southampton and America, 26 with releases to return to their homes and the rest to be reassigned to other missions. Comparable evacuations were by then in progress from all of the European missions.

Hugh Brown was now left with a half-dozen senior missionaries to effect a reorganization of operating procedures and leadership in the British Mission. A first responsibility was to explain to the local Saints why they seemed to be abandoned in their time of need, and Hugh handled this task in an editorial in the September 14 issue of the *Star*:

> The decision of the General Authorities of the Church to withdraw the missionaries was reached after consultation with the governmental officials. In making the decision the welfare of the saints and of the Church in the British Isles was uppermost in the minds of the presiding brethren. . . .
>
> Britain, while ever a gracious host, concurs in the opinion of the American ambassador, that Americans could best serve the cause by returning home. As, under the circumstances, they could not render material assistance, their presence here would tend only to increase the difficulty. An understanding guest will always go home when there is illness or trouble in the household of his host.

When he wrote to Zina Lou on August 29, 1939, Hugh expected to stay in England for some time, possibly "for the duration." On the advice of British officials, who warned of air raid dangers, the mission headquarters was transferred in September from Gordon Square to "Ravenslea," the chapel at 149 Nightingale Lane. On October 3, President Brown noted that he had received word of his family's safe arrival in Salt Lake City. Zina had rented a place at 103 F Street, the boys and the youngest girls were in school, and the family was "all again united with one exception. I shall be with them again when the war is ended."

The little band at 149 Nightingale Lane went about their tasks as well as they could during those first war months. The number of missionary elders diminished in October as three completed their two-year assignments. Because the city of London was completely blacked out, night visiting was impractical, so study classes were held both mornings and evenings. In addition to the scriptures, some of Hugh Brown's favorite volumes of biography, religion, and philosophy were read in these classes, and the course of the war was followed on a large wall map.

Within a few weeks it became apparent that the war would not soon end and that it was radically limiting the scope of the work. A letter to Mary on December 6 reported that her father expected to be home by the following March. An acting mission presidency was shortly appointed with the approval of the First Presidency; Andre K. Anastasiou held the top position until President Brown came back to London more than four years later.

One of Hugh's final tasks was to write the editorial for the issue of the *Millennial Star* which wound up its hundredth year of publication. The conclusion of the December 28, 1939, message reads:

> For one hundred years, the elders of the Church have been active in the various countries of Europe proclaiming the truths of the Gospel. 1940 sees them withdrawn from practically the whole of Europe. . . . Let us with calm courage face the future in the knowledge that after the great scourges predicted in the scriptures, there is to be a sabbath of peace and righteousness, and that they who live the Gospel of Christ will reign with Him throughout the millennium. As we face 1940, let us take courage in the thought that we are one hundred years nearer the millennium than were the gifted and courageous souls who published the first volume of the *Star.*

The mission annual reports having been completed and a farewell social having given him and his companions opportunity to give their thanks and benediction to President Anastasiou and many London Saints, Hugh Brown flew to Paris on January 12, 1940. Three days later he and Thomas E. McKay, the retiring president of the Swiss-German Mission, boarded the *Manhattan* at Genoa, Italy, for the long voyage via the Straits of Gibraltar and the Azores to New York. The cross-country railway journey brought him to Salt Lake City on January 29, where a large crowd greeted him at the station, "including my family, former associates in church and business, and also the members of the Millennial Chorus."

So ended another chapter of Hugh B. Brown's variegated career. By statistical criteria, those stressful prewar years were not notable for growth in the British Mission. The number of convert baptisms declined from 174 in 1937 to 118 in 1938 and 72 in 1939. But increases in tithepaying and acceptance of leadership positions among the local members suggest a strengthening of the branches and districts, while the public image of the Church continued to improve. With Zina's invaluable support, Hugh was performing a significant work with unusual skill when circumstances beyond his control brought his mission to a halt. Again uprooted, he faced the challenge of making a livelihood for his family while he waited for the time when he might return to England to complete his work there.

11. LDS Servicemen's Coordinator

When Hugh B. Brown returned from England in February, 1940, he entered a period of economic stress and uncertainty about the future. He had the large Glendale home, to which the family moved in March, and he had his professional training as a lawyer, but he was not licensed to practice in California. For a year Hugh and Zina conducted what was hardly more than an improvised survival exercise until the expanding scope of the war created an unexpected and challenging opportunity. The call to be coordinator of religious activities among Mormon servicemen was propitious, though its cause was a worldwide tragedy.

The reunion with his wife and children thoroughly delighted Hugh. Whatever their circumstances, the Brown family enjoyed one another and found ways of making life happy and meaningful. As in other times of transition and adversity, Zina was a stalwart. In the midst of cleaning the house on Verdugo Vista Drive, she wrote to Mary: "This is the temporary deep valley of finance that all mission presidents experience," but "soon we'll be riding high." She mentioned having just picked a red rose for "Daddy's lapel." After Father's Day she reported to Zola that "of this world's goods we have very little, but we are rich in friends and love." The letter in which she expressed similar sentiments to Mary also noted that on their thirty-second anniversary her husband gave her four dozen rosebuds — one pink, one bronze, two red. (Hugh B. Brown was never inclined to let thrift stifle sentiment. In December, 1942, he received a "fat and unexpected check," so he purchased railroad tickets for LaJune and her two little girls to come home from Texas for a visit.)

No serious attempt was made during this period to revive a law practice in Utah from a Southern California base, although a "Brown and Clarke" letterhead with a Salt Lake City address documents a brief relationship with an associate from Alberta days, P. Drew Clarke, in 1941. (During Hugh's service at BYU a few years later, the firm of "Brown and Brown" would link him and his nephew, Emmett Brown, in another short legal partnership.)

Needing an immediate source of income in the spring of 1940, Hugh Brown became an agent for the Pasadena office of the Equitable Life Insurance Association. Less successful than he had been with "eternal life insurance" in England, he soon reestablished contact with his former Utah associate, Charles S. Merrill. On August 1 he was appointed general counsel and Ogden manager for Merrill Mortuaries. The retainer was less handsome than he had enjoyed a decade before, and the work was more humble. In his memoirs President Brown wrote: "I took charge of the Ogden mortuary, leaving my family in California. I stayed in a room where I cooked my meals and slept with the 'other dead people.'" He continued this work in Ogden through the winter, sending home rather sad-sounding letters. He was constantly on the watch for a better business opportunity.

This must have been an extremely difficult time, because Hugh Brown loved his family and certainly hoped to be doing something better at fifty-seven than "batching" in a funeral parlor eight hundred miles from home. It was hard for Zina, too. She wanted desperately to take her children back to Utah, but efforts to sell the Glendale property were unsuccessful and there was nothing to do but make the most of the fleeting family reunions and keep her family close through frequent and affectionate letters.

California and Utah members of the Brown clan were pleased when Hugh was invited to give a series of five talks in the Salt Lake Tabernacle in February and March, 1941. Under the title "Divine Prophecy and World Events," they appeared in the Church Section of the *Deseret News.* The purpose was "to give some of the reasons for the hope and assurance that Christ will come again to the earth." The talks reviewed secular and scriptural history to set the stage for the latter-day restoration of the Church and the apocalyptic events to follow. Appropriate to the mood of those days in which German power was approaching its peak in Europe and the people of the United States were agonizing over their own relationship to the war is the conclusion of the last address:

> I am persuaded that we stand on the very brink of the millennial reign of Christ, and because of that persuasion and the same spirit which prompted men of old to warn their hearers, I sound a note of warning and would that I could sound it through the earth: "Repent, O ye people, for the kingdom of God is at hand." (Hugh B. Brown, *Continuing the Quest* [Salt Lake City: Deseret Book Co., 1961], p. 407.)

Such activities as this and reviewing a Churchill biography in Salt Lake's Lion House not only brightened Hugh's lonely winter but also kept him in touch with Church leaders. They probably helped to make him available for an important calling — an opportunity to serve his Church and his country and to establish a more satisfactory, if not more settled, home life.

Although the United States did not officially enter World War II until December, 1941, President Roosevelt began providing a good deal of aid to England in 1940 to help her survive the terrific onslaught of Hitler's forces. It became apparent to many that it would not be long until America became a belligerent. Congress passed the Selective Service Act in September, 1940, and thereafter National Guard and Army Reserve units, as well as individuals, were called into active duty. Some of these units contained a number of LDS men. One of the first was the Arizona National Guard, whose chaplain was a Mormon. He wrote to the First Presidency concerning the need for some type of Church oversight of religious activities in the military services. It seemed apparent that an office or agent was needed to promote organization among the LDS servicemen so that they might remain faithful and active in the Church.

Many Latter-day Saint servicemen were also in military bases in the state of Washington. Sensing their need, the First Presidency instructed Northwestern States Mission President Nicholas G. Smith to form some sort of organization, and he established a committee of civilian, military and mission leaders. Their first meetings at Camp Murray on March 9, 1941, attracted gratifying attendance. They found on investigation that over one thousand Mormons were stationed in the area and that the number was expected to increase rapidly. Of course, it was hoped that these men would attend services in the local wards when possible, but it was anticipated that many would have difficulty in doing so for reasons involving duties or distance. To encourage on-base activities and give the men leadership, Church authorities requested that the army appoint an LDS chaplain for the region, and one was assigned.

It was at this time of need that the First Presidency (President Grant and his counselors, J. Reuben Clark, Jr., and David O. McKay) announced the appointment of Hugh B. Brown to be LDS Servicemen's Coordinator. The *Deseret News,* April 28, 1941, announced that Elder Brown would assume his duties on May 1. In his journal he described what followed:

> I began my work in the new field at once and returned to my home, which I will have as headquarters. I am to visit the various camps and try to take to the men some spiritual help. Also to advise the men in the camps and the local church officers in wards and branches near the camps that each is anxious to help keep the spirit of the Gospel alive during the emergency.

The May and June 1941 issues of the *Improvement Era* featured the appointment and recalled Major Brown's service in World War I. (Hugh used the army title frequently in connection with his coordinating assignment, probably to increase his acceptability among non-Mormon military personnel and possibly also to reinforce his feeling of involvement in the great conflict.) The *Era* also reported that he would work closely with California Mission President Henry H. Blood, a relationship which was doubly agreeable because of the earlier political ties between the two Democrats.

Hugh Brown made his first official visit to a military installation on May 18, 1941. Zina accompanied him to the camp at San Luis Obispo, as she often did thereafter when he was working within driving distance of Glendale. Later in the month Elders Albert E. Bowen and Harold B. Lee of the Council of the Twelve accompanied the coordinator to San Diego and held a series of meetings. They let the servicemen talk, bear testimonies, and make suggestions concerning the kinds of programs that would be most effectual in meeting their religious needs. One officer who attended predicted that this "was the beginning of a worldwide religious organization for LDS servicemen."

For three years thereafter, Hugh Brown's life was a series of journeys, from a few days to several weeks in duration. Most of his early work was in the Pacific Coast camps, but gradually it extended into other parts of the country where Mormon military people were found in numbers — chiefly the Mountain States, Midwest and Southwest. In June, 1941, he made his first call on the Chief of Chaplains in Washington, D.C., seeking to obtain "recognition in army camps" for himself and the Church which he represented. Periodic visits to army and navy headquarters subsequently sought to increase the number of LDS chaplains and to obviate the discrimination against LDS activities which existed in some local situations. (In 1929, by appointment from President Grant, Hugh had worked briefly with Senator Reed Smoot to obtain a special allotment for LDS chaplains, but the problem was still unresolved.)

The normal pattern of a visit to a military base was to call on the commanding officer and senior chaplain, orienting them if necessary concerning the peculiar LDS enthusiasm for meetings and fellowship activities. Such meetings would be held as time, facilities, regulations and the uniformed Mormon population would sustain — Mutual Improvement Association, leadership, testimony, and counseling sessions being fitted around Sunday sacrament services and occasional specially advertised public preaching services. Local civilian leaders of the Church often provided transportation and arranged introductions for Hugh and those who might be traveling with him. Off-base chapels were used for meetings when military facilities were unavailable. As the servicemen's program expanded, business meetings with Mormon chaplains and MIA group leaders also increased. (The ordained MIA group leader was in many respects the equivalent of the bishop or branch president, except that his calling accompanied him when he was transferred and he was authorized to initiate Church activities when none existed in his new unit.)

Illustrative of the coordinator's work was a return visit to San Luis Obispo on Sunday, July 20. Hugh was invited to speak to a large audience, the commander having designated this day as Utah day in honor of the approaching anniversary of the Mormon pioneers' entry into Salt Lake Valley. Hugh was in excellent form, giving a talk on the need for military strength and physical fitness and often using the term "thoroughbred." He still loved horses, and one of the highest compliments he could give a person was to use that designation. (He often spoke so of Zina — "She was a thoroughbred." And he once confided to Zola: "Mother does not like me to compare people with horses, but some horses could teach some people a lot.") Something of his spirit can be caught in this parable, which would be retold in many places:

> A story is told of the final test to which the Arabians put their colts when selecting young stallions with which to perpetuate and improve that splendid stock. The best physical specimens were trained, while still at their mother's side, to run to the tent of their master whenever they heard a certain bell. When these colts were two years old they were confined in a corral for three days without food or water. In the evening of the third day, hay and grain and water were placed outside the gate; the bell was sounded, the gate was opened and the young thoroughbreds allowed to choose between appetite and duty. Those which stopped for food or water were rejected as unfit. Those chosen as worthy sires of future generations were the ones which were not deterred by the pull of appetite when the bell of duty sounded. (Manuscript in possession of Mary Firmage.)

This was the element in which Hugh B. Brown functioned at his best, speaking to young men facing possible combat and knowing from his own experience the dangers and opportunities of military life. The illustrations from his own missionary and army life, the humor and favorite quotations, the scriptural citations and the testimony, were variously selected and arranged in the hundreds of meetings which followed. And as in England, the hazard of saying the same thing again too soon to the same audience was forestalled by noting in the journal the main themes and stories used. The central challenge, however, never varied much from what Hugh stated to that congregation:

> If you are called upon to fight, you will be equipped with machines and arms and tanks and planes equal to the best in any land. You will be invincible as you become expert with the use of these instruments in this great scientific age, provided, and always provided, that this new technique and knowledge . . . is in the hands of men of high personal ideals, excellent social attitudes and spiritual quality — men of honor, integrity, virtue — Christian men who in the realm of personal conduct are fighting a winning battle against the forces of sin and degradation. Leaven yourselves, young men. In your highest destiny, believe in the power of truth and virtue, and taste the joy of conquest over self. (*Ibid.*)

He finished his talk with a powerful blessing for these young men who were facing new and fearful responsibilities.

Another tour of the camps along the California coast brought him again to San Luis Obispo on December 7, 1941. In his taped memoirs President Brown recalls the impact of Pearl Harbor in this way:

> When we got word of this day which President Roosevelt declared to be a day of infamy, we knew that war would be declared immediately. . . . There was a strong feeling of despair. Many of the men were despondent because they knew we were not prepared to enter into a war with Japan and Germany. . . . My mission at this time was to bring hope and encouragement and faith to the men, most of them very young, who were serving in our forces. This I am glad to say was done to some extent, and whatever the extent, I give credit where credit was due, for I was inspired beyond myself as I talked to the men and related to them many incidents in my own life that had strengthened and inspired me.

A letter to Mary two days after Pearl Harbor described the situation in more optimistic terms. "Here in the 'war zone' we are all feeling fine and itching to get at the enemy," he wrote. (Thirty years later Hugh B. Brown would tour Japan and predict that a Japanese Latter-day Saint would one day be in the Quorum of the Twelve Apostles.)

Once the United States was at war, the drafting of men was accelerated and the reserve forces were called into active duty. In order to discover how many LDS men were in the services, the First Presidency sent a questionnaire to all bishops, branch presidents, and mission presidents in March, 1942, asking how many members had been inducted from each local Church unit, how many had volunteered, and how many were in the national guard and reserve units. On the basis of these returns, President McKay reported at the April Conference that 12,206 Church members were in the armed forces at that time. These were Hugh Brown's responsibility, and their number grew daily.

Zina Brown, meanwhile, was trying to make the best of her situation in Glendale. Her letters from 1940 to 1942 are full of frustrating efforts to sell the house on Verdugo Vista Drive and longings for her husband and Utah. "I don't think that I would recommend being a 'Church widow,' " she wrote Mary in October, 1941, but she hastened to add that she would not stand in the way of her husband's work, "for I know Daddy is one of God's prophets." The dominant tone is one of cheerfulness and helpfulness, as brief visits with the married daughters are reported and support is offered in facing life's problems and sorrows. Zina Lou's marriage to Gaurdello (Gar) Brown in September, 1941, followed by only a few months her brother Hugh's departure for England and the war. Early in 1942, Manley left home for civilian pilot training in Phoenix. The last few months in Glendale saw Zina, Margaret, and Carol as the welcoming committee when Hugh Brown came home.

Finally a buyer was found for the house at the bargain price of $12,000, and on October 16, 1942, Zina wrote to Mary: "Never was more thrilled in my life than now. We are coming 'HOME'!!!" A house at 1028 South 11th East had been already purchased for $9,300, and so it came to pass that Hugh Brown celebrated his fifty-ninth birthday with his family in Salt Lake City. For a year and a half this continued to be his home.

The coordinator's position provided only a family living allowance, plus travel expenses, but the assignment was flexible enough to permit Hugh to seek supplementary sources of income. The list of possibilities alluded to in the journal and correspondence is ingeniously broad, but only one of the paths pursued was substantially profitable. An occasional law case for Merrill or others is mentioned. A July 24, 1942, entry reads: "I arranged to take over control of Baldwin Co.," but this apparently speculative venture came to naught. Visits to Washington on military matters were often combined with calls on such prominent Mormons as Ezra Taft Benson and Ernest L. Wilkinson, and for a time during late 1941 possibilities for some kind of business connection in the nation's capital were actively explored. It might mean "big money and fine contacts," Hugh wrote to Mary in November, but "we have just about decided to forget the Washington proposition" because of a desire to "make Utah our permanent home." That Zina was a major factor in the decision is apparent from a letter she wrote at the same time:

> Well, honey, I'm not exactly thrilled about Washington, D.C. . . . I want to come to Utah and stay there as long as I live and never move again. This moving one's home is a bit tragic, I think. I want to be settled. Daddy and I feel the same way about another temporary move. And we both feel Washington would be just that. We, Daddy and I, feel the partnership offer is a real compliment . . . and a big thing might come of it. But we are older now and not so prone to leap into new ventures (thank goodness). Daddy was so sweet about it all. We have discussed it at length and prayed about it a lot. Neither of us feels that any immediate decision is proper. So we are staying here this year and may move to Utah or Wash. in early spring or next summer. We only want to be where we can serve best — our family and our Church.

Nothing came of the "Washington proposition," but events would several times more disappoint Zina's hope to settle down and "never move again." Further, though the years might have tempered Hugh's enthusiasm for leaping into "new ventures," the next ten years would witness that the quest for professional fulfilment had by no means been abandoned.

The profitable economic undertaking of this period is associated with a Los Angeles promoter, Elijah L. Pilling, who first appears in the journal in the summer of 1942. Although he is mentioned as a buyer of some of the Glendale home furniture and later as a partner with Hugh in an apparently inconsequential mining venture near Silverton, Colorado, Pilling's primary connection with the Browns in 1943 was in the development of off-shore oil properties at Long Beach. Hugh provided some legal assistance and apparently also recruited investors among relatives and LDS friends. On August 13 he recorded that he had "succeeded in getting an ordinance passed by the Long Beach City Council to allow drilling on the lease which I hold." After some difficult negotiations, on November 29 he "signed a contract with Jergins Oil Co. to take over the oil leases and drill the wells on a royalty basis." Zina flew to California with Manley for the occasion. In a letter to her daughters in Utah while the outcome was still in doubt, she voiced her anxiety: "Pray for him, girls! His success will mean the financial security of so many. For he will spend all he makes to help others, as you know." The royalty contract was later transferred to another company and has been a source of income, shared with the Brown children, down to the present.

While Hugh B. Brown was busy traveling all over the United States and Canada in 1941 and early 1942, he had an ever-present concern because his older son was with the Royal Air Force in the middle of the aerial warfare that was going on over the British Isles. After returning home from his mission, Hugh Card Brown felt that he had to go back and fight for England, so he joined the American Eagle Squadron of the RAF against the wishes and perhaps the premonition of his father. While he was still in training in California, his mother wrote to Mary: "I am praying that we may find 'a ram in the thicket' — that he will not be sacrificed." When Hugh C. left for England in July, 1941, she added: "Daddy felt Hugh's leaving terribly! He was so full of grief and yearning he just had to walk away from the group several times. He knows what it means so much better than we do who have seen no war. . . ."

Pilot Officer Brown went to England in a group of twenty-nine young men who had trained together in America. Death soon began to cut into the ranks of his companions, but this did

Father and son: Hugh B. and Hugh C.

not dampen the spirit reflected in a letter he wrote while on
leave in London:

> I can't tell you a thing about where I am or what I am doing,
> but I am not where I was, and I am enjoying flying different faster
> planes with more guns than heretofore. I have been in two crashes,
> but I am 100% jake now, and I love flying more than ever. No,
> I didn't participate in that battle you heard of on the radio; in
> fact, I have been in very little danger so far. I was on leave re-
> cently in London and stayed with the Anastasious and they treated
> me wonderfully.

In commenting on that letter, Hugh wrote to Mary: "He is
keeping his chin up so well and we are all proud of him. I am
glad that he writes as he does regarding Manley's wanting to go
over there. I think it will put any thought of it out of his head.
I hope so." Manley, now twenty, was already into flight training, but the course made him a civilian pilot and he served
America's war effort by flying transport planes across the North
Atlantic and in Southeast Asia. A later letter to Mary reveals
her father's continuing concern:

> We have had another letter from Hugh, and he seems to be in
> the thick of it now. Almost every day, we think of him and pray
> that he might be protected. He says that his only regret is that he
> didn't get there sooner. I feel that he wouldn't have been happy if
> he had not gone, but really I wish I were there instead of him. If
> I were running a war, I would take all the old men and keep the
> young ones at home. When old men are killed in battle, it just
> means that the natural processes are being helped along a little, but
> to see young men go whose life is hardly started, seems all wrong.

Tragically, the parents' worst fears were realized in March,
1942, when they received word that their son was missing in
action. The message was received by Zina in Glendale while
her husband was visiting camps in Montana; he learned about
it from Manley and Zola in Salt Lake City two days later. The
bereaved mother had thus to bear the burden of the notification
without the comfort of her strong and loving husband. The
communique ran as follows:

Dear Mr. Brown:

I would like to express my deepest sympathy with you and your family on your son being reported missing. Your son has been with the Squadron since October, 1941, and since that time has shown the utmost keenness, both in the air and on the ground. He was an extremely popular member of the squadron, and it is a great loss. On the morning of the 16th he was detailed for a low patrol over the North Sea with another pilot of this unit. Some seven miles after crossing the coast conditions became extremely hazy and your son's aircraft was lost in the haze at low altitude. Another pilot called to your son on the wireless repeatedly but could get no reply, and so he returned and reported the matter and the position where your son's aircraft was last seen. An intensive search was carried out both from the air and the sea but revealed nothing. It is presumed that in the hazy conditions your son's aircraft struck the sea and disappeared. I feel that there is very little hope of your son being alive and feel that it is best that you should know the true facts which I have given. His loss is very greatly felt by us all. The whole squadron and myself offer our profound sympathy to you and your family.

> Yours sincerely,
> E. H. Thomas, Squadron Leader.

The *American Outpost,* published in London, afterward noted that Hugh was the twenty-seventh fatality among the Americans who had trained together for the Eagle Squadron, and that the remaining two were killed in action prior to Hugh's memorial service in London. This obituary tribute concluded:

> Pilot Officer Hugh C. Brown of Glendale, Calif., came to Britain the first time, an unpaid missionary of the Mormon Church. He returned the second time, a fighter pilot "to help preserve the Christian cause." As long as there are such as he, his closing words will still hold true. *"With God's help we shall be free men always."*

The desolate father hastened to Los Angeles, where "there was a brave little mother to greet me with a smile and to show me how to be a real soldier." Flickering hope that Hugh C. might be found alive was finally abandoned when April brought another message from the squadron leader expressing certainty that the young pilot had been killed instantly in the crash into the North Sea on March 16, 1942.

*Pilot Officer Hugh C. Brown and his Hawker Hurricane
aircraft.*

Letters during these traumatic weeks suggest the blending of faith and sorrow with which Hugh and Zina responded to their loss. To his son's girl friend and other friends he wrote: "I have often quoted the words of King David at the time he lost his son Absalom, but I didn't know how poignant they were or how sincere he was when he said, 'Would God that I could have died for thee!'" To Mary he expressed this comfort:

If Hugh had been given a choice of exits I'm sure he would have taken this one. He was at the wheel of his plane on scout work, not fighting or trying to kill, but defending the British people whom he loved. He was in good health as his last letters show and he flew into eternity with the smile for which we'll all remember him.

He has had an unusually full life for one so young; always adventurous, he has now known the greatest adventure of all. . . . God be thanked for such a son, and brother, and pal.

In a letter to Zola, Zina used a rather interesting metaphor for a Mormon:

Daddy and I have counted the rosary of our greatest blessings. Our children are the beads and for each one we have said a prayer. We even kissed the cross for our noble son who is not lost to us, just gone on ahead. We love to talk about him. Daddy and I live again his years with us and thank our Heavenly Father that we had him so long. . . .

The memorials to young Hugh took many forms. On Mother's Day, according to one of Zina's letters, "Daddy got up before I did and filled the house with roses," massing buds of many colors around Hugh's picture. The practice of keeping one rose beside that picture was sustained for years thereafter. Both Zina and Hugh gave expression to their feelings in poetry, she writing "My Son Passes," he, "A Father's Salute to His Son."

MY SON PASSES

My hearth is cold. The gray ash of loss is sprinkled on my brow.
The sackcloth of lost dreams will not warm my leaden heart.
I sit numb with shock. 'Til by and by memory fans to feeble life
The coals that were so dead. 'Tis a baby's smile that flickers
Through those sodden coals — his first smile in my arms.
It reveals the torch of faith I had let fall.

On bended knee I grasp that torch and hold it once again
To my sleeping hearth. It wakes to life anew,
For I have added fuel of trust. Thus kneeling,
With prayer's sweet mantle securing me from doubt's assailing blast,
I feel my spirit warm within my breast. As I lift my head
To smile at Hope, the last ash of my despair slips from my brow
And is carried away by the gentle breeze of love
That wafts itself from other hearts to mine.

O magic breeze that whispers of that Creator love that holds
Its promise of eternal joys, whose embers ever glow — embers that
Burst into light and warmth. Higher and yet higher grows the flame,

Until that shaft of Holy Fire breaks through the veil of doubt's dark wall,
And I behold the portals of that home where death has dropped his mask.
I see the spirit born anew; earthly vestures fall away
And reveal the splendor of the new-born soul.

Symphonies of light and sound pour round me 'til my whole being vibrates
To that great harmony! Exultant I see my child, a child no more,
But come to man's estate and clothed in holy robes
On which his earth life left no stain.

O, Holy One, hear my song of praise; keep bright this vision
That my steps shall tread the beam that lights my way to thee;
Nor let me step aside until I too shall join the circle of Thy love,
Where dear ones gone before will take my hand.
May this my first born son be then my guide to one of Thy many mansions
Which he was called to make ready for his own.
Forgive the clouding doubt that one instant hid Thy face from mine.
With my face toward the light I shall walk by faith until my summons come.
Dear Father, through Thy Son I pray and praise Thy Holy name.
I humbly say, "Thy Will Be Done."

— Zina Card Brown

A FATHER'S SALUTE TO HIS SON

When you asked permission in Britain to serve,
 My memory leaped over time;
The fine steel of duty had touched a live nerve
 And it hurt — but I could not decline.

"To the Saints in the mission I wish to return,"
 You said, "My duty is there."
My warnings of danger I noticed you spurn.
 You replied: "Their danger I'll share."

First as an elder with a message of love,
 You went on an errand of peace;
And then as an Eagle defending the Dove,
 You have earned a double release.

From you to the mission — to us it's the best,
 A message of courage we send;
On the Altar of Freedom our love we attest,
 As you gave your life for your friends.

Christ said such action is love at its best;
 His sacrifice haloes our loss.
To follow the Master you met the great test,
 While humbly we bow at the cross.

I put on my uniform — tunic and cap,
   And salute you, O brave son of mine!
O'er the years that must follow, faith bridges the gap;
   Holy Father, not my will but thine.

— Hugh B. Brown

At a memorial service in the chapel at "Ravenslea" in South London on August 2, 1942, the latter verse tribute was read and President and Mrs. Anastasiou memorialized the fallen ex-missionary. In his note of thanks to the British Saints after the event, their former mission president expressed a hope which would be fulfilled perhaps sooner than he anticipated — "that we may again visit with you and see you all."

Hugh Brown continued his work as LDS Servicemen's Coordinator with an even deeper understanding of the feelings of the young men he was serving. He spent much time on the road, and the *Deseret News* and Church magazines periodically carried reports of his activities and those of the Mormons in uniform.

One such account dealt with a visit to a camp in Texas. He arrived one Sunday morning unannounced and called on the chaplain, a Baptist minister with broad views and sympathetic outlook. Asked if there were any Mormons in the camp, the chaplain replied, "Come with me; I think we can find some." They went to the chapel and found forty-eight young men assembled there, singing "Come, Come, Ye Saints." Five returned missionaries were on the front bench, one presiding and the other four officiating at the sacrament table. All of them were privates. At the close of the service the chaplain said, "I know of no other case where laymen of their own volition congregate and hold religious service without the guidance of some chaplain or church leader. It is a distinct tribute to your church and its organization and discipline to find such young men carrying on when they are so far from home."

A several-thousand-mile tour from San Diego to Spokane and back in August, 1942, with Elders Albert E. Bowen and Harold B. Lee as companions, produced this comment in one of Hugh's letters: "It gave these two men a good insight into the size of job I'm trying to do and I think will result in my getting some help." Two months later Hugh B. Brown was appointed to a committee for LDS servicemen, whose chairman was Elder Harold B. Lee and third member was President John H. Taylor, of the First Council of the Seventy. With Hugh as the executive officer, this body supervised all LDS activities in the United States armed forces. In August of the following year the first assistant coordinators were appointed by the First Presidency to serve part-time in areas where Mormon military personnel were most numerous. The seven men who received this calling while Hugh functioned as coordinator were J. Orval Ellsworth, Leo J. Muir, W. Aird McDonald, Willard L. Kimball, Harry Clark, John Longden, and Riley A. Gwinn.

By February, 1943, Hugh Brown had created a very effective organization for coordinating activities in behalf of the servicemen. From his headquarters in the Church Administration Building, 47 East South Temple, with the aid of a secretary he had built a file of more than seventeen thousand names of Latter-day Saints in uniform, together with the wards and branches they came from and their last known addresses. He anticipated that when the late-reporting Church units were heard from the file would grow to more than twenty thousand names. As fast as new addresses were learned, they were sent to presidents of stakes and missions with instructions to contact the members of the Church in nearby military units and to encourage them to organize MIA groups, conduct services and maintain Church standards. Most of the missions appointed military coordinators to expedite this work.

The Servicemen's Committee also developed special directories for LDS servicemen, giving maps and worldwide Church addresses. In addition the committee published a doctrinal volume, *Principles of the Gospel,* and the Book of Mormon in handy size for soldiers and sailors to carry. Often referred to as the Compendium, the small book of Church principles and procedures contained a preface written by Hugh B. Brown and titled, "Obedience Is the Law of Liberty." As seventy-five thousand of the two-volume sets ultimately found their way to the far corners of the earth, this compressed version of one of Hugh's favorite religious themes drew much favorable comment.

A non-LDS pharmacist at the Parris Island Marine Barracks wrote that "much trouble could be saved both for the young men themselves and for we older men who have to lead them if only a copy of that article could be placed in the hands of every youngster entering the Service."

Another persuasive and popular article written by the servicemen's coordinator is "To the Girls Behind the Men Behind the Guns." It speaks to the problem of sexual demoralization so prevalent in wartime, and particularly to the new temptations confronting young Mormon women. Described by a Protestant chaplain who requested five hundred copies as "very effectively written" and "commendably non-sectarian in its approach to a problem which is troubling all creeds," the tract includes these passages:

> In this world conflict the front lines are often "behind the lines." Civilians are playing a larger part than in any war in history. It is a war against the individual, where truth and error are locked in conflict, right opposed to wrong, good opposed to evil, Christ opposed to anti-Christ. The first and most important duty of every soldier is to "choose whom he will serve." You, young women, also must decide which side you are on and then you will have ample opportunity to prove your quality. . . .
>
> Remember, the days of chivalry are not over. Men still go into the joust with their "ladies' colors fastened to their lances," and they do their best to live up to what those ladies expect of them. These men want to feel as they go out to fight that there is something in the world that has not gone to pieces. Their thought of home, family, and the verities of life include you, the girl friend, the fiancée. They want to believe that there is still something sweet and clean and pure in the world. To them you symbolize the ideal. . . .
>
> Will you young women help to stem this avalanche which threatens to engulf the future homes of our country and wreck and destroy the pillars of our society? The old cry of Cain, the murderer, "I am not my brother's keeper," cannot apply to you who are the keeper of some other girl's brother. That other girl may be with your brother now. What would you have her do for him? Then apply the golden rule.
>
> You girls behind the men behind the guns form a line of defense which must not weaken. While that line holds, the front lines will remain impregnable. There must be no compromise, no going

over to the enemy, no lowering of standards — no traitors in this line. . . .

Yes, girls, you are called to serve, and when the war is over the heroines will be as numerous and entitled to as great credit as the heroes of the war. Your medal of honor may not be pinned on a uniform but it will be the highest honor won on life's battlefield — a clean, courageous heart. God Himself will reward your valor.

"Thoughts for the Service Men's Quiet Hour" is a series of three small tracts which Hugh Brown wrote during 1942. An employee in the coordinator's office later described them as "our most popular piece of literature. I think we distribute more of them to nonmember chaplains than we do to our own people." At least fifty thousand of each were printed by mid-1944. They are rich in anecdote and such metaphorical language as this:

He who does wrong knowingly, intentionally, is a traitor to himself and to the cause he represents. It is unthinkable that any United States service man would deliberately give the advantage to the enemy by surrendering his arms or carelessly walking into a booby trap. Unnecessarily exposing oneself to danger or being the victim of self-inflicted wounds is considered cowardly and is a punishable offense in all military organizations. . . .

So in life there is a cunning, wily enemy whose whole business is to prepare booby traps and lure men into them. He not only teaches the fool to say in his heart, "There is no God," but he beguiles him into thinking that evil is desirable and inevitable. Sin is the devil's booby trap, and no amount of bravado will change the sinner's status. He who deliberately walks into a booby trap is a booby.

Do not allow either desire for the bait, nor curiosity to know the mechanism, to lure you into any of his deadly traps, which often are cunningly camouflaged to deceive the unwary. And do not be deceived if what you have been taught to recognize as such a trap does not seem to spring at the first contact. Many of them are time bombs, but there are no duds in the armory of sin.

Some men are led to think that because the punishment is not immediate, the danger of sin has been exaggerated or avoided. We may be sure that all the devil's booby traps will explode eventually with deadly and undiscriminating effect.

Between his journeys Hugh Brown managed to deliver a half-dozen Sunday morning sermons in the Salt Lake Tabernacle. These early 1943 addresses and sundry reports of other activities appeared in the *Church News* and other LDS publications. The baccalaureate address at the University of Utah on June 6, 1943, was delivered by "Major Hugh B. Brown." Entitled "Disciplined Freedom," it was a stirring speech about the need to have religious influences in the military and in the nation if it is to survive. The language of the lawyer is used to effect in this excerpt:

> You must be informed if you are to appreciate the value of your heritage, and have the power to preserve it. As to this part of your inheritance, you receive a limited estate with no right of alienation. You are to hold it in trust for others.
>
> He who receives a life estate has definite obligations to those who are to take it after him. . . . You must not allow it to fall into the hands of strangers or to be sold to the highest bidder, or be risked on chance with gamblers. Just now we are defending it from attack by alien enemies who would destroy it utterly. In its defense millions of our fellow citizens are offering their lives. This emphasizes what it costs to make and preserve a great inheritance. . . .
>
> This concept of our source, relationship, and destiny, is the strongest possible incentive to high endeavor. It refutes the false philosophy of fatalism, that whimpering doctrine of inertia and defeat which assigns control of our lives to blind impersonal forces and robs man of his power and his dignity, and accomplishes his final degradation by relieving him of responsibility for his acts. . . .
>
> The blight of war is trying men's souls today in every land as it did our countrymen in other wars, and now as then if this nation or the world under God is to have a new birth of freedom it will come by reason of the determination of the people to live in the religious highlands where Lincoln lived and died. . . . We must have a firm belief that an overruling Providence is directing the affairs of nations. And though at times truth seems to be upon the scaffold and wrong upon the throne, we must never doubt that behind that scaffold God still keeps watch upon His own.

As the number of Mormons in uniform increased, Hugh B. Brown was instrumental in opening an LDS Servicemen's Center at the former Mission Home at 41 North State Street, Salt

Lake City. Here, where Mormon missionaries had received orientation training until the demands of the war reduced their numbers to a trickle, reading and writing rooms were available and parties were held regularly for military personnel who were stationed near the city or were passing through. A similar facility was established in San Diego.

The coordinator's office was moved to the new center in February, 1943. There the volume of correspondence, mailing, and file-building expanded, as the armed forces included more than forty-five thousand Church members by the end of the year. A small-size edition of the *Church News* was added to the literature which Mormon families were encouraged to send overseas. A variety of instructional and reporting forms for LDS military groups was developed as the sheer size of the program led inevitably to a degree of bureaucratization. Contacts with higher military officials increased, and at these Major Brown was very effective. He reported that the offices of Chief of Chaplains, both army and navy, were most helpful. "Chaplains of all denominations have shown a willingness to cooperate in our operation and to locate LDS men. They have assisted greatly in helping to organize them in the various camps," he noted.

Hugh and Zina Brown celebrated their thirty-fifth anniversary and sixtieth and fifty-fifth birthdays amid these busy 1943 scenes. To Mary, whom he had for years called "Dot" and whom he this time addressed as "My Dear ☉," he wrote on the occasion of one of her husband Ed Firmage's business trips: "Hope you will not have as much of this kind of widowhood as your mother has had." On another occasion he noted that he "spent much time — too much perhaps — in retrospective musing, enjoying the roses which are kept fresh by memory." But he did not slow down, and would not for at least thirty more years.

Hugh continued as servicemen's coordinator until March 4, 1944, when he was again appointed to be president of the British Mission. He continued to be a member of the Servicemen's Committee, with the field assignment as coordinator in England and Europe. Three months after his arrival in England the *Church News* announced the appointment of eleven regional coordinators and the addition of Elder Mark E. Petersen to the supervising committee (Harold B. Lee, John H. Taylor and Hugh B. Brown).

There is no doubt that Hugh B. Brown did a remarkable job as Servicemen's Coordinator. He had the ability to mingle freely with the young men in uniform. He also had effective speaking ability, a high degree of spirituality, and a good understanding of the military. He rendered one of his greatest services during this period of his life, despite the heartache which he and his wife experienced at the loss of their first son.

12. British Mission Again

The war which sent Hugh B. Brown home from England in 1940 took him back again four years later. The Battle for Britain had been narrowly won, the United States had entered the European war, and Pilot Officer Hugh C. Brown had been among the gallant host who paid the supreme price for turning the tide toward victory for the United Nations alliance. By 1944 thousands of Americans were in England preparing for the great assault on the Continent, and the Church leaders responded to the needs and opportunities which the new situation presented. Not surprisingly, they chose their servicemen's coordinator to be the instrument of their policy.

When President David O. McKay set apart Hugh B. Brown on March 4, 1944, it was for two callings — president of the British Mission and servicemen's coordinator for the European theater of war. Hugh left Salt Lake City the same day. To his journal he confided: "The parting with my wife and family was one of the most difficult I have ever had. We have been separated much during our married life. . . . God grant that we all may be protected and permitted to meet again." Yet he wrote to Mary soon after his arrival in London: "Although my coming at this time is a sacrifice to both mother and me, I feel that it is right that I should come both for the sake of the mission and boys in uniform." He did not expect to see Zina until the war was over, and only an unforeseen circumstance brought an earlier reunion.

The journey across the Atlantic was harrowing to endure and hilarious to recall. Having secured a visa from the British consulate in New York by bypassing the front office clerks and citing his American, Canadian, and military credentials to the man at the top, he was assigned to a Greek freighter, the *Hellas*. The seventeen-day voyage paired Hugh with the only other passenger, a cigar-smoking Dutch major, in a converted medicine-storage compartment which still smelled of ether and carbolic acid. One of the severest storms Hugh experienced in his many ocean crossings battered the sixty-two-vessel convoy for several days, and the combination of heaving seas and Greek cuisine inspired some of the most vivid passages in the long letter which went home to the Brown family and to the *Church News*. For example:

> . . . When we came aboard on a Coast Guard boat we had to climb a Jacob's ladder over the side and both of us nearly got a ducking, as the Coast Guard boat decided to back away just as we were reaching for the ladder. I dangled from the end of the swinging ladder, and my room mate was a few rungs up from me. I was grateful for the very good grip which I still have in my hands, acquired when I was a boy milking cows.
>
> The following day we sailed out into the ocean and I sought relief on the deck, which proved to be exactly 12 paces long and three feet wide. We ran immediately into a heavy sea, and I got relief o.k., but it was of the more strenuous kind — in reverse — so I came docilely back to the room and took my upper bunk, where I stayed for the next 48 hours, except for staggering excursions to the bathroom which is at the end of a dark passageway as far from our room as the size of the ship will allow. This bathroom — I call it that to be polite — is minus a tub and basin and towels and a light, so you may, by a little arithmetic, find the sum total of the fixtures.
>
> The reason I am in the top bunk is that my room mate, who is fat and bald with a ring of grey hair just above the upper layer of fat on his neck, said he thought I, being so much younger than he, would not mind climbing into the top berth. This seemed reasonable, so I humored the old man; and today I learned that he will be 56 next May [Hugh himself was sixty], so I'm glad I took pity

on the poor old thing. I got more of his free cigar smoke in the upper berth than I would if he were up there and I below, as the opening for ventilation is above my cot.

The weather has been better since the third day out, but just now we are in a heavy fog which necessitates the blowing of the fog horn every two minutes, and this has been going on for 24 hours. The skipper says it will probably lift in about three days. Our room is next to the radio room, and the noise from sending and receiving of messages is very similar to that made by nocturnal cats, only it never ceases day or night. . . .

When I look at the plates . . . at the table, I seem to be using my eyes as port holes through which the pit of my stomach minutely examines each item and its analysis is assisted by an acute sense of smell, and the proffered meal is rejected without further sampling.

. . . Well, this letter seems to be in lighter vein. I never felt so light in my life. In fact, I think I'll be transparent before I get to land again. . . .

The landing was at Milford Haven, Wales, on March 29, and the next day President Andre K. Anastasiou welcomed his successor to "Ravenslea," the mission headquarters in southwest London. Since Hugh had no family to settle and little baggage to unpack, he spent a couple of days taking care of police, ration board, and U.S. Embassy registrations and then plunged into his new but not unfamiliar duties. On April 1 he was in Bristol for the first district conference of his second mission presidency.

Despite the earnest efforts of President Anastasiou and his counselors, the mission had been beset by the same problems which affected all of the European missions during the years since the American missionaries and their leaders had left. War had reduced the ranks of the local priesthood, and lack of oversight from Church headquarters had made it easier for unorthodox ideas and procedures to take root. Factionalism and improper conduct had produced difficulties in some of the branches. Only a few converts had been made by local missionary efforts, and some of the six thousand members on the mission rolls had drifted into inactivity.

President Brown's first challenge, then, was to revitalize and reorganize the districts and branches. This he did with deliberation and tact. His first editorial, written for the May *Millennial Star,* thanked the acting presidency for their faithful service and for maintaining the mission in "a healthy and prosperous condition." The district and auxiliary conferences and the *Star* were his primary instruments of leadership; Millennial Choruses and athletic teams were not feasible as morale boosters and attention getters now. Less than a half-dozen lady missionaries comprised the full-time missionary force. In June the president of the Birmingham Branch, Norman Dunn, was called to be the mission secretary and his wife, Florence, shortly became mission Relief Society president. They were Hugh's chief helpers during the following months.

Highlights of the first weeks in England included a visit to the Sunderland district, where Hugh Card Brown had spent much time prior to his death. "Many of his friends gave incidents of his activities there," the journal relates, "and all testified of his loyalty and integrity and fine sportsmanship." After a Mother's Day program at Kidderminster, the mission leader baptized a young woman who had waited four years for the event. She had sought baptism in 1939 but as she was under age and lacked her father's consent, Hugh had asked her to wait and promised that he would, if possible, return and perform the ordinance for her.

MIA conventions were held on a regional basis because of travel limitations, and several successful meetings were held with U.S. servicemen as well as local members in attendance. The Lord Mayor and Lady Mayoress of Wigan attended a conference in the movie theater there; he made a welcoming speech and they were both "most gracious." The addresses by President Brown were always received with enthusiasm. According to his journal, "Everyone seems to feel that my returning is an answer to prayer and it makes me feel humble and grateful for the privilege of serving."

Correspondence and other writing took much of Hugh Brown's time; the journal and most of the letters for 1944 are typed or written by his own hand. The *Star* carried his editorials, reports, original poetry, and miscellaneous comments and quotations labeled "Browsings and Musings." Occasional pieces were sent to the *Deseret News* and the *Improvement Era*. Many letters passed to and from the Servicemen's Committee, where

Elder Harold B. Lee was now directly involved in the management.

Early in April, 1944, President Brown called upon the chief of U.S. chaplains and received a promise of help in obtaining permission to visit LDS servicemen in the military camps in England. Among the Mormons in uniform he soon found several who had served in the British Mission before the war. Lt. J. Allan Jensen, who was stationed in London until the war ended, was particularly helpful in untangling bureaucratic snarls. (Occasional meals in the officers' club in London were a "fringe benefit" of the coordinator's calling and a happy relief from austere British wartime fare.)

By June 23 Hugh could report to Elder Lee that he had held meetings in twenty-five different places, with attendances ranging from ten to two hundred. "It is a real thrill to go into a camp and find a group of our boys assembled in a mess tent eagerly awaiting my arrival, to hear them sing lustily, to have them participate as they do in the service," he wrote. As time went on he had more opportunities to administer to the sick and wounded. The task of locating and dedicating the graves of LDS dead was another part of his assignment.

A long letter in the *Church News,* June 17, 1944, gives an encouraging report on the condition of the LDS military personnel in England. Here are excerpts:

> While the men seemed to appreciate having someone come . . . to preside and to do some preaching, the really enthusiastic meetings are where all are invited to participate in the good old-fashioned testimony meeting. . . .
>
> . . . There is a quality, a fervor, a soul-melting earnestness about these boys who yesterday have looked into the face of death and who know that tomorrow they must again brave the flack and the enemy fighters, the soupy weather, and the Channel below. When they say: "I thank God for my blessings," you know they are not just repeating an expected phrase. When they relate powerful experiences of special danger and gratefully acknowledge the protecting power of Providence, the hearty "Amen" of their comrades bespeaks the understanding of fellow pilgrims.

Hugh B. Brown's skills as a counselor were as much in demand as his platform ability. Within a month his journal was referring to confidential conversations with some of the young soldiers "re their proposed marriages to girls, many of whom have known each other for very short times." The June letter to the *Church News* reflects his thinking on the subject. Problems of cultural adjustment after the war is over are sympathetically depicted, and parents and friends are encouraged to urge their servicemen to "wait for just a short time and the waiting will pay big dividends even if finally they decide to marry the new friend." But he hastened to add: "What I have said here does not in any way reflect on the character or quality of the girls over here. I'd give the same advice to English boys if they were over there and intended to bring American girls here to live."

One of the most widely retold of President Brown's faith-promoting anecdotes relates to this period in his long career. Anticipating a visit to a camp near Liverpool, he sent a telegram to the head chaplain advising that he would arrive the following morning at ten o'clock and would like to meet all the Mormon servicemen at that time. On arrival he was greeted by seventy-five men, all in uniform and ecstatic about seeing someone from home. The chaplain introduced himself and said: "I want to congratulate you on the fact that, though I did not receive your telegram until this morning, all but one of the Mormons serving in this camp are here. What method do you use to accomplish such unusual results?"

President Brown invited him to come to the meeting to discover for himself, and the chaplain gladly accepted. As the meeting opened, Hugh asked the men how many had been on missions — and fully 50 percent raised their hands. He then designated six of these to prepare and administer the sacrament and asked another six to be prepared to speak. He noticed that the chaplain showed amazement that young men could be called out of a military unit at random and be transformed suddenly into ministers of the gospel. Asked to propose a song, the group suggested "Come, Come, Ye Saints," and a call for volunteers found several who could lead the singing and play the portable organ. There were no song books, but all seemed to know all four verses of the traditional Mormon hymn. As the youthful chorus sang the last stanza, "And should we die before our journey's through, Happy day, all is well," the chaplain wept.

Following the hymn and the opening prayer, President Brown asked one of the young men who had prepared the sacrament to ask the blessing on the bread. Kneeling, he began, "O God, the Eternal Father," and then paused for a full minute before continuing the prayer. After the meeting President Brown found the young man and asked, "Son, is something troubling you?" He responded, "Why, sir?" "You seemed to have trouble giving the blessing on the bread," the older man noted. "Why did you pause so long?" The young pilot answered:

> Well sir, a few hours ago I was over France and Germany on a bombing mission. We had made our run, delivered our calling cards . . . , and we had gained altitude and were ready to turn back across the Channel to England when we ran into heavy flack. My tail assembly was almost shot away, one of my engines was out, several of my crew were wounded, and we were high in the air. I could not see any possibility of getting back to England or doing anything other than ditching in the Channel, or landing behind enemy lines.
>
> Brother Brown, I remembered at that moment what my mother had told me and what I had been taught in Primary, in Sunday School, in seminary and in other institutions of the Church; that is, that "if you're ever in trouble where men can't help you, call on God, and he will help you." Now this looked like an impossible situation, but I remembered what I had been told, and up there above the clouds I cried out, "Oh God, if possible sustain this ship until we can get to a landing spot in England." Brother Brown, he did just that, and when we landed out here and I heard about this meeting, I ran all the way to get here — I didn't even stop to change my battle dress. That's the reason that when I knelt at the sacrament table and named the name of God again I was smitten with the thought that I hadn't said "Thank you." So I paused and under my breath I expressed my gratitude to God for hearing my prayer and bringing us back in safety.

The service became a testimony meeting. After about two hours President Brown suggested that they had better end or they would miss their dinner, but they insisted that they "could eat army chow any time." So they stayed for another two hours, and the chaplain stayed with them. When all had borne testimony and the meeting had been closed, the chaplain acknowledged to President Brown with deep feeling: "Sir, I have been a minister of the gospel for twenty-one years, but this has been the most unusual and inspiring event in my ministry. I have never witnessed anything like this in my life."

Messages which had proved effective in the United States were often used in England. Those attending an LDS service at Northampton heard the need for character stressed through the familiar parable of the Arabian horses. The experiences of World War I were particularly appropriate now, and the "currant bush" and the "unsentimental cuss" were many times recalled. That the experiences were stimulating to the coordinator as well as to those whom he served is clear. Despite homesickness and the occasional infirmities of sixty-one years, Hugh wrote to Elder Lee in September, 1944: "I'd really like to follow the troops into the Pacific after we get the Germans written off." Within days after the Allied landings in Normandy, he began working for permission to visit the Mormons on the Continent. Though this opportunity did not come for a year, correspondence from Elder Lee and others in the coordinator's office in Utah noted that Hugh B. Brown's writings were going into every war zone in the mail and baggage of Latter-day Saint soldiers, sailors, and airmen.

Less than two weeks after D-Day, the war came to Hugh Brown in the form of the V-1 flying bombs which began raining on London. The mission office was slightly damaged in one of the very first raids; between June 19 and July 1 the neighborhood experienced mounting devastation, with many injuries and fatalities. President Brown's journal gives poignant descriptions of those days when he and Norman Dunn carried on as the building on Nightingale Lane gradually became uninhabitable. A few excerpts will illustrate both the mission president's predicament and the way he responded to it:

> I again witness the rather eerie scene of flying bombs at night and with the terrible roar of the engine what seems to be a flying ball of fire strikes terror to one's heart as it seems to be headed directly toward the observer. . . . One woman who cringed as one went over her said, "Blimey, I'm glad he wound that one up a bit more." A sense of humor is really a saving grace in these circumstances. Perhaps such a sense was responsible for my starting to hum one of our hymns as I lay flat on my tummy waiting for a bomb to miss me. The

first lines of one of the verses are "When the earth begins to tremble, bid our fearful thoughts be still."

. . . There is no way of judging where they will light, as some of them dive immediately when their engines cut out and others glide for some distance before diving. . . . One wonders what he should wish or pray for. If he asks that it go over him he is suggesting that someone else be on the receiving end. In other words, is it a Christian prayer to say "let is miss me, Lord, and hit my neighbor"? I am advising all of our people to evacuate if possible and at least to send their womenfolk and children out of the city until it is over. That seems to me to be the practical thing to do rather than to doggedly "stick it," as the people here say, and ask God to save us. Sometimes it is a good thing to get out of danger even while you pray.

Now that I have said that I suppose some will wonder at my staying here in the mission home. . . . Well, just for the record, I feel that for me to go while there are saints here who cannot go would be to let them down just when they need all the moral support they can get. Many of them have expressed the faith that as long as I am in this building it will not be destroyed. Others say that this building, having been dedicated, will never be hit. For me to leave would, I fear, test the faith of some of them and cause them to question my faith. Also there is considerable church property here which should be protected. . . . I am not a bit brave but I do feel the responsibility and like the captain of a ship feel that I should be the last to leave. . . . I have really never felt that I am in danger of losing my life and therefore have not felt any fear. If I do think one is going to hit me I'll be as scared as anyone.

I think the main reason a man of my age, with his future largely behind him, does not wish to die is that he thinks there is still someone who needs him and for whom he is responsible. When one is no longer needed he should die or get some work by which he can pass on something worthwhile to those who come after him. I have looked upon several dead people today who yesterday at this time were as unmindful of their fate as we are tonight and have thought after all that is not such a bad way to go. . . .

We sent one thousand bombers over Berlin last night and dropped thousands of tons of bombs on that city. What must the Master think of CHRISTIANS who are so completely dominated by Satan that they use the inventions which have given them so much power to cause death and misery to one another. Hate is mounting everywhere and one wonders what kind of peace can follow in the wake of so much savagery. About the only Christian principle we seem to follow while bombing is the one which says "it is better to give than to receive."

At work in the British Mission office.

In the midst of this horror, Hugh Brown wrote an editorial for the August *Millennial Star*. Entitled "Justice Without Vengeance," it took issue with "those who advocate reprisals and attempt to whip up primitive impulses . . . , calling for an eye for an eye, or, if possible two eyes or four." While acknowledging the need to punish "the criminals who have caused so much misery," it emphasized that "corrections and punishments, if they are to be salutary, must be void of vengeance, made and administered without rancor, malice, or hatred." The standard proposed is Lincoln's "charity for all . . . , malice toward none."

By July 1, 1944, "Ravenslea" had been made uninhabitable by repeated bomb concussions, and the decision was reluctantly made to move the mission headquarters to Birmingham. The chapel at 23 Booth Street, Handsworth, was President Brown's base for the balance of the year. The facilities were cramped and the heated bathroom became a multi-purpose room when the temperature elsewhere in the building dropped. But morale remained high in the little missionary band, and the pattern of activities did not drastically change. As the Allied armies began to roll toward Germany the mood in England brightened. The theme of the annual conference of the priesthood and auxiliary organizations at Birmingham on August 7 was "The Morning Breaks." The poem "Autumn," a Hugh Brown contribution in the October *Star*, ignores the war and evokes the cycle of the seasons to dramatize the challenges of mortality and eternity:

AUTUMN

Did you ever wander through the countryside of England in
    September,
Where the beauty of the colorings, ripened grain and heavy dew
Warn that summertime is merging into crisper days of Autumn,
While just offstage stands winter, waiting for his chilly cue?

Have you felt a wordless longing for the scented early blossoms,
And the beauty of the springtime with its fleeting days of youth?
Have you almost wished for "static" time requiring no adjustments
And resented Nature's "move along and go in search of truth"?

While there's beauty in the blossoms quite apart from fruits to
  follow,
It's beauty that's prophetic of a harvest day.
For if spring were made eternal, there would never be a harvest;
If all the days were planting days, all nature would decay.

Let's be grateful for the seasons with their trials and contribution,
For the sternness of December and the tenderness of June;
Drab indeed would be existence if God's pictures were not moving—
We even welcome sunset just to see the harvest moon.

Those of us who know the pathos of the leaf when "sere and
  yellow,"
We who, in life's garden, feel that frost is in the air,
Often think of early springtime and look back instead of forward,
As the coming of life's winter brings its whiteness to our hair.

There's no turning back to harbor once we've launched upon the
  voyage;
We must sail with dauntless courage and with faith to chart the
  way.
We'll be judged, not by the speed with which we travel,
But by the cargo we've collected from the ports along the way.

There's no landing port triumphant for the ship that stays in
  harbor.
It must sail, and in its sailing ne'er look back from whence it came;
Nature's bugle call sounds "forward," there's no glory in retreating;
Life calls for stamina and courage, and asks only, "Were you
  game?"

There's no calm upon life's ocean, where no engine throb is needed,
Where the sails may all be folded and vigilance suspended;
There's adventure on the journey from home port to port of land,
And then another journey will begin when this is ended.

Yes, there's need for spring and summer, for autumn and for
  winter,
Both in the seasons of the year and in the life of man;
But spring should think of autumn as it plants the future harvest,
For autumn crops depend upon the way the spring began.

And just as in the seasons, springtime always follows winter,
So the twilight of life's evening is the harbinger of morn;
And in the resurrection we'll be thankful for the voyage,
And for the testing of our timber since the day that we were born.

—Hugh B. Brown

There were many moments of loneliness as Hugh Brown faced the rigors of war and English weather thousands of miles from his family. "Guess I'm too old to be away from my mama," he wrote to Mary in April. Manley (recently married to Grace Bowns and based in New York) flew into Scotland occasionally on Air Transport Command missions, and the telephone chats with his father were welcome contacts with home. Zina's frequent letters kept her husband informed of the activities of children and grandchildren and assured him of her love; his letters to all of them have been treasured through the years. To Mary he sent this encouraging report on his health:

> My skin is clear and my hair is curly and I walk two hours per day regularly and sleep like a baby, so when you see mother tell her to stop worrying about my reduced waist line as that is the best thing which has happened, and many a man and woman, who could take a shower bath without getting their knees wet would envy me my streamlined torso.

Another letter contains this wistful comment, which is better psychology than prophecy:

> Think when this mission is over I'll just take one big holiday for the balance of my time on earth and sort of glide into port with the engines turned off while I listen for the "Pilot's" voice as He guides me to a landing. I begin to realize that the air in which I now fly at "60 altitude" is lighter than it was at other levels and therefore has less lifting power. But up here there are not so many cross currents, it is less hazy and one seems to fly with less effort. This I suppose because one has stopped trying to climb or do stunts and can take time to enjoy the scenery and his companions — if any — and is less concerned with the style or make of plane in which he sails than in making port without a crack-up.

President Brown was temporarily grounded at the end of 1944 when his old nemesis, tic douloureux, attacked relentlessly. He was first afflicted at Merthyr Tydfil, in Wales, while conducting a conference on December 2. He completed the assignment with difficulty and then returned to London for medical help. For the balance of the month he sought admission to a British military hospital for surgery, finally gaining the necessary clearance with the help of Lt. Jensen and U.S. Ambassador John

Winant (whose wife was also a tic sufferer). A doleful holiday was spent in pain, only Christmas dinner with the solicitous Dunns interrupting the loneliness.

No more remarkable document exists among the voluminous papers of President Hugh B. Brown than the one he enclosed in a letter to his family as he sat alone in the flat in Birmingham on Christmas Eve. The three-page essay (typewritten, single-spaced) is titled: "An Unprofessional Analysis of 'Tic Douloureux' by a Surviving Victim." The letter confesses that "the thing is not really as bad as this description paints it but I'll be glad to say goodbye to it forever." Here are excerpts:

> One is subjected to various kinds of attack, individual, in pairs, fours, groups and battalions. Each imp is armed with special and different instruments of torture and each vies with the others to see which can inflict the most exquisite pain and keep the victim conscious. All the nerves of the side of the head and face seem to be fully charged with electric wires which can be turned on one at a time or all together according to the whim of the head imp. . . .
>
> Now a new device is tried. This little fellow is equipped with a grappling hook made of needles which are kept quite hot and are attached to an electric cord for super-shock. . . .
>
> This little fellow thinks the others were all too humane . . . so he undertakes to put on a show which will win a decoration. . . . His instruments seem like trip-hammers with the power of a pile driver, the speed of a machine gun and the point of a needle. . . .
>
> The boss imp himself takes on the next spasm as though to show the others up. . . . He sets a slow but intense fire inside this big nerve and heats it to boiling, then shoots small jets of steam into each little nerve separately until they all sing out in unison . . . and each imp takes up the chorus. . . . But the Big Boy is not to be outdone. He carries on with the big nerve, convulsing, exploding, tearing apart, pulverizing, pounding with terrific sledgehammer blows, drawing each separate nerve like the string of a bow and releasing it to quiver back into the cable against the others. . . .
>
> So this, a gross understatement, will give you some idea of what the TIC is like. It is inflicted only on those whose pre-existent wickedness was such as to warrant punishment beyond anything which justice could demand for any sin of which a mortal could be guilty. Think what I must have done to merit eighteen years of it. And now for three weeks I've had to wait for a hospital bed and one more week to go and then out comes the nerve and we live happily ever after.

> I sought the relief promised by the use of the ether which was to be inhaled. The instructions on the bottle said "a few drops on gauze to be inhaled when in pain." Thinking if a few drops would help, a few more would be better, and knowing of the natural reserve of the English, I took the stopper out and saturated the gauze and put it to my nose and mouth and shortly went to sleep. . . . When I told the lady of the house who makes my bed of how I had secured a little sleep she looked horrified and the next time I reached for the bottle of ether it was missing. . . . But anyhow I shall insist in the future when I have operations that I am an experienced anesthetist and thus save one fee.

By now the First Presidency had advised him to come home for treatment, and when the British operation was postponed again he secured an Army air priority and flew from Prestwick, Scotland, to Utah. His two Zinas, Mary, Margaret, Carol, and other kin were there to welcome him, and "it was a great reunion." After an administration by Elder Harold B. Lee and Drew Clarke, Hugh was operated on at the LDS hospital in Salt Lake City on January 17, 1945. Scar tissue from years of pain-dulling alcohol injections complicated the surgical procedure for Dr. Reed Harrow, but the afflicted nerve was finally severed and the tic was relieved. After ten days' hospitalization Hugh returned to his home where, according to his journal, "I had the loving attention of my wife and family and I recovered rapidly."

Despite his announced intentions, Hugh did not return to Europe for several months. Zina wrote to the British Saints that his first conscious expression after the surgery was: "Now I can soon return to England to finish my mission — I want to go back." President Brown confirmed this desire in a letter written while still in the hospital, and he also addressed himself to the concerns of those prayerful men and women who may have wondered "why He didn't heal me and allow me to remain at my post":

> I think always we should pray with the feeling that we do not know really what is best for us; that He does know, and that we should express the desire that He do for us what is best. . . .
> There is no question in my mind but what I could have been healed, but I am convinced the Lord had a purpose in the program

which, it seemed, inevitably had to be followed. I make this explanatory statement that none of you may feel that you, or any of us, lacked faith, or that the Lord was not willing to hear our prayers. He certainly did hear, and has answered in His own way, and His way, as always, has proved to be right.

Assignments for the Servicemen's Committee detained Hugh in America until May. While in the East he visited with Manley and Grace, who were then expecting their first child. The birth of the "fine baby boy" is noted in the journal. "This is the first of our grandchildren to bear the Brown name and we are grateful for him." The purchase of buildings for servicemen's centers in Marysville and Oakland took him to California, and at San Diego he addressed two large audiences of military personnel. Zina was with him in Southern California and a happy week was spent with Zola's family and other relatives and friends.

V-E Day ended the war in Europe on May 8, 1945, and two days later Hugh entrained for England. This time Zina, Margaret, and Carol were to follow as soon as schools were out and travel arrangements could be made, so the farewells were less anxious and sorrowful. The journey from New York to Ireland was by well-appointed seaplane, with sleeping accommodations, and the trip was reported to Zina in fascinating detail. Always delighted to be in the company of notables, President Brown wrote a vivid description of the appearance and bearing of one of the other passengers, the Baroness de Rothschild:

> I learned that the charming lady who shared the seat with me was the Baroness de Rothschild. We hit it off as well as though she had been a farmer girl from the next quarter section in Alberta. While we were in the British "Caribou Club" in Newfoundland I sat at a table writing letters and she came and sat opposite and wrote several long cables, and it was there that I studied her appearance for the curiosity of the girls.
>
> I really had a good chance to gaze without detection. While I wrote I used my eyebrows for a screen through which to peer without rudeness and this is part of what I saw. On the third finger left there was the grand-daddy of all the diamonds set in wonderful gold mountings. The broach was set with various stones of obvious quality and on the right wrist was a watch of the most exquisite and curious workmanship, especially designed and hand

made. The "hair do" was distinctive and set off with some jeweled
combs which were dazzling. She was dressed in a traveling suit of fine
grey with a black hand-bag and in every move and word and action
there was evidence of culture, refinement and breeding.

I have gone into this much detail only to please the girls and
to suggest to them that they can be just as lovely without the money
it took to make her seem so charming. In fact each of them has
more to start with than she had, as nature has been more kind to
them than to her. But somehow one sensed a refinement of spirit
which after all needs no outward adornment to make the soul beautiful. I learned part of the secret of this as I talked with her and
learned that she had been exiled and separated from her husband
for five years. She has two children, six and eight, and says they
together have suffered much during the war years as the Daddy was
in a German concentration camp. . . .

President Brown reached London on May 22, to find that
"Ravenslea" had been repaired and reopened. He found too
that the mood of the people was vastly changed, as he expressed
in that same letter home three days after his arrival:

I have just come in from a walk through the Wandsworth
Common where I used to walk last year, and it is really wonderful
to feel the difference in the very atmosphere. There is a spirit
everywhere of good cheer and the kind of happiness which is known
only to those who have suffered much and lived in fear, who have
known dread and sleepless apprehension and are then released,
freed, liberated and made to feel that all is well.

It was raining yesterday and the clouds were heavy, but today
the sun is out, the skies are clear, the birds are singing and all seems
well with the world. The traditional reserve of the British is still
in evidence but there is a quiet "shining through" of the spirit
which betrays a wealth of emotion, a depth of gladness the studied
restraint of which is almost tragic. I think it would do the whole
nation good if the people would just break through the restraining
dykes which have held back the flood through the centuries and
allow the parched social fields to be flooded and refreshed.

Hugh now plunged into the business of consolidating and
reorganizing branches, holding district conferences and a servicemen's convention, acquiring and disposing of property, and
preparing for a visit to the Continent. News of the death of his
old and dear friend Heber J. Grant had reached him en route to
Europe, and the contributions of the late Church President were

the theme of many of his addresses during this period. A letter
to Zola cheerfully asserted that the "operation on my head seems
to have released something which was holding me back and
now I seem to be able to really get things done." But he mentioned how much he missed his wife. "I have been thinking of
her a lot this month which is our month of roses and of memories.
Hope we will not spend another June apart." This hope would
be fulfilled; they would yet be often separated but the remaining
twenty-nine of their sixty-six anniversaries would be celebrated
together.

The long-awaited visit to the Continent brought Hugh B.
Brown into his first contact with many hundreds of Mormons,
including one of the authors of this book. It began with a
flight to Paris on July 20 and a stay at the Hotel Terras, where
"American food with the flavor which only French cooks could
give" merited special mention in the journal. A ballet at the
Paris Opera and a servicemen's field day in the Bois de Boulogne
were followed by a conference in the Hotel Louvois. Three
hundred and fifty persons, including Chaplain Eugene E. Campbell, attended the public meeting, the largest LDS meeting that
had ever been held in the French capital.

The circuit through Basel, Lausanne, Geneva, Bern, Lucerne, Zurich, and back to Basel in company with Swiss Mission President Max Zimmer almost took on the aspect of a
triumphal tour. The enthusiasm with which the local Latter-
day Saints welcomed a spokesman from Church headquarters
after five years of separation is typified by the meeting at Bern.
The journal describes it thus:

> At the opening of the meeting three little Swiss children, a
> boy and two girls, in native costume came onto the stand and sang
> a Swiss song and then presented me with flowers and presents to
> which purchase the saints had made contribution. Some Gleaner
> Girls sang a welcome song in English and then I spoke to them
> through an interpreter and they drank like thirsty men on a desert.

After a suffocating return to France in an overcrowded
train compartment, Hugh toured the battlefields between
Rheims and Liege and met with Church members, military and
civilian, in both cities. Then he was off to Marseilles, where

arrrangements had been made for a conference of servicemen. Arriving ahead of schedule, he was forced to improvise arrangements for a night's lodgings, and his experience at the "Wagon Lits Hotel" — a French Pullman car on a siding in the railroad yard — is colorfully described in his journal. A servicemen's outing the next day, with lemonade, ice cream, and "real American dough-nuts" revived his spirits.

The series of meetings in the Marseilles area on August 5 must have been unique in the annals of the U.S. armed forces. President Brown addressed five audiences in thirteen hours, traveling by jeep from one location to another with a small entourage of LDS chaplains and MIA group leaders. Three of the gatherings were interdenominational and two were LDS sacrament and testimony meetings, described as "very enthusiastic."

Waiting for Hugh in London were Zina, Margaret and Carol. They had arrived by air the day before his return, eager to hear his report and to play an active part in the remaining portion of his mission presidency. Hugh's reactions are recorded in his journal:

> My own joy upon their arrival can be assumed by the fact that for nearly eight years we have been separated more than we have been together. We now hopefully look forward to an era of teamwork, with mother, as usual, in the furrow. (To those who were not raised on a farm as I was I should explain that the 'furrow horse' is the one which walks in the furrow when plowing, and the one which keeps the rest of the team, two or many, true to the course marked out by the Gardener.)

Margaret was called to serve as a missionary in the office, handling *Millennial Star* circulation. Carol went to school and established a place in the teen-age set; she could not understand why some of the English in this pre-Beatles era disliked "jiving." Zina moved back quickly into the role of "mission mother," an assignment which expanded in scope as the number of missionaries from England and America gradually increased. She traveled with her husband to most of the conferences, and she confided to Mary that she was often homesick but always "very proper" in her relations with the British Saints. Enduring friendships were formed with several English elders and lady missionaries, some of whom later emigrated to the United States.

In October the Church purchased "Valerian," a house on Ravenslea Road, and the Browns moved from their lodgings in the nearby mission headquarters on Nightingale Lane. It was a cozier accommodation as the cold English winter approached. On the eve of the move Hugh celebrated his sixty-second birthday, noting, "I am growing older but life seems to have more interest for me than at any time before, and for this I am grateful." At Christmas the festivities were shared with several servicemen, and by a long, thoughtful letter with the children in America. "Too much turkey has made many philosophers," Hugh wrote, "a sort of turn-about process where first the turkey is stuffed with sage and then the sage is stuffed with turkey." He added, "Mother has come through as usual after carrying the main burden, but she does too much and does not realize that having a grand-dad for a husband usually means one is getting older. . . . We're very happy together and were never so completely in love. . . ."

Long before the war ended, Hugh Brown had become concerned with the problems of adjustment which American military personnel would confront as they returned to civilian life. He wrote to Elder Harold B. Lee on August 16, 1944: "As I see it, the most devastating and far-reaching of all the effects of war has to do with its effect upon the souls of these men, upon their thinking, their ideals, and upon their willingness to be led." An article in the *Relief Society Magazine* of September, 1943, "To the Parents of Servicemen," urged families to keep in close contact with their members in uniform. "They must know — and you must tell them — that they are trusted. . . . They will spread their wings to the lifting power of your faith in them." A letter from London appeared in the *Improvement Era*, December, 1944, under the title, "To the Veterans of World War II." Tapping his experience after World War I, Hugh invited the prospective new crop of veterans to share what he had learned:

Do you remember how when the first thrill of our newly found
freedom was over, it dawned upon us that we were still subject to
discipline. . . , that we had not, and could not, escape from the
necessity to obey. . . .

How gradually we came to realize that the law of cause and effect
was still in operation, and that we would reap as and what we had
sowed. . . . That from our homecoming to the end of life we should
need to devote ourselves to the work of reconstruction and that with
self-imposed discipline we would strive to be worthy of the country
and the freedom for which we fought. . . .

"An Old Veteran Speaks" is an editorial from the July,
1945, *Millennial Star* which speaks to the expectations of the
men then coming out in thousands from the victorious armies.
Among other things, it said, they wanted release from routine
and regimentation, a chance to finish their education, and freedom within the law to think and speak without fear. They
wanted "a world in which beauty has real value" and "a world
brotherhood where their children and their children's children
may live in peace." The editorial by President Brown concludes:

They want a little of the earth's surface which they may call
their own, upon which they may stamp the imprint of a coat-of-arms
which they themselves have fashioned, a little home to which they
may retire for the enjoyment of family life, a few good books, some
music, and a radio. A place where they may shut out or bring in the
outside world at will and where at night they may draw the curtains
and invite the Prince of Peace to bring his benediction to a Christian
family in a Christian country in a world where the principles of the
Prince of Peace have replaced the mad attempts of would-be dictators
to rule the world!

And thus do old men dream dreams while they pray the young
men may see visions. (*Continuing the Quest,* pp. 427-431.)

The month before that, President Brown was less optimistic
in the first *Star* editorial he wrote after returning to England.
Noting scriptural prophecies concerning the last days, he continued: "We doubt if we are justified in believing that this is
the last or final war, that universal peace has come to stay. . . . "
Yet he sustained the same hopes for international law and cooperation that he had expressed before the war, and he attended
some of the meetings of the new United Nations Organization

in London in January and February, 1946. (His appointment as a delegate for the National Order of Women Legislators was arranged by a Utah friend.) His editorial in the February *Star,* "The Birth of the United Nations," acknowledges the concerns which some critics were expressing about the possible surrender of national sovereignty. "But if the object of that surrender is to secure and protect and guarantee the continued life of that nation without the ruinous and tragic cost of recurring wars, then will the arrangement be seen as an investment and not a sacrifice."

Pursuant to a letter from the newly reorganized First Presidency (George Albert Smith, J. Reuben Clark, Jr., and David O. McKay), the head of the British Mission wrote an editorial for the October, 1945, *Star* entitled "Church Policy on Emigrating." The letter declared that "missionaries should not hold out inducements to the Saints to gather to Zion on the score of bettering their material interests. . . ." The editorial called for willing acceptance of the counsel to build up the Church in Great Britain, with the promise that "whether or not we are permitted to gather to Zion we shall have earned the blessed privilege of eternal association with the Saints. . . ."

In February, 1946, Elder Ezra Taft Benson of the Quorum of the Twelve came to London to preside over the several European missions and particularly to direct the work of rehabilitation and reorganization among the Church members on the Continent. He apparently brought word that the Browns would soon be released. Writing to Zola, Zina noted:

> Elder Benson is a fine man. He and Daddy are good friends of long standing. . . . President Benson's wife sent me a pair of sheer hose and a pound of home made caramels. . . . I thought that was surely kind of her. Daddy just had such a sweet letter from Harold Lee. All such expressions of real friendships are a real lift to morale.

Two months later, the notice came from the First Presidency that Selvoy J. Boyer had been appointed to head the British Mission. President Brown's release would date from the arrival of his successor, and the departure from London was tentatively scheduled for the latter part of May.

One of President Brown's favorite anecdotes dates to these last weeks in England. An aggressive correspondent for one of the British newspapers came to him for an interview preparatory to writing "a series of articles against the Mormons." Using his experience as a lawyer, Hugh soon led the journalist to the admission that he knew very little about his subject. The next step was to challenge the man to "take thirty days to investigate and study the Mormon doctrine and then write your articles." Informed that the resources were available at "Ravenslea," the correspondent accepted. The predictable conclusion has been retold in these words:

> I thought it only fair to warn him that if he spent thirty days in that library reading on Mormonism he would ask for baptism. When I told him that, he said a lot of things I couldn't repeat. . . .
>
> He went into the library; he read and studied; and, as he afterwards told me, he prayed, because in his reading he had read in the Book of Mormon, that anyone who wants to know can ask of God and He will reveal the truth of it unto him.
>
> I went home in the meantime and was teaching at the Brigham Young University when I received a cable. . . . It said, "I think you will be interested to know that I am being baptized next Friday." (*The Abundant Life,* pp. 30-32.)

The Boyers arrived in mid-May, and Hugh and Zina spent some time acquainting them with the affairs of the mission. At the end of 1945, the number of full-time missionaries, including two Browns, was only nine, and the year had witnessed only twenty-four convert baptisms. But the flow of elders from America, some of them war veterans who had been stationed in England, was resuming, and the prospects for the British Mission were bright.

The Brown family sailed from Liverpool on June 4, 1946, on the *Benjamin Brown French.* They had made reservations on the *Queen Mary,* but a strike had forced them to seek other transportation. For seventeen days they were assigned to segregated sleeping quarters on a freighter which was quite without the amenities for ocean cruising. Fortunately, the food was good and the weather, except for a few days, was very favorable. According to Hugh's journal, the journey, "though a bit tedious, gave opportunity for relaxation and quiet reading." From Pensacola, Florida, to Salt Lake City, was another tedious three days of travel. At Provo, Margaret and Carol were met by boy friends with cars, so Zina and Hugh made the last part of the train trip alone.

The interrupted nine-year mission was now over. In the journal the homecoming is thus described: "We put the house in order and were happy to return." An evaluation of the wartime work of Hugh B. Brown had already been written by his friend and colleague, Harold B. Lee, in a letter to England in July, 1944:

> Our prayers are constantly for you to be blessed of the Lord, and strengthened for your great responsibility, which perhaps is greater than is being carried by any missionary now in service. That you are fitted and qualified by native endowments, and by spiritual strength given you of the Lord, gives us great satisfaction and much joy, and we glory in the opportunity for service that you now have. There is no doubt in my mind that when this war shall have ended, Latter-day Saint boys will call your name blessed because of your kindly and effective administrations in behalf of them and their fellows.

13. Professor at Brigham Young University

Hugh B. Brown's brief career as a college professor came at the opening of a new era in the history of the Church and its university, the nation, and the world. Within a few months in 1945, Harry S. Truman succeeded Franklin D. Roosevelt, President George Albert Smith succeeded Heber J. Grant, Howard S. McDonald succeeded BYU President Franklin S. Harris, and World War II came to an end. The GI Bill of Rights assisted thousands of Mormon veterans to attend Brigham Young University, and the ex-mission president and servicemen's coordinator soon moved into the center of the action. The 3½ years in Provo (1946-1950) were among the happiest in the lives of Hugh and Zina Brown.

"No doubt I will be instructed as to what the Presidency has in mind for my future activities." So wrote Hugh to Elder Harold B. Lee in August, 1944, about his post-war prospects. That BYU might have a place in that future appears to have occurred to a number of people in the following months, for on October 5, 1945, Hugh wrote to Mary and Ed Firmage, "We have not lost sight of the possibility of someday being at the BYU ourselves. A letter from President McDonald this week indicates that such a matter has been mentioned in upper circles.

This is on the Q.T." He added, "Keep your eyes open for a good house down there and for a good horse for an old man to ride. . . ."

Given Hugh B. Brown's experience and wide reputation, his circle of friendship among the Church leaders (who were BYU trustees), and the prospective needs of the university, it is not surprising that the idea of converting President Brown into Professor Brown found favor, though the lack of an academic pedigree may have seemed an obstacle to a faculty appointment. (While the matter was still up in the air, Zina wrote to Mary, "I want to come to Provo and have Daddy in B.Y. as a scholar if not as a teacher. . . . *I want him to get his degrees* — it is one of the secret longings of his dear heart.")

As the end of the mission in Great Britain approached without a formal offer, Hugh's hopes sagged a little, but finally the happy news came late in April, 1946. "God is good; He has heard our prayer," is the way Zina expressed her feelings to Mary. Though final approval by the board of trustees was still required, Mary was soon charged to begin house-hunting in earnest, and her mother spoke with delight about the possibility of their taking classes together. As for Hugh's feelings, "Daddy is really *awfully pleased!*"

Since the appointment as Veterans Counselor and Associate Professor of Political Science and of Religion began July 1, 1946, there was barely time for unpacking at the Salt Lake City home before Hugh had to report to Provo. He rented a room near the campus and spent the balance of the summer school term handling veterans affairs from an office on the lower campus. He and Zina had a commuter relationship until a house was found in Provo and she joined him before the start of his first teaching term.

The appointment of Hugh B. Brown was fortunate for both the man and the school. BYU needed someone with his military and religious insight to counsel the two thousand LDS servicemen who had enrolled or would soon do so. Many were experiencing problems of faith, President Brown remembers. "They had difficulty in harmonizing the idea of God with what they had seen" during the war. Antoine K. Romney, his predecessor as veterans adviser, told the school newspaper, "We are all happy to have Mr. Brown become the Veterans Coordinator. No other man in the Church is so qualified to do this work." The same interview on July 30, 1946, conveyed Hugh's enthusiasm for his new assignment:

> The response of the veterans to the offer of the government to help them continue their education is one of the most heartening experiences to come to us who are interested in the returning servicemen. There is a zest and a hunger among the men that brings a promise of achievement in the field in which courses are offered. We hope to give them help and guidance as they pursue their quest.

The calling satisfied Hugh Brown for several reasons. First, he needed the position so that he might provide for his family. Second, although he was not a certified teacher, he loved to speak. Manley has aptly observed, "On the platform he was at his peak, where he could draw strength from the experience — from the crowd." Third, he loved students. When interviewed by the *Y News,* he acknowledged: "I have long had a desire to get back into the schools. The contact with the young people is a good thing for a man. It helps him to believe that there are great things ahead; to look forward instead of backward — to keep from arriving." The brief journal summary of these teaching years, written in 1952, notes:

> As I travel about the country several years later, I meet young people, most of them now married and making their way in life, who uniformly express appreciation and make assertions as to values received during those fruitful years. This is a source of real satisfaction.

Although he never earned a college degree, Hugh was able to bring to BYU a scholarly perspective. His inquisitive mind and thirst for knowledge made up for the lack of formal education. In the memory of one of his faculty peers, he was "a brilliant and well-read man with a marvelous gift of words," superbly suited for the classroom. Zina told a yearbook reporter that her husband was "one of the greatest bookworms" she had ever known. As will be shown, Hugh Brown was a memorable figure on the campus during the period in which the Church-sponsored university grew from 3,500 to 5,800 students and approached its seventy-fifth anniversary.

Although he was assigned to the Political Science Department, religion had been the vocation of Hugh B. Brown for almost a decade, and it was soon apparent that it would be his primary calling at BYU. In 1947-1948 Hugh held the post of Director of Religious Instruction, and the next year he was promoted to Professor of Political Science and of Religion; and he was Chairman of the Department of LDS Church Organization and Administration and Director of Religious Activities during the remainder of his time at the university.

Realizing that his teaching gift was to motivate rather than to convey information, Hugh Brown preferred to teach the introductory courses in religion. Veterans advisement warranted a reduced teaching load in the fall quarters of 1946 and 1947; in 1948 that responsibility was transferred to another faculty member. Otherwise Hugh taught five two-hour classes each quarter, and all but six sections (out of fifty-six) were lower-division courses in LDS principles and doctrine. They were taught mostly at eight and nine o'clock in the morning, and as their popularity grew they were regularly scheduled in the largest classrooms in the still new Joseph Smith Building. Occasionally sections were moved into the auditorium to accommodate the auditors and visitors who came in increasing numbers and the students who persuaded Professor Brown to lift the space-imposed ceiling on enrollment. Sections were consistently between 100 and 150 students during Hugh's last two years at the university. (The largest enrollment was 160 in the winter quarter of 1950, and when the instructor left for Canada before the quarter was over, whoever inherited the task of completing the record gave 155 A's.)

In an effort to recapture the real Professor Hugh B. Brown, a limited number of his former students were asked to respond to a questionnaire prepared by one of the authors. Twenty-six of forty-two replied. Nine remember his teaching vividly; eleven, more than most of the BYU instructors; four, rather vaguely, and only two — not at all. Eleven took more than one class with him. Respondents were asked to try to "base your replies

on your college experience and not upon other contacts with
or impressions of President Brown." A sampling of comments
confirms what one student recalls after twenty-five years: "He
was a 'natural-born' teacher. We felt he was sincerely interested
in us and in our spiritual growth."

Among the one-sentence responses to the question, "What
do you remember most clearly about the class(es)?" were these:

> "Hugh B. Brown could communicate better than any other
> teacher I have studied with."
>
> "His broad background of experiences tended to enrich the
> class discussions. . . ."
>
> "His seemingly endless knowledge, his flatout testimony, his ex-
> periences in the Church."
>
> "I remember that he never looked at a note or a book during
> his lecture, but that later when I read the book we were using he
> had covered every point in the chapter, using not only the material
> in the book but his own personal experiences and materials as well."

The question, "What was the subject matter of the
class(es)?" elicited various references to LDS doctrines and
principles and was left blank by quite a few respondents. The
upper-division classes were Church organization and government, advanced theology, and Mormonism for non-Latter-day
Saints. But like the lower-division classes, they had a functional
emphasis. "Helping us to live each day as the Gospel taught,"
is the way one student described the subject matter. Another
made this very perceptive comment about Professor Brown:
"Looking over my notes, I can see that he taught himself, and
his view of life primarily; the course title was only an excuse
or the vehicle."

The format of the classes apparently changed as the enrollment increased. One upper-division section is remembered
as "a combination of lecture and discussion, with an informal,
easy feeling." A student who has preserved his class notes recalls
that Professor Brown "talked most of the time. Not like a formal
lecture, but sharing informally the wisdom of life he had gained.
He stood, sat on the edge of the desk, walked about a bit, but
did most of the talking." Apparently non-Mormon students were
sometimes invited to tell about their beliefs and culture; in ad-

vanced classes students might be called to speak impromptu. Questions and discussion were invited, and the teacher had no hesitancy in digressing from the assigned subject if the discussion warranted. Yet his own skill as a "spellbinder" tended to inhibit discussion. Wrote one student, "No one wanted to take time from Brother Brown. We wanted him to speak." The blackboard was sometimes used for listing scriptures or text assignments, but there were no other visual aids except the teacher's power to quicken the imagination.

Asked to characterize the objectives of the classes, students were virtually unanimous that promoting spirituality and building testimony were uppermost. Said one: "Even at an age when one did not easily turn to spiritual things, Brother Brown made it happen. *Inspirational* is the word most frequently used to describe class quality, with *entertaining, exciting,* and *informative* the next most popular adjectives.

Few students remember any kind of class outlines. Printed lists of topics and text assignments apparently were occasionally used, but sometimes the blackboard served for that purpose. President Brown replied to a recent inquiry about lecture notes in these words: "Knowing my habits of a lifetime, . . . I know that I lectured 'off the cuff,' and any meager notes that I may have made were not preserved." Student class notes which have come to the attention of the authors are consistent with this impression; there is structure in the courses, a degree of paralleling with the text assignments, a certain amount of repetition from one quarter to the next, but a high degree of spontaneity and variation in individual class periods.

Textbooks do not loom large in student recollections. Lowell Bennion's *The Religion of the Latter-day Saints* was used much of the time in the principles and doctrines classes, and one comment is to the effect that Hugh "showed respect and appreciation for the text." In the unavailability of John A. Widtsoe's *Priesthood and Church Government,* James E. Talmage's *Articles of Faith* was used in the Church organization class. There was heavy reliance on the standard works, inspirational passages being cited rather more frequently than proof-texts. Years later President Brown gave this advice to missionaries: "I hope you will not try to hold too closely to the texts of the lessons which have been prepared. One is much more effective when he simply speaks from his heart, tells what he knows and believes, and gives reasons for his faith."

Assignments were not extensive: Hugh B. Brown's were not "hard" courses. Students were required to keep a journal of class notes, and in it they were encouraged to record their own thoughts about some of the subjects under consideration. There is solid evidence that students actually did so. Term papers were apparently required in some of the advanced courses. Hugh did some of his own grading, but as enrollments increased he had student help. These mechanical aspects of academia were not seen as profoundly important. The primary assignment in every Hugh Brown course, as one student remembers, was "to pray, study, and live the truth."

Those who remember the tests at all remember that they were generally multiple-choice, identification, or other objective and semi-objective questions. Small classes had some opportunities to tackle discussion questions. There is general agreement that the tests were neither frequent nor difficult. Hugh is quoted as having told one class that he didn't believe in tests in religion but was required to give them by departmental policy. On one occasion he observed cheating on a final examination. Remarking to one of the student veterans who was taking the test nearby, "I would not have believed it if I could not see it myself," he walked out of the classroom and did not return.

Student comments corroborate the testimony of the grade reports in the BYU archives. Hugh Brown's grading was "fair," "somewhat easy," "not preferential" and "high." Student assistants handled most of the paperwork after the first year.

"Was Professor Brown accessible outside of class?" Even those who had no outside contacts believed him to be accessible, and many students sought him out. Ex-GI's particularly enjoyed "picking his brain," and his office in the Joseph Smith Building was always open to them. Among the student comments are these:

"On several memorable occasions I had the privilege of chatting with him on such subjects as the Negro problem, Church organization, . . . marriage and pre-existence. He greatly impressed me and I fully expected him to be an apostle."

"I remember him picking me up in his car to give me a ride to campus. He questioned me extensively about who I was and who my parents were . . . and told me of fond recollections of his associations with them."

"We used to hurry to walk with him up the hill."

"He always made you feel welcome. . . . Conversations were never hurried."

Inquiry into "the basis of this popularity" which Hugh B. Brown enjoyed at Brigham Young University produced a gamut of quotable responses:

"He did the same in his classes as he did in sermons — he held the audience in his hand."

"His broad background of experience and training which he shared. I know many have been impressed by his currant-bush experience."

"He was a person of such dignity and stature, with such a commanding appearance. He spoke with such conviction and authority that we hung on every word. . . ."

"Primarily his lectures. They were classics. You could never leave his classes without feeling better and more determined to stay close to God."

It is clear that Hugh B. Brown's forte was neither doctrinal analysis nor scriptural exegesis. He is quoted at the start of a freshman course as saying: "I will not give you a creed to learn. I am hoping that we may come to feel religion and that it may influence us for good." The application of principles was everything. One of his most often-repeated sentences was: "You are sentenced to live with you throughout all eternity."

He was remarkably sensitive to the religious needs of the young, the curious, and the disenchanted. Wrote one young veteran, "His lectures were down to earth, simply stated, inspiring, and perfect for college students." Another student remembers an instance:

Professor Brown was lecturing on God's creation of the earth and its life forms as if that act were the only way it could possibly have happened. I raised my hand, was recognized, and asked why our world could not have appeared spontaneously, an idea which then, as now, made more sense to me. He answered my question as if he understood perfectly the agony of a young man not yet sufficiently experienced to be assured of the rightness of any question. His answer began with an analysis of my argument, and with an ability to meet my thoughts like one who had already wrestled with them.

This patience with troubled, skeptical, and critical students was a hallmark. "He who has never doubted has never thought," is a quotation in more than one set of class notes, and President Brown to this day likes to cite Will Durant: "No one deserves to believe unless he has served an apprenticeship of doubt." How to cope with the perilous passage from naïveté to mature faith was a major thrust of Hugh Brown's instruction. One who experienced it remembers it now in these terms: "I felt at the time the leverage, the prying, the invitation to reach out, to expand, to enlarge, to define in broader terms my view of truth, life, religion and good."

Professor Brown's classes were taught that the process of growth is endless. He gave them this definition of intelligence:

The combined powers of man *choosing* those things that are for his best — *ever* growing by experience — *ever* changing by development — *never* reaching an optimum point of progression. There is no such thing as a non-progressing intelligence, if the word *intelligence* is used to mean that it is eternal — and it *is* eternal.

The leaven of humor was freely mixed with the other ingredients in Hugh Brown's teaching, and he recommended it to his students. "Religion is not measured by the length of the face," he declared. He illustrated an appeal for humble faith with this suggested prayer: "I shall continue to row, God. You guide the boat." And he delighted to share with his classes a comment which he attributed to a student final exam; the question was, "What are the duties of the General Authorities?" and the answer was, "They go about appointing and disappointing members of the Church."

It is not surprising that a strong unit on marriage and the family found place in all of Professor Brown's classes. Indeed, two of the students listed "marriage" as the remembered subject of the advanced class in LDS organization. Here is the recollection and tribute of another:

> He told us vividly of his love for his "companion," his dear wife. He told us of how he would often pick her a flower from the garden before work. He told how she had said that after many (I can't remember how many it was at the time — but enough to really impress me) years of marriage her heart still did a 'flip-flop' when she heard his step on the path.
>
> Since I had come from a broken home, I wondered if love could ever endure. Their example of love and devotion, which he fervently declared had increased ten-fold over the years, was a source of great inspiration to me. I set my goals on this type of marriage and I can say gratefully after twenty-two years that our love also has grown and continues to grow sweeter each day.

Home for Hugh and Zina Brown during their Provo years was a comfortable old house at 313 East 200 North, about a mile from his office in the Joseph Smith Building. Recently remodeled, it had a spacious living room and fireplace, but its overall size and style matched the family and income of the Browns, both of which had diminished since the days on Stratford Avenue. One prized possession was a large oriental rug whose dimensions dictated one of Zina's housing requirements. A living room which would accommodate the carpet was ideal for entertaining faculty, student, and church groups, and such activities were frequent.

Three of Hugh and Zina's children were in Provo during these BYU years. Mary and her mother shared many activities, though their hope to take classes together never materialized, for their two families represented too many competitive claims on time. Margaret married Clinton Jorgensen in August, 1946, and the newlyweds lived a few blocks from her parents while they attended the university. Carol was thus the only daughter left at home, and she lived in an apartment with other coeds for part of the time she was in school. (Perhaps she felt the need for an independent base of operations after a fellow explained that he had asked her for a date "because I wanted to meet your father.")

Zina Lou, Zola, LaJune, Manley, and their families were often in Provo, and Hugh and Zina frequently visited their children in Salt Lake and Southern California. Letters supplemented the personal contacts, sharing experiences and conveying love and support in times of difficulty and sorrow. Hugh's practice of writing birthday letters was extended now to the older grandchildren. One notable message to "My dear Birdie" (Zina Lou) in April, 1947, comments on the challenge of teaching religion to young people, and adds: "In my own family I have tried to avoid a too dogmatic treatment of the subject in the hope that the living of the gospel would better indicate my faith than any amount of precept." Enclosed with the letter is a statement which was eventually sent to all of the children. Its purpose, Hugh wrote, was "to outline in general form some concepts which, to me, seem to form a basis upon which to build faith; faith in the meaning and purpose of life and in the ultimate decency of things." Preserved in the correspondence files of several of the Brown children, the four-page statement reflects on science, philosophy, art, and religion as approaches to life's big questions:

> . . . May we just sit down together and think of this experience which we call life and see whether out of such thinking we can reach helpful conclusions.
>
> Sometimes during the war, young men were asked to fly over enemy territory and to parachute out and land in unfamiliar surroundings. I have talked with many of these lads and have asked them how they felt when they landed and what their duties were.
>
> It seems that the parachute troops were given definite instructions as to their procedure upon arriving at their appointed stations. First, they were to orient themselves, to find out where they were, and in the light of the purpose for which they came, to try to determine the best means of reaching their objective. Secondly, to consult their maps if they had them, their compasses or other means of orientation. Then with the aid of radio equipment, they attempt to establish contact with headquarters to report on their whereabouts and their activities, and to get further instructions.
>
> After we leave those early years when we were inclined to accept as true all the statements that are made to us by those in whom we

had confidence, after we reach the age of maturity and are able to think more clearly and act more purposefully, most of us find ourselves, figuratively, in the same position as the man who jumped from the airplane into unfamiliar territory.

We look about us and try to orient ourselves. We become aware of the fact that we are a part of the universe, a universe which is friendly. We discover that we have landed in a fruitful country where provision has been made for our needs. As we think more deeply, we become aware of the fact that not only is it a friendly universe, but a universe in which there is solicitude and love.

We can, also, feel with Sir James Jeans, one of the greatest of modern philosophers, that this is a universe of thought and that therefore its creation must have been an act of thought. We acquire a sense of belongingness, a sense of at-home-ness in a universe which somehow has produced persons — a personal universe, and we have a desire to be in harmony with the nature and destiny of the universe and the central figure of that universe. . . .

As we pursue the quest and come in contact with science and with beauty, with philosophy and with thought, at first the sense of loneliness and helplessness is accentuated.

Science introduces us to a universe of astronomical space measured by light years, and at the other extreme to a universe of the infinitesimally small. "Between these two universes of the infinitely extended and timeless and the infinitesimally small and transient, man maintains his extremely tentative hold upon life within a very limited habitat and a brief moment of time. It is no wonder that when he stops to contemplate his place in such a universe he is humbled and overwhelmed and filled with a sense of utter loneliness and helplessness."

I think the ancient Hebrews with their limited knowledge of the heavens, of astronomy, and science must have felt this loneliness when one of the greatest of them was led to say, "When I consider thy heavens, the work of thy fingers, the moon and stars, which thou hast ordained, what is man that thou art mindful of him and the son of man, that thou visitest him?"

These ancients were, I think, sustained by their belief that above the universe there was a God and that somehow he was their God, that they were related to him and therefore an integral part of the whole plan and pattern.

As we discover that there are persons in the world and that personality is the most important of the things we contact, we seek a more personal approach to the universe. In other words, we feel that personality came from personality. We look behind the achievement in search of the achiever.

Religion is one approach to an understanding of the universe. Like science, philosophy, and art, it interprets the universe in terms of its own point of view. "Science approaches reality in terms of the organization of matter and energy bound together by a tissue of antecedent and consequent." Philosophy makes its own approach, as does art, but religion approaches reality in terms of practical values of the satisfactions of needs and aspirations for a more abundant life.

"Who shall say to which of these approaches reality yields itself more completely. May it not be that reality is so complex that it requires all of these approaches and perhaps still others of which we do not know as yet to apprehend its many facets which it exposes to man's intelligence, his appreciations, and his far-reaching desires? It is probably true that our *real* world is for each of us our world of values. . . .

"In any case, by whatever route he arrives at the conviction, the religious man finds in the universe more than a mechanism, more than a structure of ideas, more than a mathematical formula. He believes himself to be an integral part of and participant in a universe that responds to intelligence, to a sense of values, and to creative purpose, and which is, therefore, to that extent at least personal, rational, and moral. For him religion is one method of adjustment to reality. He readily concedes that it is not the only method. Science represents one adjustment to reality. So does rational thought. So does aesthetic appreciation and expression. But religion approaches reality from the viewpoint of the supreme value of persons."

Well, folks, I have perhaps wearied you by this dissertation, . . . but I feel sure, as time goes on, as life brings varied and trying experiences to you, you, too, will delve back into yourselves in search for answers to questions, questions which will not forever remain unanswered, questions, however, to which, while we are mortal, there may not be full answers, but the very upsurge of these questions causes thinking men to believe there is an answer.

Faith in God, faith in oneself, faith in the general proposition that there is purpose in life and that that purpose is not achieved in mortality — these great and fundamental concepts are indispensable to abundant living. I commend to you the reading of the most recent books on philosophy and religion. The best minds we have in the world are concerning themselves with possible answers to these questions. Their findings may not satisify completely our longing, but they may be as guide posts along the way pointing us to a destination.

Hugh B. Brown's reputation as a speaker preceded him to Provo and he was soon in demand for sermons, service club talks, and special assignments. Carol still remembers his public dialogue with a visiting rabbi. An address to a BYU student assembly on December 10, 1946, raised the question: "Do the young people of the world need to be taught religion?" He warmed up the audience with a playful comment on a current event:

> I may observe that during the coal strike a great many people have heaped anathema on the head of John L. Lewis; many would have heaped coals of fire if they could have found the coals. But I am wondering whether some of us ought not to make friends with him; some of us, when we die, may have to go to the lower regions and if we do . . . we'll need a coal strike.

He responded to those who questioned the requirement of religious instruction at BYU by citing his experiences in England, where friends had expressed deep concern about the absence of religious commitments and moral standards among the young. Great names in science and philosophy were quoted on the relevance of religion. The mixture of anecdote, authority, and testimony was typical of Hugh B. Brown.

A recurrence of tic douloureux made it necessary for his talk, "Teach Ye Diligently," to be read for him at the Sunday School Conference in the Salt Lake Tabernacle on October 6, 1946. The facial nerve which was severed in 1945 had apparently grown back together. The upshot was a trip to the Mayo Clinic, where, on November 2, surgery removed a section of the main trunk nerve, ending the pain but leaving one-half of his face devoid of all feeling. The side effects of the operation would be a source of some embarrassment for the rest of his life, but Hugh handled the situation with typical humor, observing in a letter to Zola that "the numb side of my head is not much worse than the other side, which is dumb."

A series of radio addresses, titled "Rational Faith" and delivered over radio station KSL on Sunday evenings from September 7 to December 28, 1947, is the most comprehensive systematic treatment of Mormonism to be found among the writings of Hugh B. Brown. They reflect much of the style and content of his BYU courses, but they are more tightly organized than his classroom lectures and are directed primarily toward the unconverted in his audience. Their general tone is set in the "Introduction":

I come to you as one who invites his friends to accompany him on a quest, the kind of a quest which implies curiosity, a desire to know, a certain teachable humility — all of which are prerequisites to a successful search for truth. . . .

Inasmuch as we shall be seeking to discover, to interpret, to evaluate — we must be open-minded, unprejudiced, and unafraid. There will be no disposition on the part of the speaker to say dogmatically, "This is it — no more and no less." Rather he will undertake to give some reasons for certain convictions which he entertains. . . .

I have said that this proposed quest will require faith. Any honest consideration of the vast and controversial subject of religion calls for faith — for an inner vision. . . . When we come to the edge of knowledge the scientist as well as the religionist leans on faith and, if courageous, will follow its tender light. . . .

Dismissing the "religious rationalizers" and the "irreligious rationalizers," who muster evidence to support a priori positions, Hugh Brown aimed his radio talks at the "religiously inquisitive." For them he mustered poets and scientists, philosophers and prophets, in support of the basic affirmations of the LDS faith: There is a God and Christ is his Son. Man is immortal, free, and capable of becoming Godlike. The word of God is available through revelation, past and present. The speaker endorsed prayer in terms particularly relevant to a time when world war was a recent memory and the "cold war" was a looming threat:

Let us learn some bigger prayers than we said as little children. Let us shift the emphasis from ourselves and our next of kin and enlarge the scope of our interest and our supplication. We should continue to pray for the safety and the guidance of our loved ones and to believe those prayers are efficacious. But we must enlarge our outlook and have faith that prayers to God for our country and the world will be heard and answered. . . . We must recognize him as the universal Father and not a mere tribal god who would help one group or section at the expense of another. . . .

Let us pray and praise and worship — secretly — in our families — and in Church. Let us give thanks for all our blessings and seek forgiveness for our follies. Let us pray for those who love us, for our leaders, church and state. Let us pray for those who need help and support our prayers with service. Let us pray for health and strength and wisdom. Pray for faith to carry on when our strength seems insufficient, and the answer is delayed. Let our prayers go out as well as upward. We must work as well as pray. Let us pray for peace and concord, in our hearts, our homes, and country. Let us pray for other nations — enemies as well as friends. Thus may we make our little corner of the Garden a productive spot of beauty, with no wall or fence or hedge between us and our neighbors. Prayer will rid our hearts of hatred, it will chasten our ambitions, until with love of God and neighbors we shall keep His two commandments. Let us pray.

Four of the talks dealt with the LDS concepts of salvation and exaltation and with the first principles and ordinances which relate to their realization. The last two addresses had commemorative significance. "The Christ Child" presented a Christmas message of hope, and "Pioneering Our Second Century" marked the end of the centennial observance of the Mormon entry into the Salt Lake Valley. Hugh's benediction on the century and on the radio series was in these terms: "May He who guided both ancient and modern Israel sustain and direct us that we may have faith in Him, in ourselves, and in our destiny."

Like most of Hugh Brown's "prepared" talks, these radio addresses were delivered from detailed notes rather than finished texts. The transcripts reveal the familiar rhetorical style; they should be read as addresses, not as essays. They were published in pamphlet form soon after their delivery and they later appeared, slightly revised, in the first published volume of President Brown's speeches and writings, *Eternal Quest*.

Evidence of the high regard with which the Church leadership regarded Hugh B. Brown as a speaker was his appointment to speak on the CBS "Church of the Air" series. The address from the Salt Lake Tabernacle on June 6, 1948, was a "Baccalaureate Sermon to American Students":

> Washington warned us long ago to "indulge with caution the idea that morality can long survive without religion". . . .
>
> If your generation fails to live and to teach the Christian way of life, you may expect your children to forsake the American way of life. If the children of Christian parents come to maturity without Christian beliefs and convictions, there will be a resultant agnostic vacuum into which false and foreign ideologies will rush with devastating consequences. . . .

> If we live and preach "the gospel of the kingdom" with the con-
> viction and enthusiasm of a Peter, John, or Paul and if we catch
> the fire of their zeal, there will be no need to fear the advocates of
> atheistic "isms."

When Hugh came to the university, he wrote to Zola that
he thought it would be "wrestful as well as worthwhile employment." The pun was fulfilled both ways. Although he taught
Sunday School classes at times on the BYU campus and in the
Provo Fifth Ward, he held no major positions of ecclesiastical
leadership during these years. The days were free for teaching
and counseling, and the evenings were less locked into meetings
than they had been during most of the previous twenty-five years.
There was time for trips, for riding, fishing, and golf, and for enjoyment of many campus activities. House and garden parties
brought many people of all ages to the Brown home, and family
and friends were available to help celebrate the thirty-ninth,
fortieth and forty-first wedding anniversaries. Hugh sometimes
taxed his strength (and Zina's patience), but he wrote to Zola in
1947: "I have never had a time when I could give so much
thought and do so much reading along lines which intrigue me.
It is fortunate that we can be here at our age and have work
which is not too hard and feel that we can still be useful."

Had the pay been better, Hugh and Zina might have remained in Provo indefinitely, or until the call to be a General
Authority came, as so many BYU students expected it would.
But the professorial salary crimped Hugh's impulsive generosity
and inhibited the life style which he desired for his family, and
neither the token law partnership with his nephew Emmett nor
a fling at real estate with his bishop, Daniel D. Bushnell, provided adequate relief. So he left Provo in 1950 for what appeared to be greener pastures in Canada, as will be noted in the
following chapter.

The break with Brigham Young University proved, however, to be only temporary. From the moment of his return
to Utah as an Assistant to the Council of the Twelve, he was in
demand for assembly, fireside, and other addresses on the
campus.

The propositions which Hugh had taught to hundreds of

students in the late 1940s were brought to tens of thousands as BYU reached an annual enrollment of twenty-five thousand during the years that he was a member of its board of trustees. To a Leadership Week audience in 1956 he gave this challenge:

> Awareness, like creation and salvation, is an on-going process and the quest for truth is eternal. . . .
>
> God bless us that, as individual members of the Church, we may catch the vision of the restored gospel and realize that education is part of religion and that, therefore, a man cannot be saved in ignorance any more than he can be saved in sin. . . . (*The Abundant Life,* p. 263.]

Some suggestions on how to "Learn Continually" were spelled out in a telecast devotional in 1964. "The Lord never puts a premium on sluggish thinking," President Brown remarked, in urging his auditors to "acquire a working knowledge of the classics in literature and in current thought." The lives of great men and the thoughts of great minds were commended from the perspective of eighty years of companionship with books. He said:

> While making a lifetime study of the standard works of the Church, one should also become familiar with the classics, with Shakespeare, Milton, Tennyson, and Wordsworth. He should read something of the philosophers and scientists, should find out how boundaries of knowledge have been altered and extended in religion and in literature. One should know something of the writings of Plato, Aristotle, Socrates, and the later philosophers, who, while they err in many respects, will start a man thinking independently and courageously on the meaning of life and its purpose. . . . (*The Abundant Life,* p. 107.)

"Be Aware — Beware" was the title of a baccalaureate address at BYU on May 24, 1962, the day before the institution bestowed on him an honorary Doctor of Humanities degree. The keynote was, "Be dauntless in your pursuit of truth and resist all demands for unthinking conformity. . . . Tolerance and truth demand that all be heard and that competing ideas be tested against each other. . . ." In calling for optimism in life's "battle between fear and faith," President Brown added this counsel:

One must have a sense of humor to be an optimist in times like these. And you young women will need a sense of humor if you marry these young men and try to live with them. Golden Kimball once said in a conference, "The Lord Himself must like a joke or he wouldn't have made some of you people." But your good humor must be real, not simulated. Let your smiles come from the heart and they will become contagious. . . . Men without humor tend to forget their source, lose sight of their goal, and with no lubrication in their mental crankshafts, they must drop out of the race. Lincoln said, "Good humor is the oxygen of the soul." (*The Abundant Life*, p. 50.)

Brigham Young University audiences heard two of the talks which, as tape recordings, have become Mormon classics. "The Profile of a Prophet" (*Eternal Quest*, pp. 127-135) and "Father, Are You There?" (*Vision and Valor*, pp. 232-253) combine the retold experiences of missionary and other earlier days with the pulpit magnetism and convictions of full maturity. The testimony which he gave to a ten-stake fireside in September, 1969, on the eve of his eighty-sixth birthday and a few months prior to his release from the First Presidency, is a fitting monument to the love affair between Hugh B. Brown and Brigham Young University which has spanned more than a quarter century:

My young friends, with all the sincerity and vigor of my soul, I testify to you tonight that Jesus of Nazareth is the Son of God, the Redeemer of the world. I know that as well as Peter knew it when in answer to the question of Christ, "Whom say ye that I am?" he said, "Thou art the Christ, the Son of the Living God." And the Savior said, "Blessed art thou; flesh and blood did not reveal this unto thee, but my Father which is in heaven."

My testimony to you tonight is not that I know it because of what people have told me. I know it because of the revelations from Almighty God that have come into my life, and I thank him for it, humbly. I leave that testimony with you with a blessing.

O God, bless this congregation of the cream of the membership of the Church; bless their parents, that they may know of the influence under which their children are working; bless the parents and the children that they may work together in harmony, that the children may never get the idea that their parents are getting old-fashioned and out of date.

O God, bless these young men and women that they may realize that they are the temples of God and that the Spirit of God dwells in them and remind them, O Father, occasionally, that any man who will defile the temple of God, him shall God destroy.

O my young people, beware — be careful of your associations, keep your conduct, your words, your actions together on such a high plane so pure and undefiled, that you would not be ashamed to have them written in fire in the heavens, told to everyone in the world! Let your light so shine that men seeing your good works may be led to glorify Him. (*Vision and Valor,* pp. 230-231.)

14. Prospecting in Canada

Early in 1950 Professor Hugh B. Brown received a phone call from Ed Preston, a Texas businessman, that was to change his life for the next three years. Preston, who represented the Richland Oil Company, of Houston, reported that his company was interested in moving into Alberta, where oil and gas had recently been discovered. He added, "We want a man who has practiced law in Canada and in the United States, and you have been recommended to us. I am phoning to ask if you will be available to come to Alberta, join our firm, incorporate a new company and become its general counsel." Hugh's initial reaction was that he could not leave because he was teaching at BYU. Preston's response was overwhelming. "I don't know what you are getting at the university," he said, "but whatever it is, I will multiply it by ten if you will come." President Brown went immediately to Salt Lake City and conferred with members of the First Presidency. When told of this offer, they said, "Go, by all means."

Given Hugh Brown's earlier connections with oil leasing and with Alberta, it was natural for him to take note of the reports of oil and gas discoveries which came from the Canadian province in 1947. What followed is described in a journal entry written in Edmonton in 1952:

> Having previously lived in Canada, my interest was aroused and at the request of a group of Texas oilmen I flew to Edmonton to investigate possibilities of obtaining a franchise for the export of oil and gas. I continued to teach at the "Y" with occasional visits to Canada, until 1950, when, due to increased obligations with oil and gas companies, I resigned from the University and have since that time spent most of my time in Alberta.

At the time the assignment was pending, his nephew N. Eldon Tanner was Minister of Lands and Forests, Mines and Minerals in the Alberta provincial government. No one knew better than he the qualifications Hugh Brown would bring to the position should he be chosen to spearhead the Richland enterprise, even though he was then in his sixty-seventh year and twenty-three years removed from the practice of law in Canada.

Hugh Brown was excited with the new project. It would give him a chance to achieve that affluence for which he had been striving at different periods in his life, and especially to get out of debt and be able to help his family. As he put it in a letter of March 4, 1950, he anticipated that it would soon be possible "to surprise each of you occasionally with a little check for 'pin money'."

The departure from Provo in February 1950 was rather precipitate. Classes were reassigned, a disappointment remembered by many students. Zina was to follow when the situation in Alberta clarified, but it proved to be more than two years before she moved to Edmonton. (It is possible that she was no more enthused about moving back to Canada than Zina Card had been in 1908 about Hugh's taking her daughter back to the same region.)

His journal and correspondence establish that the initial interest of Hugh Brown's business associates was in the transportation of natural gas rather than the production of gas or oil. Hugh's role, comparable to his work with Elijah Pilling in Southern California in 1937 but on a far grander scale, was to recruit capital and handle the legal arrangements necessary to incorporate the venture in Alberta. The previously mentioned family letter notes that his Houston associates "are now operat-

ALBERTA AREA INCLUDED IN
HUGH B. BROWN'S ACTIVITIES

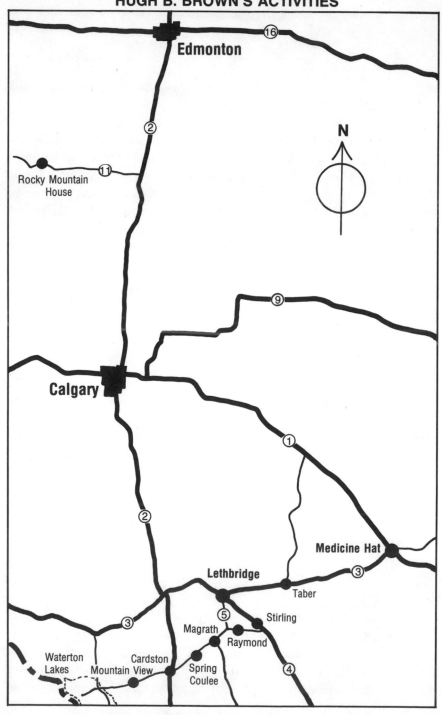

ing gas pipe lines in many parts of the U.S.A.," and that the proposed project "will cost from $300 to $400 million dollars and involve several years of work." To insure "an equal chance with other applicants for export licenses and franchises" it was necessary to enlist some Canadian capital, so Hugh had already met in Winnipeg and Calgary with businessmen from both sides of the international border. The plan at that stage was to "organize two corporations, one American and one Canadian, to handle the deal."

"To indicate the interest awakened in the project" — and the excitement and exhilaration which Hugh Brown, at 67, still felt in dealing with people of influence in a major project such as this — part of the March 4 letter follows:

> I may say that our group consists of a prominent lawyer from Boston — in addition to the prominent lawyer from Salt Lake — an oil man in the multi-millionaire class from Houston and Dallas, a high rating engineer also from Houston who has built several gas pipe lines, and finally one of the largest investment banking houses in New York, who are prepared to underwrite the deal up to half a billion dollars.

> The other group, without mentioning names, consists of one of the largest banking houses in Canada, . . . an engineer from Vancouver, a lawyer from Edmonton who is a director of the Royal Bank of Canada and also is head of the gas company in Alberta, a very prominent businessman from Winnipeg who has great influence in Dominion and Provincial political circles.

> These men came into Calgary by plane from New York, Texas, California, Montreal, Winnipeg, Edmonton and Vancouver —and Salt Lake — and a more animated and professional discussion would be difficult to arrange.

> . . . If the project goes through we will build a gas pipe line from Texas and the south to Montreal and other Canadian cities in the east and from Alberta to Spokane, Seattle, Portland and other points in the Pacific Northwest and the Rocky Mountain area. This will provide gas for the cities in those areas totaling 800,000,000 cubic feet per day. This gives you some idea of the project we are trying to get under way. There is of course always the chance of a sudden blow up but now it looks like we are going to get together on a deal.

Unfortunately, these grandiose plans did not materialize. The Alberta Conservation Board reviewed all applications and did not give the necessary permits to any company, American or Canadian. The shipment of Canadian gas by pipeline into the United States has not yet become a reality and a pipeline from Alberta to the eastern Canadian provinces did not materialize until after Hugh B. Brown had become a General Authority. Interestingly, the Trans-Canada Pipe Line Company, which constructed the project in the late 1950s, was headed by N. Eldon Tanner, later a counselor with his uncle in the First Presidency.

Organizational work and the solicitation of capital nevertheless kept Hugh Brown busy through 1950, and his letters to his children remained optimistic. One written to Zola from Edmonton's Corona Hotel in July declares, "My business here continues to be encouraging and I hope for such success as will enable me to do for my children what I have always wanted for them — security and relief from financial worries." Two months later he wrote "that business continues good and I'm enjoying the work in spite of the fact that it keeps me away from Mother so much." He added:

> In all our married life she has never complained once about being left alone — and she's had more than her share of separation.
>
> It is really wonderful that we should have our best years financially after I have passed the retirement age. We both give thanks all the time to Him who has made it possible for us to make our loved ones happy. I feel the presence of other loved ones often when I am lonely. Perhaps this is the answer to a prayer I've breathed often this year: "Please let my mother and my son who are with you, be messengers to guide, inspire, caution and encourage so that I may be able to bless those whose welfare means so much to them and to me and I'll divide every dollar I get."

The disappointment with natural gas lines led Hugh and his Texas associates to move into exploration for oil. Articles of incorporation for the Richland Oil Development Company of Canada, Ltd., were filed in 1951, according to the 1952 journal entry. The firm was capitalized at $1,000,000, with one million shares of no-par-value stock, and one of Hugh's responsibilities was to promote investment. Under drilling contract, the company acquired "a 70 percent interest in approximately 8,000 acres of petroleum and natural gas leases in the Ram River area," 150 miles southwest of Edmonton. This site near Rocky Mountain House represented "a very promising opportunity," according to President Tanner. (As a resident of the Alberta capital during these years, he was in frequent touch with Hugh and, of course, was aware of his business plans and aspirations.)

Subsequently Hugh acquired the oil and gas rights to some adjoining land and arranged to consolidate the two properties for development purposes. This, according to the journal, made it possible "to interest capital with which to undertake a drilling program." In March 1952 Hugh flew to Miami to negotiate with Harry W. Knight, a Toronto banker. The upshot was an advance of $200,000 to Richland, a firm offer to take $400,000 in shares when they were placed on the market, and options to purchase additional shares later.

Up to this point, Hugh noted in the 1952 journal entry, his relationship with Richland had been advisory and promotional. Now, at the request of Knight, he assumed the position of president and managing director of the company, with headquarters in Edmonton. A base camp was established on the leases near Rocky Mountain House in order to begin drilling in earnest in the summer of 1952.

This was the turn of events which apparently convinced Zina that Canadian oil was more than a profitable will-o'-the-wisp. In 2½ years her husband had traveled over two hundred thousand miles, mostly by air. While the inveterate sightseer could describe his visits to most of the American states and Canadian provinces as "educational and profitable," they had made him something of a gypsy. His abode in Edmonton had been at first a hotel and then a rented house. Here Zina had visited during the summer of 1951, and his journeys to Utah and California had provided additional brief reunions, including a family Christmas in 1951. Now at last he and Zina could purchase a home and settle down, the comforts of affluence offering some compensation for the distance separating them from most of their loved ones. (Hugh noted in June, 1952, that Zina Lou, Zola, and LaJune were then living in Southern California, Manley, Mary, and Carol in Provo, and Margaret in Ogden,

Utah. Carol had married Douglas Bunker the year before. Grandchildren numbered eighteen.)

The spring and summer of 1952 marked the peak of Hugh Brown's fortunes in Canada. Although the Richland Oil Company had so far produced more prospectuses than petroleum, Ed Preston's promise to the BYU professor struggling on a $4,500 salary had been more than literally fulfilled. President Brown remembers, "The remuneration I received . . . relieved me . . . from the bondage of debt." When the Knight investment converted what was essentially a paper organization into a going concern, the new president and managing director wrote to one of his daughters that he was "grateful for the blessing of relief from financial worries and for the joy that comes from lifting a bit of the loads which our own are carrying."

April and May were spent recruiting additional investors, including some of Hugh Brown's own friends. From a San Francisco hotel he wrote to "Birdie" (Zina Lou), "The wheels turn and the pot boils, and I enjoy the game." To "Blossom" (Zola) he wrote the same day, "Your old Dad is some stepper these days, but perhaps after we get settled in Canada in June we can quiet down to a pace more suitable to our ages." A similar yearning, lightened with humor, is in the letter to his oldest daughter, in which he remarks, "I did not consider the volume of correspondence entailed by large families or we might have limited the number." He speaks of a coming trip to Los Angeles with Zina, and adds:

> Our grandchildren will remember us only as sprites on the wing unless we can stay long enough with them to get acquainted. Sometimes I fear even our own children do not know us really as we are in the evening of life, and that is too bad, as we are anxious to have them see us in the softer afterglow which tends to blend the colors into more beautiful harmony. Guess I feel poetic this A.M. so will go down to breakfast and see what ham and eggs will do to esthetic flights.

That Hugh's patient wife cherished similar yearnings, plus an affection undiminished by time or separation, comes clearly through these "Lines Written by Zina C. Brown While Crocheting an Afghan for Her Husband on the Occasion of their 44th

Wedding Anniversary." For more than two years Hugh had lived in Salt Lake only when between trips to Canada and California, Zina's relationship with him being reminiscent of the days when he was on the road as servicemen's coordinator. Now they were together and anticipating moving into a permanent home. On June 17, 1952, she wrote:

> This is the coverlet I have woven for my love.
>
> The hook is the shuttle that gives pattern to my dreams. Dreams of our togetherness, here and *always*.
>
> Shall we be living on that hill where once our dreams were dashed?
>
> We went forth from this garden to toil and carry yet another Cross. Ah! so much we've learned since then! A long way we have come. We seek Thee still. Then who showed the way to turn the Cross to a Crown of Glory? . . .
>
> Are there but the Light and the Dark? How could one be without the other? . . .
>
> The Great Artist did not mean it so. These hours of deep hurt and of loss, which seemed so very dark and almost without hope, have rested us from the overmuch of sun. The sun alone, that is offtimes counted as Success, cannot give us the reward of those great words, "Well done."
>
> And now the resplendence of this New Day in our later lives finds us prepared to use its hours in spreading this bright month of happiness so that many will feel its glow of warmth. . . .
>
> The gliding shuttle sees one who stands at the head of a house and home, whose only quest is to guide the pattern of our lives away from black despair or wasted time that might tangle the weave, or leave the design scarred or unlovely to God's gaze, and blight our days with the sadness of regret. . . .
>
> God bless the Master of my Dreams, the Companion of my youth and my days of maturity and now of Life's fading years — years which he makes so bright by the help which God gave his courage and his faith. My heart is in complete accord with Browning's lines: "The best is yet to be," for we are now reaping the gladness of those "Best Years." The yearning of my heart is that we will be together all the way. . . .

With the launching of the drilling program at the Ram River property, Hugh Brown's primary responsibilities shifted from promotion to management — getting supplies, supervising

workers, and maintaining records. He divided his time between
Rocky Mountain House and the Richland office in Edmonton.
Some traveling was still required, and the journal notes that
Hugh "met many distinguished and successful men and had the
opportunity of discussing with them the principles of the Gospel."

Among those recruited for the Richland work force were
Zina Lou and her husband Gaurdello Brown, who moved from
Los Angeles and lived in the basement apartment of the Hugh
Brown home at 13511 101st Avenue from the summer of 1952
until the autumn of the following year. Gar was a helper in the
oil drilling operations, and Zina Lou acted as the company secretary.

For a month in the summer of 1952 Richland's work force
also included Hugh and Zina's oldest grandsons, Ed Firmage,
Mary's boy, and Dick Hodson, Zola's son. They had a delightful experience at the drilling camp, with only two or three visits
to Edmonton. Richard Hodson remembers the drive to the camp
with Gar Brown in these terms:

> We had good roads to Rocky Mountain House and then it took
> us several hours to go the 39 miles into camp. They told me that
> . . . on one occasion 12 hours were required to drive that distance
> because of the roads and the spring thaw. The roads were very
> muddy and slick, but it was not mountainous nor was there too
> much forest. No car would attempt to go up there without a winch.
> They would winch themselves literally from tree to tree all the way in.

The boys were assigned to a cabin in the camp and they
ate in the cookhouse with the workers. Food was plentiful and
included bear and deer meat on occasion. When their grandfather came to the camp, they would stay up far into the night
talking with him of philosophies of life, religious questions, and
many other things. It was a memorable experience for the two
high school youths. Ed Firmage recalls it in these words:

> As a young man of sixteen full of questions about life's mean-
> ing and my particular place in it, I was most grateful to be with
> one who was not only full of wisdom and experience but who took
> seriously my questions, however adolescent they may really have been.
> Throughout those long summer evenings in our bunkhouse we talked
> into the early morning hours often, on matters ranging from religion,

philosophy and life's purpose to the selection of a profession and the life of the law. Never did he answer childish questions with an abrupt or abrasive rebuke, never did he respond with an authoritarian, mind-chilling refusal to speculate, explore, or reconsider. While I never remember a time in which I did not simply assume that I would at some time fill a mission, I think I made the commitment firmly to myself that summer, sufficient to accept the call when it came.

Business travel precluded a major administrative role for Hugh Brown in the Edmonton Branch of the West Canadian Mission, but he taught Sunday School and High Priests quorum classes in the branch, and Sunday School in the Institute of Religion adjacent to the University of Alberta. When the branch was divided, the members were so upset at the prospect of losing their teacher that Hugh finally agreed to teach Sunday School classes in both branches as well as in the Institute. His teaching ability contributed to the popularity of the classes, and he took great care with preparation; stenographic transcripts which his daughter Zina Lou made of two lessons are evidence. He also spoke in other wards and branches, including some in southern Alberta which he had known as a stake president twenty-five years before. He was also invited to speak at the Sunday School general conference in Salt Lake City on April 6, 1952, and his address there, "The Voice of God Is Heard Again," appeared in the September issue of the *Instructor*.

"Mother and I were very happy during the time we were in Edmonton in spite of the fact that our ventures were not as successful as we had hoped they might be." This is the assessment which Hugh Brown included in a two-page "continuation of my journal" which he wrote in Salt Lake City on January 26, 1954, just a few weeks after he had left Canada to become a General Authority. The story of the last year of business activity in Alberta is summarized in these words:

> In my last entry I mentioned that as President and Managing Director of the Richland Oil Development Company . . . we were undertaking an ambitious drilling program. This program was continued and carried out during the following months and until the summer of 1953. We drilled on two locations in the Ram River Area to a depth of 4900 feet but did not encounter commercial production

of either oil or gas. Some good showings were had and encouraging indications, but the cost of drilling, together with the inaccessibility of the area, made it uneconomic to continue.

There is something poignant about the title, "Almost a Millionaire," under which an early narrative account of Hugh B. Brown's last episode as an Alberta lawyer-businessman appeared in print. (See *The Abundant Life,* pp. 265-271.) Within a very few years many who were prospecting around Edmonton became millionaires, but in the fall of 1953 Hugh and Zina were alone and the prospects for Richland were quite uncertain. Operating capital, including some invested by Hugh and his close friends, was running out. On the eve of his seventieth birthday Hugh B. Brown apparently experienced a feeling of uncertainty — of unfulfilled destiny — comparable to that which he had noted in his journal thirty years before.

The question of whether or not to persist in that quest for "real money" which had been for half a century a counterpoint to the main themes in his life was very much in Hugh's mind on that October morning when he "went into the mountains and talked to the Lord in prayer." What followed is recorded thus in his dictated memoirs:

> I told Him that although it looked like I was going to become wealthy as a result of my oil ventures, if in His wisdom it would not be good for me or my family I hoped He would not permit it to come to pass.
>
> That night I drove from the camp up at Rocky Mountain House down to Edmonton still spiritually disturbed and depressed. Without having dinner that night, I went into the bedroom by myself, told my wife that she should stay in the other room as I felt I would not have a good night's rest. All night long I wrestled with the evil spirit. I was possessed with the spirit of wishing that I could be rubbed out of existence. I had no thought of suicide, but wished the Lord would provide a way for me to cease to be. The room was full of darkness, and an evil spirit prevailed, so real that I was almost consumed by it. About three A.M. I was barely able to call to my wife. She came in and asked what was the matter. Upon closing the door, she said, "Oh Hugh! What is in this room?" And I replied, "The Devil." We spent the balance of the night together, much of it on our knees. The next morning upon going to the office (and there was no one there, it being Saturday) I knelt in prayer

again and asked for deliverance from the evil spirit. I felt a peaceful spirit come over me and phoned my wife to that effect.

That night, while I was taking a bath about ten o'clock, the telephone rang and she called me and said, "Salt Lake City is calling."

Upon going to the phone, I heard a voice which said, "This is David O. McKay calling. The Lord wants you to spend the balance of your life in the service of the Church. The Council of the Twelve have just voted that you should take the place made vacant by the recent death of Stayner Richards, and you are to become an Assistant to the Twelve."

The currant bush had been pruned again. Now, at the close of a normal life span of threescore years and ten, Hugh B. Brown knew what the Gardener wanted him to do.

15. Assistant to the Twelve

When Hugh B. Brown was sustained as an Assistant to the Council of the Twelve at the general conference in October, 1953, it was a long step toward the fulfillment of a cherished dream. He had been a teen-age farm boy in Spring Coulee, Alberta, when the dream was instilled in him by an incident involving his mother, Lydia, and a visitor in the Brown home, Elder Francis M. Lyman. Following the visit the apostle went to Cardston to preside at the stake conference, and the prophetic promise which ensued is remembered by President Brown as follows:

> Mother and I went to conference . . . in the horse and buggy. As we were coming home she told me of an experience she had had while Francis M. Lyman was addressing the conference. She said: "As I looked upon him he ceased to be Francis M. Lyman and became Hugh B. Brown and I saw you as occupying the position he then held. I know as I know I live that that's what is going to happen to you. If you will just behave yourself and do what is right, the time will come when you will be called into the Council of the Twelve."

Close as they were, it is not surprising that Hugh's mother often reminded him of this experience and reaffirmed her faith in his future. He comments, "I thank God for the fact that she, in her prophetic mood, warned me in time to save me from the pitfalls that threatened me."

When President Brown received the call from President McKay, he and Zina reflected back on some of the other incidents in which Hugh's potential for leadership had been assessed by some of the great men in his life. One that especially impressed him was a visit with his maternal grandfather, James S. Brown, just before Hugh left for England in 1904. The white-bearded, one-legged veteran of seventeen missions expressed regret that none of his sons had manifested a comparable zeal for proselyting. Then, looking at young Hugh, he said: "My son, I feel that to you will come the calling that will culminate the work that I have wanted to do for the Church. You, I believe, have been chosen by the Lord for great things in the Church. I want you to remember it and keep yourself worthy, so that when the time comes you will be called."

The blessing which the young Hugh Brown received from Patriarch John Smith contained a comparable promise: "You will sit among the leaders of the Church and the Lord has his eye on you." President Brown says that he did not interpret this to mean that he would become one of the General Authorities, but after giving him the blessing the patriarch pointed to him and said, "Young man, you will someday sit among the highest councils of the Church."

The episode in England when Heber J. Grant predicted that one of the group of missionaries would become a member of the Council of the Twelve has been noted in an earlier chapter. Years later President Grant told Hugh that he had considered him for an appointment to the Twelve, but the problems associated with the Liquor Commission made it inadvisable at the time. Several of the apostles confirmed President Grant's statement to Hugh, and Elder John A. Widtsoe is remembered as having stated, "The time will come when you will be in that group."

Certainly Hugh B. Brown had enjoyed the tutelage and fellowship of a remarkable group of Church leaders. In addition to three presidents, Joseph F. Smith, Heber J. Grant and David O. McKay, he was at one time or another on terms of personal friendship with Anthony W. Ivins, B. H. Roberts, Albert E. Bowen, J. Reuben Clark, Jr., Richard R. Lyman, J. Golden Kimball, James E. Talmage, Melvin J. Ballard, Harold B. Lee, Marion G. Romney, and others of the General Authorities. Interestingly, both of Hugh's counselors in the Granite Stake Presidency moved into Church-wide leadership positions: Marvin O. Ashton became a member of the Presiding Bishopric, and Stayner Richards, as noted, preceded President Brown as an Assistant to the Twelve.

In view of the prophecies dating back to his youth and the intimate contacts which he had had with Church leaders, it is possible that part of the depression which President Brown felt on that early October day in Edmonton reflected a feeling that he was nearing his seventieth birthday and seemed further away from the center of the Church and the fulfillment of his destiny than he had been for many years. On one occasion in London his son Charles Manley had asked if he wouldn't like to be a General Authority, and his reply was characteristic: "No, I have much more freedom as a mission president. . . ." Nevertheless there can be little doubt that Hugh B. Brown was thrilled when he received the call from President McKay. His memoirs note his reaction in this way:

> Although Mother and I had spent a wakeful night the night before, and a terrible night it was, this night we stayed awake as well, but rejoicing in the thought that the Lord would reach out to touch us in time of need. We were not seeking for position or place but were happy with the thought that we might be able to serve the Lord and his Kingdom.

Among President Brown's papers are some interesting sidelights on this turning point in his life. One is a clipping from *The Albertan,* dating back to his first call to the British Mission presidency. The non-LDS columnist speaks favorably of both Hugh Brown and the Mormons and adds, "Knowing Mr. Brown as well as I do, I am quite sure that he will before long be very near the highest position in his church, if not indeed actually occupying it." Other documents record two occasions on which President Brown has told groups of missionaries that one among them, if he lives faithfully, "will stand where I now stand as a member of the Council of the Twelve."

Edmonton was too far from Salt Lake City for the Browns to attend the closing sessions of the October conference, but within a few days the new General Authority met with President McKay and his first counselor, Stephen L Richards, to be set apart and receive instructions. The eighty-year-old President of the Church performed the ordinance and told Hugh B. Brown that if he would be true and faithful there would be other callings lying ahead. He attributed the deep depression which had been experienced in Alberta to the influence of Satan, pointing out that many of the General Authorities had had comparable tests prior to receiving their appointments. He and President Richards reviewed some of their own experiences as LDS leaders and previewed what Elder Brown might expect in his labors in the ministry. It was a profoundly impressive introduction to what a journal entry of January 26, 1954, describes as "a calling which I undertake with humility, with some misgivings, and with deep gratitude. . . ."

The home in Canada was quickly disposed of, and 1117 Alpine Place, Salt Lake City, became the base of operations for Hugh and Zina Brown for the next eight years. According to the journal, the couple were enjoying "reasonably good health, although we begin to feel the effects of approaching age." He passed his "70th milestone" on October 24, 1953; she was sixty-five and their marriage was in its forty-fifth year. In addition to the seven living children, the proud patriarch noted, "We have twenty-one grandchildren and find great joy in visiting with them whenever possible." A very early highlight of the new calling was the opportunity for the Browns to attend the ceremonies at the laying of the cornerstone of the Los Angeles Temple. Zina Lou, Zola, LaJune, Manley and Margaret were all living in Southern California at the time, and a joyful reunion was held.

Elder Brown noted that his duties consisted "in the main of filling appointments to attend and preside at stake conferences of the Church, to ordain and set apart officers in various capacities, officiate in the temple in marriage ceremonies, sealings, etc., and in other ways act as an assistant to the Council of the Twelve." Often Sister Brown accompanied him to conferences in various parts of the country and the world, on tours of missions and on special assignments, and her testimony was heard by many congregations. These were happy times of togetherness, and President Brown remembers them as some of the most rewarding in his life. In fact, he recalls that he enjoyed being an Assistant to the Twelve perhaps even more than being an Apostle, because he did not feel quite the same burden of responsibility and could simply enjoy the assignments which gave him a chance to travel, meet many wonderful people, observe the rapid growth of the Church, counsel with the local leaders, appoint new leaders, and try to help people with their problems. A family letter, dated May 27, 1954, conveys this enthusiasm:

> Just a line to report in after our tour of the Northern States Mission. Both Mother and I returned in good health, both grateful for the opportunity we had to partake of the missionary spirit again and to meet so many new friends and so many old ones. During our trip we traveled 2,000 miles within the mission, held 27 meetings, dedicated 6 chapels and did all the interviewing, advising and administering, etc. that goes with such work. Altogether it was a glorious event. . . .

A very important assignment which came to Hugh B. Brown at this time was the screening of applications for cancellation of temple marriages. He remembered the call this way:

> About one year after I came down from Canada, President McKay called me into his office and said, "We have a number of applications from married people for cancellation of their temple sealings. This involves the inquiry into the causes and results of civil divorce. I would like you to take it over if you will. Investigate all of these cases and, with your legal background, advise me as to what should be done in each case. . . .

The discharge of this assignment, which continued after President Brown became an apostle, took a great deal of time and careful attention. Several hundred cases were reviewed, and where sufficient evidence of infidelity was found, or conclusive evidence of the hopelessness of reconciliation, a recommendation for cancellation of the sealing ordinance was usually made. President McKay explained when making the assignment that the fundamental ground for cancellation was sexual immorality on the part of one of the parties concerned. He also advised that

when a couple had obtained a civil divorce and one or both partners had foreclosed reconciliation by remarrying, and especially
when no children were involved, requests for cancellation might
be granted.

Elder Brown made it a rule to call in the parties concerned
if they were in the Salt Lake area, or if they were in the neighborhood of a stake conference he was visiting. He would talk
with the couple, first together and then separately, to find out
the cause of the civil divorce. Often he found that it was basically lack of communication, and he was sometimes able to affect
a reconciliation if there had been no intervening marriage. He
realized that he did not have the training and experience necessary to help all of these people, and he frequently referred them
to psychologists, physicians, psychiatrists, or marriage counselors
for aid in restoring their marriages. President Brown remembers
that some cases presented such difficulties that he simply recommended that no action be taken on the sealings, leaving the
issues to be resolved in the resurrection. Over the years he became very understanding of people's needs and feelings and often
said, "If I make errors I want them to be on the side of mercy."

President McKay was so impressed by the handling of this
delicate assignment that he sent this handwritten note on March
24, 1956:

> My Dear Brother Brown,
>
> Having just completed most of this day on applications for can-
> cellation of sealings, I feel impelled to send you this note of apprecia-
> tion for your masterful attention to this arduous duty. Your careful,
> intelligent consideration in each case merits the highest commenda-
> tion and praise. Your assistance to me in this important phase of
> Church work is immeasurable. Please be assured of my deep grati-
> tude. God bless you.
>
> Affectionately,
> David O. McKay

Out of this work, plus experience as adviser to servicemen,
missionaries and students and fifty years as husband and father,
came the popular and still current book *You and Your Marriage*.
Published in 1960, the volume is dedicated to Sister Brown — "a

most successful matrimonial mariner," who "has valiantly stood at the helm beside the 'Captain' through high seas and stormy weather, without flinching or complaining. She now nestles with him in the harbor and sweetly whispers, 'It was worth it. I'd do it all again.' " "The excuse for writing," declared the author, "is the conviction that a large percentage of marriage failures could have been avoided if, figuratively, the drivers — both front- and back-seat drivers — had taken some elementary instructions and passed some simple tests before being allowed to 'take the wheel.' "

The contents of this volume, the only one written by Hugh B. Brown for publication as a book, are arranged under five topics: "Marriage Instituted by God, Therefore Eternal," "Pre-requisites — Education for Marriage," "Postrequisites," "The Family," and "The Ripening Years." In chapters bearing such titles as "Purity is Priceless" and "In-laws Get Off the Boat" are found such homely and profound observations as these:

> Marriage is an enterprise for adults. They who do marry in infancy — and some infants are more than twenty years old — find themselves in almost constant conflict. (P. 26.)
>
> . . . religion, if sincere, is fundamental, and wisdom would suggest in the interest of peace and happiness that not only Latter-day Saints, but men and women of other faiths, should marry members of their own church. (P. 42.)
>
> The way married couples meet and cope with life's problems, and with each other's weaknesses, idiosyncrasies, and foibles, will determine in large measure how their own children will solve the age-old and continuing problems of human relationships. (P. 49.)
>
> One of the cornerstones of happy married life, so often disregarded by parents as they train their children for future wedlock, is the necessity for harmonious sexual activities between the parties thereto. Each couple should, with reverence, intelligence, and consideration, build solidly and skilfully on this stone in the foundation of the temple of the home. The man who seeks physiological or biological satisfaction without regard to the effects of his conduct on the highly sensitive physical, mental and spiritual personality of his wife, fails to realize how fundamental proper sex behavior is to future happiness. . . . (Pp. 74-75.)
>
> Let all young pilgrims know that God is a Loving Father who stands ready to assist them. He understands the weaknesses of His children, and, if they fall and sincerely wish to rise again, they can

rely upon His love and mercy and obtain the blessings that follow true repentance. . . . (P. 83.)

It is not only what we do that tends to break up our marriage, but what we fail to do. . . . I think it was a Scotsman who said, at his wife's bier, "She was a good and lovely lady and once I almost told her so." (Pp. 98, 101.)

How unfortunate it is that so many of us put on our worst behavior in the home. (P. 117.)

It takes self-discipline to select a good book rather than a western on the TV, to enjoy a home evening with the family rather than go to a second-rate movie, to keep the mind in gear rather than let it idle. . . . (P. 129.)

The Latter-day Saints believe in large families wherever it is possible to provide for the necessities of life, for the health and education of their children, and when the physical and mental health of the mother permits. . . . The parents with the largest families are, generally speaking, most successful in life's battle. (Pp. 135, 136.)

Marriage should be a complete and a genuine love-inspired partnership, where each ascribes to the other not only maturity but also intelligence. For a man to deny his wife her right to examine the joint balance sheet occasionally, is to imply that it is not jointly earned, or that she is not intelligent enough to understand it. . . . No husband would stand for it if their respective roles were reversed. (Pp. 148-149.)

Worry is more exhausting than work. (P. 179.)

This program of enjoying things together, which begins in courtship, should not lapse, but continue through the early, middle, and later married years. The couple should not wait until the days of their active parenthood are past before undertaking their joint project of enriching life. If they have not learned along the way to be delightful, lively, interesting, and inquisitive, then when their active parenthood days are past, there is danger of their seeking the chimney corner, where, as querulous old people, they may huddle and commiserate. (P. 107.)

One of Elder Brown's most exciting assignments as an Assistant to the Twelve was to represent President McKay at the laying of the cornerstone of the new temple being erected in New Zealand. He was instructed "to take my wife with me and to tour some of the South Sea missions en route." The couple left Salt Lake City on December 5, 1956, and spent three months visiting the LDS branches and absorbing the scenery in New Zealand, Australia, and the Hawaiian Islands. At the cornerstone ceremonies on December 22, "the Maori people sang beautifully, and the various services held were not only well attended, but enthusiastic."

President Brown also visited the West Canadian, California, Canadian, Southwest Indian, and Central American missions between 1953 and 1958. A highlight of the visit to Central America in January of the latter year was the opportunity to travel with his missionary grandson, Richard Hodson, Zola's oldest child, who was assigned by the mission president to act as an interpreter during part of the tour. President Brown recorded that he was very proud of Richard, whose "Spanish was excellent." It may be assumed that Elder Hodson was also very proud of the grandfather whom he had come to know so well in the prospecting camp near Rocky Mountain House a few years before.

The speaking ability of President Brown was an important and recognized asset during his years as Assistant to the Twelve. In addition to the almost weekly stake conference visits and the mission tours, he was frequently called upon by the First Presidency to represent the Church on national radio broadcasts. "The Living Christ" was his Christmas message on the CBS "Church of the Air," December 19, 1954, and "History's Most Eventful Week" was his Easter sermon on the NBC "Faith in Action" series, April 3, 1955. Under the title "Whom Say Ye That I Am?" he delivered five testimonial addresses on the divinity of Christ over Radio Station KSL between December 26, 1954, and January 30, 1955. (*Continuing the Quest,* pp. 81-118.) Interesting insight into Hugh B. Brown's sensitivity to his audiences may be found by comparing two Easter Messages which he delivered on April 6, 1958. The first, over NBC, expressed his testimony in terms of broadest appeal: "We join with other Christians in celebrating this miraculous event. . . . We humbly proclaim not only the reality of his resurrection, but the certainty of his second advent." (*Ibid.,* p. 447.) The second, given before the Tabernacle congregation which that day sustained him as a member of the Quorum of the Twelve, was in categorically LDS terms:

The announcement of the Church today, and let all people heed as they hear, is that this same Jesus has appeared again, established his kingdom, organized his Church with apostles and prophets and set in motion a great missionary system by which the gospel of Jesus Christ shall be carried to all the world as a witness, and then the end shall come. (*Ibid.,* p. 80.)

The first volume of Hugh B. Brown's speeches and writings, edited by Charles Manley Brown, appeared in 1956. Its title, *Eternal Quest,* reflects one of President Brown's favorite themes: "Awareness, like creation and salvation, is an on-going process. The quest for truth is eternal." The selections range from *Millennial Star* editorials and articles for other Church publications to radio addresses, talks at BYU devotionals and leadership weeks, and general conference sermons. The first selection is his poem, "I Would Be Worthy," which was later set to music by Lowell Durham and performed by the Tabernacle Choir:

I WOULD BE WORTHY

I thank thee, Lord, that thou hast called me "son,"
And fired my soul with the astounding thought
That there is something of thee in me.
May the prophecy of this relationship —
    Impel me to be worthy.

I am grateful for the covenant birth;
For noble parents and an ancestry who beckon me
To heights beyond my grasp, but still attainable
If with stamina and effort I cultivate their seed —
    And prove that I am worthy.

I am grateful for a companion on this Eternal Quest.
Whose roots and birth and vision match my own;
Whose never-failing faith and loyalty have furnished light
        in darkness,
    Inspire me to be worthy.

I am grateful for the cleansing power of parenthood,
With its self-denial and sacrifice — prerequisites to filial
        and parent love;
For each child entrusted to our care, I humbly thank thee;
If I would associate with them eternally.
    I know I must be worthy.

I am grateful for the one who was recalled in youth,
For his love and loyalty and sacrifice.
May the memory of his clean and manly life keep resolute
        the hope
That I may renew companionship with him — and thee;
        For this I would be worthy.

I am grateful for the children of my children
And, in anticipation, for others yet to be.
Keep alive, I pray, within my bosom, a sense of obligation
        unto them.
To pass a name unsullied as it came. To become an
        honored sire.
        O make me worthy!

I am grateful for the lifting power of the gospel of thy Son;
For the knowledge thou hast given me of its beauty, truth
        and worth.
To attain its promised glory, may I to the end endure,
And then, forgiven, let charity tip the scales and allow me
        To be considered worthy.

                                                    — Hugh B. Brown

The book, now out of print, is inspirational and often entertaining reading, yet many who remember hearing some of
the talks agree that the essence of Hugh B. Brown is not captured on the printed page. J. Reuben Clark, Jr., recognized
this in a card of thanks which he wrote to Hugh and Zina Brown
acknowledging their 1959 Christmas greeting. To the man
who one day would succeed him as a counselor in the First
Presidency, President Clark said: "I want to congratulate you
upon the great gift which God has given to you of the power
of speech, of real oratory. The Saints of the Church love to
hear you, as do others. May you continue to be an inspiration
to them for many years to come."

A master of arts candidate at Brigham Young University
once used magnetic tapes of several BYU addresses as the basis
for "An Analysis of the Speaking Style of Hugh B. Brown, Mormon Orator." William E. Morgan, Jr., came to the unstartling
conclusion that "one major reason that Hugh B. Brown is so
well liked as a speaker is that he constantly uses many of the
principles of effective public speaking as taught by today's speech
teachers." (M.A. Thesis, BYU, 1968, p. 237.) The principles

had not, of course, been learned from textbooks but from sitting at the feet of such oratorical giants as Brigham H. Roberts, Orson F. Whitney, John W. Taylor, and Melvin J. Ballard, and from practicing before soldiers, jurors, Mormon congregations on two continents, and among the patient pines on the southern Alberta frontier. One of Morgan's findings is of particular interest in view of the partial facial paralysis caused by the surgery for tic douloureux. "President Brown had no pronunciation problems in these speeches. He did have a slight number of errors of articulation, which were mainly due to his desire to deliver a more appropriate word [and not] because of any sluggishness on the part of his articulators." (*Ibid.*)

One clue to President Brown's popularity as a speaker is provided by a bedraggled envelope with a 47 East South Temple return address. On it he once pencilled several witticisms — whether because he had just heard or invented them or because he planned to use them in an upcoming talk is not clear. Among them are these:

> To get chap off lips, slap face.
>
> I'd be satisfied with my walk in life, if I didn't have to shovel it.
>
> A boy should not ask a girl for her hand unless he's able to remove it from her father's pocket.

His platform humor carefully avoids the broad puns and earthy wisecracks which have tickled the Brown children and grandchildren and sometimes led Zina to scold "Oh, Hugh!" But President Brown has no qualms about reaching for a laugh in order to engage his listeners, even if they are a congregation in the Salt Lake Tabernacle.

That public speaking was a joy to Hugh B. Brown was recognized by Zina and the children during the Cardston days. The delight did not diminish with the years, nor did the obvious ability to move audiences diminish the self-image. As President Brown frankly acknowledged only a few years ago, "Every man is supported by the public's opinion of him." Yet he recognized the hazard when the gift was combined with the calling of a General Authority. His taped reminiscences contain this answer

to a question about what he learned from traveling around the
Church as an Assistant to the Twelve:

> I think the main lesson I learned was humility. When one is out
> speaking, representing the General Authorities, he is eulogized and
> almost idolized. What is said is taken as gospel and what he does
> is an example to all. . . . Sometimes men in such a position are in-
> clined to think that they themselves are the object of this adulation
> when in fact what the people are doing is indicating their respect for
> the authority the man holds and the appointment that he has re-
> ceived. If we can keep in mind that fact and never arrogate to our-
> selves the honor which belongs to the office, we will be safe. . . .

President McKay's promise that greater assignments lay in
store for Hugh B. Brown was fulfilled to a degree when he
announced in the April, 1958, general conference that Elder
Brown had been called to fill the vacancy in the Council of the
Twelve caused by the death of Adam S. Bennion. The new
apostle wrote in his journal:

> This calling was very humbling indeed, but in fulfillment of a
> life long ambition of my beloved mother, who predicted it when I
> was but a boy. I was ordained an apostle in the Salt Lake Temple
> in the meeting of the Council of the First Presidency and the Quorum
> of the Twelve, by President David O. McKay, on April 10, 1958.

Sister Brown, writing a birthday note to Zola five days
after the conference, exulted:

> My joy was so great — a real shock of joy — that I'm just get-
> ting over being stunned by it. And now it looms so large and so
> beautiful, and so great that my life has been illumined anew and I
> feel like I had had a glimpse into heaven.
>
> Daddy is almost overcome with the wonder of it all. . . .

Thus, a new opportunity came to Hugh B. Brown to serve
the Church he loved.

16. Apostle and Counselor

The five years following his appointment to the Quorum of the Twelve Apostles must have been among the most exciting and fulfilling years of Hugh B. Brown's life. They were accented with worldwide travel, which members of his family often shared. His health was remarkably good, and his beloved Zina was able to enjoy many of the memorable experiences with him. His financial worries were over and the members of his family were generally comfortably and happily situated. To be ordained an apostle, a special witness of Jesus Christ, was the crowning event in his life. And to be chosen as a counselor in the First Presidency must have been particularly gratifying. These were years in which the Church was prospering and growing, and there were many opportunities for Hugh B. Brown to render the kinds of service for which his varied experiences in life had prepared him.

His reminiscences give details on the manner and circumstances of his call and ordination to the Twelve. President McKay asked to see him in the Tabernacle office of the General Authorities immediately after the Sunday morning session of the April 1958 general conference. There the Church leader said: "The Lord wants you to be a member of the Council of the Twelve. How do you feel about it?" President Brown remembers saying, "Well, if I was ever justified in criticizing what the Lord wants, I am in that position now because I feel that I am unprepared." President McKay answered: "We don't agree with you. We have submitted it to the Twelve and they have approved, and now we want you to tell us whether you will accept." The reply was predictable. "Of course I will accept any call that comes from the Lord, and I will do the best that I can. . . ." The new apostle was invited to address the conference after being sustained, and he pledged to devote the balance of his life to trying to justify the faith of the Brethren in him.

Following the ordination in the Temple on April 10, 1958, Hugh B. Brown received his charge as an apostle from President McKay. This charge, according to President Brown's memoirs, included the commitments to give all, both of time and means, to the building of the kingdom of God, to keep pure and unspotted from the sins of the world, and to support the decisions of the Council of the Twelve and the First Presidency. The new apostle was given to understand that, in his calling, he had freedom to speak his own mind on all problems of concern to the Church, but he must be willing to accept decisions of these quorums and thereafter support them by word and deed. Not every action of these councils in the ensuing years reflected the personal preferences of Hugh B. Brown, but he remained faithful to this commitment.

As an apostle, Elder Brown continued to screen applications for cancellation of temple sealings, and he spent many hours in his office counseling members of the Church who sought his advice. He also instructed and set apart missionaries, visited missions, presided at stake conferences and made personnel changes, spoke at funerals, dedicated chapels, and acted as host to important visitors who came to Salt Lake City. Sister Brown's letters to her children record that these were busy times. "He awakens early — sometimes 2 a.m. — this time he spends reading and writing in bed," she wrote in one letter. And in another: "Daddy is typing — working on his Conference talk. This is the fourth one he has written. . . ." She added, "Daddy needs your prayers for this very strenuous time. . . . Oh, Zola, he is surely a man of God."

Quorum of the Twelve, April 1958: l. to r. (seated) Joseph Fielding Smith (president), Harold B. Lee, Spencer W. Kimball, Ezra Taft Benson, Mark E. Petersen, Henry D. Moyle, (standing) Delbert L. Stapley, Marion G. Romney, LeGrand Richards, Richard L. Evans, George Q. Morris, Hugh B. Brown.

HUGH

1908

ZINA

Grow old along with me;
The best is yet to be,
The last of life,
For which the first was made.

—Browning

FATHER

1958

MOTHER

Fiftieth wedding anniversary — program pictures.

*June 11, 1959, Elder Brown bends to kiss Sister Brown
as they receive the Master M Man and the Golden
Gleaner awards.*

The fiftieth anniversary of the marriage of Hugh and Zina Brown was celebrated at a reception in the Garden Park Ward chapel on June 12, 1958. The "before and after" pictures on the program show that the years had matured but not marred the loving couple. The program's quoted lines from Browning had begun to appear in their correspondence at least twenty years before:

> Grow old along with me:
> The best is yet to be,
> The last of life,
> For which the first was made.

These were some of the best years for Zina Brown. Although her health was not always good and the petite figure which once caught Hugh Brown's eye had long since taken on matronly dimensions, she was a poised and participating partner in many of her husband's activities. She was also called upon for talks, particularly to Mormon young women, and she enjoyed the monthly "Wives' Luncheons" in the Lion House, at which the partners and widows of the General Authorities enjoyed a unique and amiable relationship. Visits with the children and grand-children were frequent, and even more frequent were the letters to them, full of comfort, nonmalicious gossip, encouragement, family tidings, admonition and praise.

To bring their home closer to his work, and to reduce her household tasks, in late 1958 the Browns moved from Alpine Place to what one of his letters refers to as "our little love nest" at the Eagle Gate Apartments. There he would often come home for lunch and a quick nap afterwards. But what at first seemed cozy was soon too cramped for the entertaining of family and friends, so early in 1960 they purchased a home at 1002 Douglas Street, on Salt Lake City's east bench. Here they shared the last fifteen years of their earthly partnership. And here, on Christmas Day, 1962, Hugh gave to Zina a diamond such as he had coveted for her for more than half a century. The note which accompanied it read:

Sweetheart:

Fifty-five years ago I was looking forward to June when you would become my bride. I bought the best gem my meager means would permit.

Since then you have given me eight of the most precious jewels of earth or heaven.

Only a diamond can symbolize the enduring love which has grown through the years.

God bless and spare you to me and us that our love may continue to grow throughout eternity.

Your own forever,
Hugh

On the evening of June 21, 1961, Hugh B. Brown received a call from President McKay asking that he come to the President's office the following morning. There the leader of the Church, then in his eighty-eighth year and himself somewhat impaired in health, said that because of the illness of President J. Reuben Clark, Jr., and the volume of work that was dependent on the First Presidency, he felt it necessary to call an additional counselor. He proposed to recommend the one-time Spring Coulee cowboy for the position. The journal records, "I was, of course, overwhelmed, but inasmuch as the call came from the President of the Church, I had but one course to take and that was to humbly accept the responsibility."

At the ensuing meeting of members of the Council of the Twelve and the First Presidency in the Salt Lake Temple, President McKay's nomination was unanimously adopted. Then, according to the journal, "the President of the Church, with President [Henry D.] Moyle and members of the Council of the Twelve, laid hands upon my head and the President set me apart as a Counselor to the First Presidency." (In his dictated memoirs President Brown calls attention to the significance of the preposition "to" in this ordination: "The revelation says that the Quorum of the First Presidency shall consist of three high priests. If you put another in as a member of the quorum or counselor *in* the First Presidency, you are enlarging that quorum, but if you make them counselors *to* the First Presidency, you could add a hundred if you wanted to."

President Brown served in this capacity for less than four months before the death of President Clark on October 6, 1961, necessitated a reconstitution of the presiding quorum of the Church. President McKay selected Henry D. Moyle and Hugh B. Brown to be the new first and second counselors, and the proposals were approved and the two men set apart in the Salt Lake Temple on October 12. President Brown's journal notes that both the June and October announcements brought "literally hundreds of letters, telegrams, telephone calls, etc., in which the people generally expressed confidence and support." He further noted, "However, I undertake the work with grave misgivings and trepidations, but with faith in God and in His promise to help those whom He calls to labor to accomplish the work which he assigns to them."

The first public functioning in his new calling was on October 22 — "a last-minute appointment, because of the illness of President McKay, to dedicate the Ogden Stake Center." The journal notes that "the spirit of the occasion was most remarkable," and it adds, "Sister Brown accompanied me on this trip and, by invitation, we visited President and Sister McKay at their lovely home in Huntsville, where we had dinner together and an enjoyable visit." More than a half-century before these two charismatic men and exemplary women had enjoyed a camping trip together at Waterton Lakes, Alberta. Their lives had frequently intersected and interfaced, and now they were linked together in a relationship of profound importance to the Church which they had loved and served for so long.

Two days later Hugh B. Brown celebrated his seventy-eighth birthday. His journal records it thus:

> The employees of the office here gave me a party in my large office, which now is downstairs in the Church office building, all at the instigation of my capable secretary, Norma Ashdown. They made it a surprise party by getting me out of the office for a time until they could assemble. The birthday itself was a very busy day because President McKay was ill and President Moyle in Europe. . . .

Most days were busy in the months which followed. "My present duties in the office require about 12 hours a day of my time," he noted in March, 1962, "but I am thoroughly enjoying them and enjoying reasonably good health." In addition to the duties which he had as an apostle, he was now assigned the chairmanship of the Genealogical Society, with general supervision of all the temples and of the Data Processing and Electronics Committee, which had oversight of revolutionary changes in the Church's record-keeping and information systems. He was also appointed to be vice-president and director of the Beneficial Life Insurance Company, Zions Securities, KSL, Utah-Idaho Sugar Company, Z.C.M.I. and the Hotel Utah.

President Brown's journal passes lightly over the fact that he was working "twelve hours a day in the office" in addition to the numerous speaking engagements he accepted in the evenings. His years of hard work and self-discipline made it possible for him to survive such a schedule and his brilliant mind and charismatic personality enabled him to counsel stake and ward leaders, young people with problems, college leaders and professors, business executives, married couples on the brink of divorce, and Church members seeking answers for tragedies in their lives. It required strong reserves of physical, mental and spiritual energy.

Speaking of his self-discipline and his working habits, his secretary Vera Hutchinson wrote:

> I think President Brown has always set himself goals. As I can see his youthful experience herding those cattle in Canada, he was not about to let them stray, while others of his family were not quite that demanding of themselves. He did the job at hand, but always his goal for that job was a little higher, or much higher, than the job demanded.
>
> I found this to be the case when I first worked for him while he was in the Presidency from 1966 to 1970. He never took a day to forget it all. I didn't say rest, because I know he observed the Sabbath insofar as it was possible, and he did spend as many evenings as possible in his home with Sister Brown. But he was always at the office at 7 a.m. and in fact accomplished more during that first hour than most people do from 8 to 5. His mind went so fast, and things began to pop the minute he walked into the office. He knew right where he was going.

President Brown's travels during the years 1958-1963 were very extensive. It seems amazing that a man of his age could survive the assignments, including the long plane rides, the different bed almost every night, the variety of foods, and the pressures associated with his position as a spokesman for the Church, but he seemed to thrive on them. As president of the British Mission he had learned to replenish his strength by occasional sightseeing journeys, and this practice was repeated as a General Authority. The companionship of members of his family and the opportunities to squeeze vacation interludes into many of the journeys lightened the burdens, and Hugh B. Brown's unquenchable enthusiasm for seeing new places and meeting new people is reflected in the letters and reports which each trip produced.

The first major trip was to Europe in August and September, 1958. Accompanied by his wife and three daughters, Zina Lou, Zola and Mary, President Brown combined business with sightseeing in New York City, Norway, Switzerland and France. In Bern they visited the Swiss Temple. In Paris President Brown had the unhappy responsibility of working with the president of the French Mission to check an apostate movement which had made some inroads among the missionaries and members; the excommunication of several young men and women was the sad outcome. A visit to the Brussels World's Fair and a tour of The Netherlands Mission led up to the climax of the trip, the dedication of the British Temple by President McKay on September 7. After these inspiring services the Browns returned to America on the S.S. *United States,* a restful finale to what the journal describes as "a glorious trip for all of us."

Visits to many stake conferences and tours of the Central Atlantic, Western States and West Central States Missions preceded the next overseas journey — to Europe and the Near East in the summer of 1960. This time the objective was primarily sightseeing, and the traveling companion was LaJune. Much had transpired in the lives of father and daughter since she had chauffeured for him on some of the senatorial campaign trips in 1934, and the journal records that "the opportunity to

With daughter LaJune on 1960 Near East trip.

have an intimate visit" made this "a memorable trip for both
of us." From New York they flew to Lisbon, Madrid and Rome,
enjoying the cities but disliking the Spanish bullfight. Then they
did the tourist circuit of Cairo, Beirut, Baalbek, Damascus and
the Holy Land. La June remembers that her father almost had
a heart attack climbing a pyramid. Athens, Basel, Bern, Geneva,
Paris, London and Edinburgh followed in rather rapid sequence,
with a pause in Manchester "where we held a stake conference
in the new and first stake in Europe and met many old friends
and former associates." Father and daughter parted in Glasgow,
he for New York and she via the polar route for Los Angeles.
Long afterward their letters still referred to each other as "The
Sheik" and "The Queen of Sheba."

Another major Church assignment took Hugh B. Brown
to Europe and Africa early the next year. Accompanied by
Sister Brown he left Salt Lake City on February 22, 1961, traveling with President and Sister McKay via New York to London.
Others in the party were Elder N. Eldon Tanner, then an Assistant to the Twelve, his wife, Sarah, and Elder Alvin R. Dyer. All
participated in the dedicatory services for the impressive Hyde
Park Chapel and in the organization of a stake in London. The
McKays then returned to America, while the three other General
Authorities organized stakes in Leicester and Leeds, England,
and in The Hague, Holland. President and Sister Brown then
flew to Johannesburg, South Africa, for a month of touring the
mission and enjoying the scenic and zoological wonders of The
Wilderness and Kruger National Park. They left for home on
April 27, with stops at Dakar, New York, and Washington and
a brief visit with Carol's family in Silver Spring, Maryland.

Always sensitive to the danger of overreaching zeal, President Brown spoke to a seminar for mission presidents a few
months later on questionable proselyting tactics which were ap-
pearing in some areas. Reassurance for both missionaries and
the missionary parents is in these words which later appeared in
the *Improvement Era:*

> These young people under you are like colts. They are purebreds
> but all are not intended or fitted for the same kind of work. . . . We
> do not expect a Hambletonian to be a good plow horse nor a plow

Elder Brown in typical pulpit pose in Manchester, England, at organization of the Leeds Stake, 1960.

horse to be a good racer. So with these young men. Classify them and
do not yoke them together unequally. Do not expect the same speed
or pulling power from each. Beyond all else, inspire and save them.
Do not allow competition to become the chief incentive to work.
Encourage them all, of course, to do their best, but let your competition from now on be with your own mission, your own past record,
and not with any other mission. . . . Encourage them to be humble
and prayerful. Do not downgrade them with unfavorable compari-
sons. Preserve their self-confidence and self-respect. . . . In your
enthusiasm to increase the flock, be careful you don't lose the shep-
herds. (*Continuing the Quest,* p. 64.)

During his two years as second counselor in the First Presidency, President and Sister Brown made two trips to Hawaii, one
to dedicate buildings at the Church College at Laie, and another
quick visit to Samoa and Australia. He also made an extensive
tour of Alaska, accompanied by his good friend Milton Weilenmann, then president of the Alaskan-Canadian Mission. The
journal duly notes meetings with servicemen, students, missionaries, civic leaders, and Mormon congregations, but the words
"exciting" and "fabulous" are reserved for the fishing. The
two days flying out of Anchorage with a bush pilot produced
"the best fishing I have ever known anywhere in the world."
(Of course, some of President Brown's most notable fishing feats
were in 1962 still in the future.) The beautiful polar bear rug
given him by the members of the mission and the Alaska Stake
was accorded a featured place in his office.

Special assignments also included the dedication of the
Visitors Center at Sharon, Vermont, the birthplace of Joseph
Smith, a visit to Illinois to help organize the Nauvoo Restoration
project, and participation with President McKay and other
General Authorities in the ground-breaking for the Oakland
Temple. In June, 1963, President Brown visited Fort Lewis,
Washington, where he was made an honorary colonel in the
United States Army and "treated with great deference." It
brought back many memories.

Europe called the Browns again in October, 1962, this time
with two of Hugh's sisters, Roumelia Hartley and Verona A.
Hamblin, as traveling companions. Their hosts in London were

the N. Eldon Tanners, who were presiding over the West
European Mission at the time. (Elder Tanner had been sustained as a member of the Council of the Twelve at the general
conference just completed.) President Brown described the
"hospitality as matchless and the rest as very much worthwhile."
Two stake conferences conducted by President Marion D. Hanks
of the First Council of Seventy, then serving as British Mission
president, particularly pleased the former British Mission president because of the "evidence of renewed interest and growth."
Meetings in Paris, Geneva, Bern, Zurich and Vienna followed.
Despite the Cuban missile crisis, the scheduled LDS serviceman's
conference at Berchtesgaden, Germany, was "a wonderful convention," with over eight hundred in attendance. A side trip
to see "Mad Ludwig's" palace at Chiemsee produced the verdict,
"the most fantastic building I have ever seen, and undoubtedly
one of the most costly." Church business then required President
Brown to fly back to Salt Lake City, while Zina, Roumelia and
Verona came by boat to New York and reached home in late
November.

President and Sister Brown made several trips to Alberta
during this period, including a motor trip with Mary and Ed
Firmage which featured sightseeing in the Canadian Rockies
and the dedication of a new stake center at Edmonton. Three
weeks later the Browns flew back for Cardston's seventy-fifth
anniversary celebration. On July 4, 1962, the man who had
come to Alberta in 1899 to seek his fortune — and find his
wife — shared the platform with Canadian Prime Minister John
Diefenbaker. It was a particularly exciting time for Sister Brown,
one of the first children to be born in the town which bore her
father's name. The *Lethbridge Herald* carried a feature article
which she wrote for the special anniversary edition. President
Brown took care of some business relative to Church property,
including the Cochrane Ranch which had figured so prominently
in his youthful efforts at farming and stock raising. The special
issue of the *Herald* printed pictures of the Browns and commented on President Brown's impressive career and his position
in the Church. It also carried a picture of the first class to
graduate from grade twelve in Cardston; two of the members

were Glenn Nielson, who became president of the Husky Oil Company and a very good friend of the Browns, and Nathan Eldon Tanner.

Some of Hugh B. Brown's finest sermons and addresses were produced during these busy and exciting years. "Fit to Live" was the title of his appeal for physical and all-around personal development on the CBS "Church of the Air," June 14, 1959. "Man . . . is only fully alive and capable of enjoying life if all aspects of his complex nature are kept healthy and growing," he declared. The NBC radio audience heard a thoughtful analysis of Mormon doctrine on the "Covenant" program, March 10, 1963. The vernacular of the media was employed by President Brown in explaining one of the Articles of Faith:

> . . . because of our faith in the universal and unchangeable love and justice of God, we cannot believe that in some dispensations His Church will be blessed and led by what in television parlance might be termed "live" revelation and that in this, the dispensation of the fulness of times, our distraught and imperiled world is left with only the recorded messages of ancient prophets, some of which were given for specific purposes or to meet special conditions. We believe that revelation, both live and recorded, is now and will continue to be available to men.

By special appointment from President McKay, who had received an invitation to address the students at the Presbyterian Theological Seminary, President and Sister Brown flew to Pittsburgh in February, 1962. Following meetings with missionaries and members in the area, he gave the seminarians a two-hour discourse on LDS organization, history and doctrines. The talk was published in the *Deseret News* and later as a pamphlet for general distribution throughout the Church. It bore the simple title, *Mormonism*.

The appearance of *You and Your Marriage* in 1960 has been previously mentioned. Parts of this volume had previously been used in addresses and periodical articles, and the treatment of personal morality was substantially expanded for an address to a three-stake fireside at Brigham Young University a few months after an honorary doctorate was bestowed on the author.

On September 22, 1962, President Brown asked several thousand collegians, "Shall we then think together about such subjects as dances, dates, and danger; parties, people, and petting; rules, regulations, and religion; self-denial, self-esteem and sanctity; about honor, home and heaven; about truth, triumph, and tranquility; about sex, self, and salvation?" His tactful but trenchant response to these alliterative questions has enjoyed wide circulation in pamphlet and magnetic tape form under the title *Purity Is Power.* (*The Abundant Life,* pp. 55-74.)

Representative of another favorite Hugh B. Brown theme is his address to the Relief Society General Conference on September 27, 1961. Women's paramount roles are affirmed to be homemaker and mother, but the roles are not to be performed in the demeaning context which gives impetus to movements for "liberation." Here are excerpts:

> The work in the home, as well as in the Church, requires that women, as stated, shall stand side by side with their husbands, not in front of them, not behind them. . . . Service, love-inspired service, is the symbol of womanhood. It is the emblem of Relief Society. But, and we tell our brethren this quite often, service does not and must not mean servitude. . . . When the Lord made provision for men to have the priesthood and gave the sacred honor and glory of motherhood to women, he divided not only the responsibilities but the blessings of life equally between men and women.
>
> Through the divine institution of celestial marriage, with all its privileges, obligations, joys, trials and sacrifices, men and women, joined together by the Holy Priesthood, may through their faithfulness attain immortality, eternal life, and eternal increase; that soul-satisfying state of eternally becoming, forever achieving. When we speak of eternal increase, we speak not only of increase of posterity, we speak of increase of knowledge and the power that comes with knowledge; increase of wisdom to use that knowledge and power wisely; increase of awareness and the joy that comes through understanding; increase of intelligence, which is the glory of God; increase of all that goes to make up Godhood. (*Continuing the Quest,* pp. 4-6.)

To emphasize his point and to pay tribute to his partner of more than half a century, President Brown concluded his sermon with a poem which Sister Brown had written while they were together in England, "Woman Exalted":

Ye chosen ones, list to his word:—
"Man is not without the woman in the Lord,"
Think ye, then, that Gods are half-Gods, not whole,
And reign, and make these orbs of light, and live
        incomplete, alone,
And in celestial might make harmony with harps
        half-strung?
The answer's thine already. Thou hast it in thy heart.

Twas Mary knew from angel bright that she was
Chosen to clothe the Spirit of our Lord.   Her heart
Sang its exquisite joy!   Told she this to the other
Honored of the Lord.   And found believing response
        from this
Her woman kin.

Followers of our Savior and his church were women.
How great their love, how complete their trust in him!
E'en when the cross the Son and Master bore, and
        lifted, tortured,
Broke the chains that bound the mortal man and
        bade him sleep forever.
How great, I say, in that trusting humility, like unto
        a child's—how supreme!
Last at the cross were they—first at the tomb—
        heralds of the Risen Lord.

"Not honored," say you, and "below your brother man"?
Open thine eyes and see what place is given thee, O
        woman fair!
Hold high thy head to wear its crown.   Kneel thou,
        too, in
Reverence to thy Lord.   For thank offering remember
        thou his word—
"O be ye clean that bear the vessels of the Lord."
Prepare thy souls to bear the souls of men.

When the spirits of the dark shall stalk the earth to
        stay his second coming's time,
Fear not to array thyself in armor white, as symbol
        of thy state,
And rise in power and womanhood.   At the portal of
        thy home
Guard that which is dearer than life itself.   By thy
        companion's side
Uphold him in his priesthood and godly power.

Remember thou art high priestess of the home—the
        home,

The heart of all the world, and the altar at his throne,
The heart whose throbbing life holds in its power, the
     molding of good or ill.
And sends forth the sinner or the saint, or weak ones
     'tween the two.
Sends the mortal-clad spirit, born of woman, to sow
     discord, hate, and greed

Or be messengers of light, who seek to guide their
     fellows
Back to him where only harmonies abide.
O be ye strong, and let not the weak ones grope and
     find him not.
Be thou a woman whole and pure, with that militant
     love
That fights for her own, and God's.

Take then thy seat in nations great and small.
Still not thy voice when its clarion call should speak
     for him
To thy sisterhood the world around,
Thou champions of righteousness, thou mothers of
     his little ones,
Thou believers of his Word. Lend to his priesthood
Thy powers of purity and love that falter not,
And that faith that makes their faith more strong.

Daughters of Zion, ye mothers of men, hold fast these
     gifts of thy calling great,
Lest they be lost—these priceless pearls of purity and
     purpose holy.
Know ye not that thy place is at the side, and not
     below,
This companion to whom thou art given of the Lord?
Thou woman exalted, thou first to forgive and last
     to forsake,
Thou priestess, queen,
Thank thy God who made thee thus, that thou wast
     born
A woman.

                                        — Zina Card Brown

The happy years of shared activities continued. One memorable entertainment occurred on August 10, 1963, when the family
had a reunion to celebrate Sister Brown's seventy-fifth birthday,
President Brown's eightieth birthday and the couple's fifty-fifth

anniversary. The journal says with understatement, "We had a wonderful time together. . . . "

A month later Presidents Moyle and Brown hosted a party honoring President McKay's ninetieth birthday. All the General Authorities and their partners were invited, and the trophies of President Brown's recent trip to Alaska were featured on the menu. He said of the fifty-pound salmon which was the main course, that it was the answer to the fisherman's prayer, "Oh, Lord, help me catch a fish so big that I won't have to lie about it." It is noted in the journal, "I, of course, did not catch the fish, but some people got the idea that I had."

On September 18, 1963, Henry D. Moyle died suddenly while attending to Church business in Florida. This able and strong-minded man had been a friend and frequent colleague from the days in the 1930s when he and Hugh B. Brown worked for the New Deal in the Utah Democratic Party. Now his passing produced a vacancy in the First Presidency and a new calling for the son of Homer and Lydia Brown.

At the ensuing October conference, President Brown was named first counselor to President McKay and Elder N. Eldon Tanner was sustained as second counselor. President Brown was delighted with the choice of his nephew, although President McKay surprised him with the nomination. The new first counselor needed a strong and sympathetic colleague, because the President of the Church was now frequently ill and much of the burden of leadership fell on the broad shoulders of Hugh B. Brown.

17. First Counselor in the First Presidency

Hugh B. Brown was within a few days of his eightieth birthday when he was set apart as first counselor to President David O. McKay. But he was young compared to the venerable President, who had already passed his ninetieth birthday. President McKay's health was such that President Brown was obliged to assume more responsibility than normally would have been his, and he was thus in a position similar to that which had tested and demonstrated the powers of two earlier great first counselors, George Q. Cannon and J. Reuben Clark, Jr. Like them, Hugh B. Brown was capable and rendered wonderful service, but he necessarily functioned within a priesthood context in which the final earthly authority is the President of the Church. Sometimes President McKay was well enough to be fully engaged in Church business; at other times he was hospitalized or home-bound and of necessity the processes of deliberation and decision-making were delayed or diverted. President Brown loved and honored the aging leader and was very sympathetic to his infirmities, but the day-to-day administrative problems were nonetheless ever pressing; and while the responsibility gravitated to the two counselors, their inability to obtain the

1964 picture of First Presidency: President David O. McKay with counselors Hugh B. Brown and N. Eldon Tanner.

necessary decisions combined with their lack of complete authority to act was bound to be at times frustrating.

In meeting the challenges of his calling, President Brown was handicapped also by the serious illness and incapacity of his beloved wife, Zina, and by some physical problems of his own. But despite the difficulties, the six years and three months he served as first counselor were filled with thrilling experiences and major accomplishments. He continued to savor the delights of new lands, new people, and new adventures, and his wisdom and testimony were heard by literally millions.

The 1960s were years that placed heavy demands upon the LDS leadership. The nation was in a state of turmoil brought on partially by discontent among blacks and other American minorities. The Vietnam War turned many young people, especially in colleges and universities, against government policies and society in general. There was a serious revolt against sexual morality, family solidarity, patriotism, and other traditional values and standards. As the expanding missionary program accelerated the Church's transformation into a worldwide faith, responses to these challenges had to be developed.

Perhaps it was because he was already deeply involved with some of the problems and frustrations that Hugh B. Brown's mood in the days prior to his new appointment was sometimes depressed. Just after the death of President Moyle he wrote to a friend, "You don't know how much good your letter did me, arriving as it did at a time when I am under very heavy stress with some uncertainty and apprehension." He continued:

> Were you ever in a desert or wilderness where it seemed that you were alone in the world? . . . It is a challenging feeling but it is greatly relieved when some friends take time to shout a friendly "hello" and an encouraging "keep it up". . . .
>
> I guess we must just carry on as best we can until the time comes for us to do as President Moyle did, just lie down and go to sleep and have no concern for the wilderness, the desert, or the world.
>
> Does this sound like a rather gloomy letter? I think perhaps it is inspired by my deep concern for the duties that lie ahead in the next few days. Eight major speeches, several on very short notice because of President Moyle's death, would be a sizeable assignment for a really capable man, but for me it is almost overwhelming.

One of the immediate problems with which President Brown was engaged in October, 1963, was a product of the accelerating civil rights movement. Although since the early history of the Church the priesthood had not been held by its Negro members, this did not become a national issue until after World War II. As blacks moved toward equal legal and political rights, the Church became a target since it seemed to some critics to symbolize the concept of white supremacy. Mormons who disapproved of the practice called for change, and some non-Mormons demanded that change be forced upon the Church. The civil rights march on Washington in August, 1963, produced increased public discussion and then rumors that there might be an important policy statement in the October general conference.

The first of the two official pronouncements on civil rights which bear Hugh B. Brown's name as a member of the First Presidency came at the closing session of the October 1963 general conference. He read this statement defining the LDS position:

> . . . We would like it to be known that there is in this Church no doctrine, belief, or practice that is intended to deny the enjoyment of full civil rights by any person regardless of race, color or creed.
>
> We say again, as we have said many times before, that we believe that all men are the children of the same God and that it is a moral evil for any person or group of persons to deny any human being the rights to gainful employment, to full educational opportunity, and to every privilege of citizenship, just as it is a moral evil to deny him the right to worship according to the dictates of his own conscience. . . .
>
> We call upon all men everywhere, both within and outside the Church, to commit themselves to the establishment of full civil equality for all of God's children. Anything less than this defeats our high ideal of the brotherhood of man. (*The Abundant Life,* p. 235.)

Utah NAACP leaders responded that this statement was "in accord with the highest principles of Christianity and democracy and that it represents a significant first step in helping to solve the problems of race relations here in Utah and across the nation." (BYU *Daily Universe,* October 7, 1963.)

As the decade progressed and attacks on the priesthood issue focused on the Church missionary program and Brigham Young

University, President Brown repeatedly reaffirmed this civil rights position. Protests against BYU within the Western Athletic Conference died out as reason replaced emotion and the national temper changed in the early 1970s. Amid the stress and excitement another statement of the First Presidency was issued in December, 1969, over the signatures of Presidents Brown and Tanner. It declares "that we believe the Negro, as well as those of other races, should have his full Constitutional privileges as a member of society, and we hope that members of the Church everywhere will do their part as citizens to see that these rights are held inviolate."

At the other end of the political spectrum, the categorical opposition of the Church to communism provided a basis for some Mormon involvement in the ultra-conservative political movements which were a domestic response to the Cold War. President Hugh B. Brown was emphatic, both as an individual and as a spokesman for the First Presidency, in cautioning against the dangers of political extremism, both of the left and of the right. He frequently cited the 1936 statement of Presidents Heber J. Grant, J. Reuben Clark, Jr., and David O. McKay, which concluded: "We call upon all Church members completely to eschew Communism. The safety of our divinely inspired Constitutional government and the welfare of our Church imperatively demand that Communism shall have no place in America." To the general priesthood meeting on April 7, 1962, he added: "I think I can authoritatively say to you that the position of the First Presidency has not changed since that time." In a general conference address a year later he added this denunciation:

> The threat of Communism is sinister and its dangers relentlessly imbued with the satanic ideology that the Fatherhood of God, the Saviorhood of Christ, and the brotherhood of man are stupid myths, that religion is nothing but a tranquilizing opiate. They seek to deprive men of physical, mental, and spiritual freedom while endowing the state with monstrous supremacy. This relentless indoctrination is but a continuation of the war that began when Satan's plan of force was rejected by the Father. We live in the most dangerous period of all history. The sixth chapter of Ephesians was never more applicable than today:
>
> > "For we wrestle not against flesh and blood, but against principalities, against powers, against the rulers of the darkness

of this world, against spiritual wickedness in high places. —
Ephesians 6:12"

The Church is the main bulwark against Communism. . . . (*The
Abundant Life,* p. 155.)

His own political liberalism, his commitment to an open
market in ideas, and his awareness of the wide range of political
backgrounds and allegiances which were represented in the
worldwide Church led President Brown to oppose the extremes
of anticommunism which seemed in the 1960s to be making some
inroads among the members. To the April 1962 general priesthood meeting he issued this warning:

> . . . Brethren, beware that you do not become extremists on
> either side. The degree of a man's aversion to Communism may not
> always be measured by the noise he makes in going about and calling
> everyone a Communist who disagrees with his personal political bias.
> There is no excuse for members of this Church, especially men who
> hold the priesthood, to be opposing one another over Communism;
> we are all unalterably opposed to it but we must be united in our
> fight against it. Let us not undermine our Government or accuse
> those who hold office of being soft on Communism. Futhermore,
> our chapels and meeting houses should not be made available to
> men who seek financial gain or political advantage by destroying faith
> in our elected officials under the guise of fighting Communism. We
> call upon the priesthood of the Church to stand together with a solid
> front against everything that would rob men of their God-given
> freedom. (*The Abundant Life,* p. 196.)

A few months later similar counsel was expressed in a statement signed by Presidents David O. McKay, Henry D. Moyle,
and Hugh B. Brown that specifically mentioned one of the
militant anticommunist organizations which had found some
acceptance among Latter-day Saints:

> We deplore the presumption of some politicians, especially offi-
> cers, coordinators and members of the John Birch Society, who under-
> take to align the Church and its leadership with their partisan views.
>
> We encourage our members to exercise the right of citizenship,
> to vote according to their own convictions, but no one should seek or
> pretend to have our approval of their adherence to any extreme
> ideologies.

> We denounce Communism as being anti-Christian, anti-American, and the enemy of freedom, but we think they who pretend to fight it by casting aspersions on our elected officers or other fellow citizens do the anti-Communist cause a great disservice. . . . (*The Messenger,* Presiding Bishop's Office, February 1963.)

Efforts to suggest an official Church endorsement of the John Birch Society produced a crisis somewhat later when it became known that an issue of the organization's *American Opinion* was being prepared for the press with a picture of President McKay on the cover. Prompt action within the Church leadership prevented this from happening.

Through correspondence, interviews, and public addresses, Hugh B. Brown strengthened LDS resistance to political extremism of both right and left through his years as first counselor. A commencement address at BYU, May 31, 1968, is perhaps the best expression of his philosophy and advice on this subject:

> I want to speak of another matter briefly but sincerely. You young people are leaving your University at a time when our nation in engaged in the abrasive and increasingly strident process of electing a president. I wonder if you would permit me, one who has managed to survive a number of these events, to pass on to you a few words of counsel.
>
> First, I would like you to be reassured that the leaders of both major political parties in this land are men of integrity and unquestioned patriotism. Beware of those who feel obliged to prove their own patriotism by calling into question the loyalty of others. Be skeptical of those who attempt to demonstrate their love of country by demeaning its institutions. Know that men of both major political parties who guide the nation's executive, legislative, and judicial branches are men of unquestioned loyalty, and we should stand by and support them. This refers not only to one party, but to all.
>
> Strive to develop a maturity of mind and emotion, and a depth of spirit which will enable you to differ with others on matters of politics without calling into question the integrity of those with whom you differ. Allow within the bounds of your definition of religious orthodoxy a variation of political belief. Do not have the temerity to dogmatize on issues whereon the Lord has seen fit to be silent.
>
> I have found through long experience that our two-party system is sound. Beware of those who are so lacking in humility that they cannot come within the framework of one of our two great parties. Our nation has avoided chaos like that which is gripping France today

because men have been able to temper their own desires sufficiently to seek broad agreement within one of the two major parties, rather than forming splinter groups around one radical idea. Our two-party system has served us well, and should not be lightly discarded.

At a time when radicals of right or left would inflame race against race, avoid those who preach evil doctrines of racism. When our Father declared that we, his children, were brothers and sisters, He did not limit this relationship on the basis of race. Strive to develop that true love of country which realizes that real patriotism must include within it a regard for the people of the rest of the globe. Patriotism has never demanded of good men hatred of another country as proof of one's love for his own. Acquire for others, including those of different political belief or race or religion, the tolerance and compassion appropriate to the heavenly parentage which all mankind have in common. (*Vision and Valor*, pp. 207-208.)

Transcending the partisan and political enthusiasm of Hugh B. Brown was his intense patriotism, tested in two wars and in decades of civic activity. In the First Presidency it found expression in admonitions to loyalty and observance of the law and paeans to his re-adopted native land. His first general conference address after his release as First Counselor followed a world-circling tour of missions; "I return," he declared, "with an increased appreciation for our beloved America, its freedoms and opportunities."

As demonstrations and civil disobedience became prevalent, he charged the Relief Society General Conference on October 2, 1963, "to teach our people to respect authority, both in church and state, to obey the law, and be made amenable to discipline." A general conference address in the same period criticized "those who advocate breaking the law as one means of calling to the attention of the nation that some have not been given the full benefit of the law." "No orderly society," he declared, "can be established on such a theory." When the prolonged conflict in Vietnam produced questions, particularly among some young Mormons, the First Presidency (Presidents David O. McKay, Hugh B. Brown, N. Eldon Tanner, Joseph Fielding Smith, Alvin R. Dyer) issued a statement in May, 1969, which did not waver from this position:

. . . We make no statement on how this country can or should try to disengage itself from the present regrettable war in Vietnam; that is a problem which must be solved by our governmental officials, in whom we have complete confidence.

We believe our young men should hold themselves in readiness to respond to the call of their government to serve in the armed forces when called upon, and again we repeat, we believe in honoring, sustaining and upholding the law." (BYU *Daily Universe,* May 19, 1969.)

From what has already been noted, it is apparent that President Brown's concept of loyalty was not parochial. As a leader in a worldwide church, he reminded Mormons "wherever they may live in other Christian countries to be patriotic and loyal to their homeland." Yet he fully shared the LDS view that "America is a chosen land, preserved and discovered under divine inspiration," and in his general conference address in October, 1965, he became almost rhapsodic:

I cannot leave this subject without a sincere and heartfelt prayer that the Spirit of Almighty God shall be upon all men everywhere. May our lofty institutions, our matchless Constitution, our love of freedom and liberty be noted by other nations and, insofar as they can be made applicable, be adopted by them that all men everywhere may join us in singing what might well become an international anthem,

"Our fathers' God to thee,
Author of liberty,
To thee we sing.
Long may our land be bright
With Freedom's holy light,
Protect us by thy might,
Great God, our King."

(*The Abundant Life,* p. 354.)

There were, of course, many other kinds of concerns and opportunities during his years as first counselor. One of the more painful tasks came when John F. Kennedy was assassinated and President Brown was called to represent the Church at the funeral services. This was a particularly difficult assignment because just two months earlier, on September 26, 1963, he had helped to entertain President Kennedy in Salt Lake City, taking him to President McKay's suite in the Hotel Utah where they had breakfast together. President Hugh B. Brown's tributes to the young chief executive, whom he much admired, have been described in an earlier chapter.

The last months of 1963 were filled with exciting activities. On the day before his eightieth birthday, President Brown accompanied Ambassador-at-Large W. Averill Harriman to BYU, where the ambassador gave a public address on the recently negotiated nuclear test-ban treaty. President Brown received birthday greetings from the Rocky Mountain Conference of International Relations Clubs and strongly endorsed the United Nations, whose official birthday coincided with his own. (The birthday was celebrated with his family, and the journal contains this cryptic note: "Apparently time is passing.")

Hugh and Zina Brown were honored at a special meeting on December 8, in which the Granite Stake paid tribute to all past stake presidents. Two weeks later he gave an address in the Music Hall in Boston and the same day NBC carried his Christmas message nationwide in its "Faith in Action" series. He and Sister Brown spent Christmas in Cambridge with daughter Carol's family and toured parts of the New England Mission with President Truman Madsen and his wife, Ann.

In April of 1964 President Brown was required to conduct most of the general conference meetings because of President McKay's illness. His address at the opening session, "The True Gospel in the Modern World," was directed at least in part to the non-Mormons in the radio and television audiences. It contains these thoughtful statements about the nature of man and God:

> Our doctrine of man is positive and life affirming. We declare unequivocally that by his very nature every man has the freedom to do good as well as evil, that God has endowed him with a free moral will and given him the power to discern good from evil, right from wrong, and to choose the good and the right. We refuse to believe, with some churches of Christendom, that the biblical account of the Fall of man records the corruption of human nature or to accept the doctrine of original sin. We do not believe that man is incapable of doing the will of God, or is unable to merit the rewards of divine approval; that he is therefore totally estranged from God and that whatever salvation comes to him must come as a free and undeserved gift. We never tire of proclaiming the inspiring

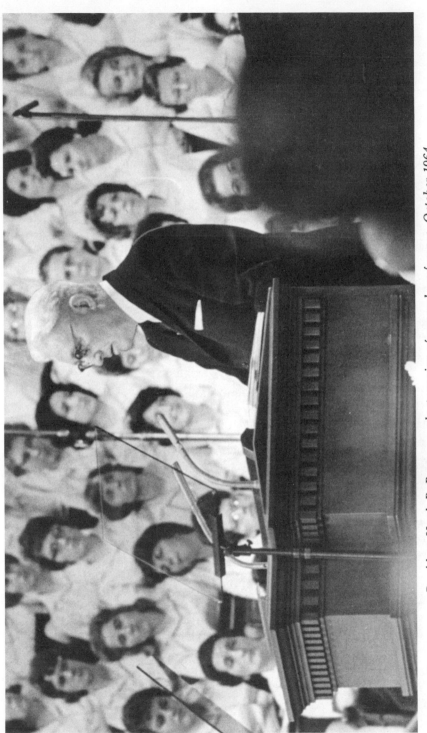

President Hugh B. Brown conducts session of general conference, October 1964.

truth of the Gospel that man is that he might have joy. For us the so-called Fall of man placed the human spirit in a world of experience and adventure where evils are real but can be overcome, where free moral decision is a constant requirement, and where choices, freely made, determine the quality of life and the eventual condition of the soul. . . .

For us God is not an abstraction. He is not just an idea, a metaphysical principle, an impersonal force or power. He is not identical with the totality of the world, with the sum of all reality. He is not an "Absolute" that in some way embraces the whole of reality in His being. Like us, He exists in a world of space and time. Like us, He has ends to be achieved and He fashions a cosmic plan for realizing them. He is a concrete, living person, and though in our finite state we cannot fully comprehend Him, we know that we are akin to Him, for He is revealed to us in the divine personality of His Son, Jesus Christ. (*The Abundant Life,* pp. 18-19, 21.)

A visit to Nauvoo, Illinois, in July involved discussion with Dr. LeRoy Kimball and others about "the advisability of the Church spending money to acquire certain properties there in memory of the activities of our pioneer leaders." At intervals during the next decade President Brown would return to the little town on the banks of the Mississippi to dedicate or discuss other projects of Nauvoo Restoration, Inc.

Two eventful weeks followed, in which President and Sister Brown flew to Europe where he dedicated a chapel in Crawley, England, and then presided at a mission presidents' conference in Geneva. En route home on July 23 they met with the Tabernacle Choir at the White House, where they "were cordially greeted by President Lyndon B. Johnson." The next day they attended Utah Day at the New York World's Fair.

Following the October conference the Browns spent a ten-day vacation in Hawaii, where he celebrated his eighty-first birthday at a lunch with Averill Harriman and others. President Johnson's campaign visit to Salt Lake City made October 29 newsworthy. A newsmaker now in his own right, Hugh B. Brown still delighted in the companionship of influential people, almost as if a little bit of the Lake Breeze farm boy were still in him seeking confirmation that he had, in fact, "made his mark" in life.

NBC interview.

Journeys, mostly official, highlight the survey of events in President Brown's journal for 1965. The first was a whirlwind air tour of some of the South American missions, with President A. Theodore Tuttle of the First Council of the Seventy, and Sister Tuttle as traveling companions. In eleven days in March the Browns visited Peru, Chile, Argentina, and Uruguay, attending conferences, dedicating four chapels, holding missionary meetings, and thoroughly enjoying the sights and the hospitality of the people. The David O. McKay School in Viña del Mar, Chile, was particularly interesting. Held in the local branch chapel and comprising 120 students, according to the journal, this elementary school "is operated by the Church and is doing a wonderful work, both in educating the young people and in making friends among nonmembers." Later President Brown visited two similar schools in Santiago, one of which was named in his honor.

In connection with the April general conference a special tribute was paid to President and Sister Brown at a reunion of elders and lady missionaries with whom such ties of affection had developed in the British Mission. His talk to the Primary Conference expressed understandable nostalgia for the freedom and flexibility which had prevailed before programming, timing, and media requirements imposed constraints upon the conference speakers. "This is," he mused, "an occasion when one would wish to take his sermon from his heart rather than from his pocket."

Another enjoyable trip was to New York in May to participate in the honoring of the Browns' good friend Lorena (Mrs. Harvey) Fletcher, as American Mother of the Year. Honors for President Brown followed during the summer as he presided at the baccalaureate exercises at BYU, spoke at similar services at Utah State University, and spoke and received an honorary Doctor of Laws degree at the August commencement of the University of Utah. Interspersed were trips to Hawaii, the World's Fair, and the Hill Cumorah Pageant, dedication of the stake center at Taber, Alberta, and a brief tour of LDS missions and activities in Mexico. *The Abundant Life,* the third volume of

Hugh B. Brown's collected speeches and writings, also appeared in 1965.

Following the October conference, President Brown and Elder Thomas S. Monson were assigned to tour the Pacific missions. Hawaii, Samoa, New Zealand, Fiji, Tonga, and Tahiti were on the itinerary, but ill health forced President Brown to return home from Auckland, New Zealand. Inspirational meetings were held with LDS congregations, missionaries, and students in the Church schools. The official report to the First Presidency mentions a visit with the Chief of State of Western Samoa and includes this glimpse into the meeting with the students and faculty of the Church college at Apia: "The school children were enthralled as President Hugh B. Brown spoke to them on true life's application of the little story about the engine who said, 'I Think I Can.' "

The New Zealand Temple, where Hugh B. Brown had laid the cornerstone nine years before, the Church College of New Zealand, the extensive Church farm at Hamilton, and stake centers for Auckland, Hamilton, Wellington, and Hawkes Bay were visited. In a special interview on October 26, Prime Minister Keith Holyoake "spoke in favorable terms of the work of the Church in New Zealand and expressed his desire to be of any assistance." The report in the Wellington *Evening Post* quotes President Brown as having said that the Church has no immediate plans to go into Russia, but "we will eventually."

The official report describes two remarkable incidents in connection with the visit of Elders Brown and Monson to the Samoan Islands on October 17, 1965:

> For many days prior to our visit, the members of the school faculty and children at our school in American Samoa had been fasting and praying for moisture. Since the water supply is totally dependent upon rainfall and the accumulated storage of water, a severe drought had caused our reservoir to be depleted, even to the point of establishing emergency lavatory facilities. During our early morning conference sessions [at Pago Pago], the heavens opened and literally produced a deluge of rain. . . . We spoke to the pilot and navigator of a plane which arrived shortly after the downpour. The

pilot commented, "I have scarcely seen such an unusual type of rain-
fall. The only place where rainclouds hovered was over this particular segment of American Samoa." Those who had been fasting
and praying could explain the significance of this fact.

Arrived Apia, Western Samoa, in the late morning and met with
1322 members of the Apia Stake and surrounding missionaries. . . .
At the session, each speaker was supplied a translator, so that the
remarks made in English could be translated for the members who
spoke only Samoan. As President Hugh B. Brown commenced speaking, a translator was provided. As President Brown concluded his
introductory remarks, a counselor in the mission presidency leaned
forward and spoke to the stake president, these men being native
Samoans. They had observed that the congregation was receiving the
message of President Brown without the aid of interpreter. The interpreter was, therefore, excused from his assignment, and President
Hugh B. Brown spoke for a full 40 minutes, with his remarks being
understood by English- and Samoan-speaking members alike. All
assembled felt the inspiration of this divine gift of the interpretation
of tongues.

While President Brown was in the South Pacific, President
McKay added two counselors to the First Presidency. Given the
precedents for enlarging the Presidency and David O. McKay's
failing health and strength, the action is understandable. The
selection of the President of the Council of the Twelve, Joseph
Fielding Smith, was logical in view of the likelihood that he
would succeed to the leadership of the Church. The second
added counselor was Thorpe B. Isaacson, an Assistant to the
Council of the Twelve. Elder Isaacson suffered a disabling illness shortly after his appointment and so was unable to function
in the position. The appointment of another Assistant to the
Twelve, Alvin R. Dyer, as a counselor to the First Presidency in
April, 1968, brought to six the membership in the presiding
council of the Church during the last part of Hugh B. Brown's
tenure. President McKay also ordained Elder Dyer an apostle,
although a vacancy did not exist in the Council of the Twelve
at the time.

During these years President Brown had the responsibility
of coordinating the activities of the First Presidency when President McKay was unable to do so, and of conducting the Thursday meetings of the Presidency and the Twelve in his absence.

Most of the meetings of the First Presidency from 1965 to 1970 were held in the Hotel Utah apartment of President and Sister McKay. As many of the counselors as were available met with the President several mornings a week when his health would permit. In the intervals informal contacts had to suffice and some matters of consequence were unavoidably delayed. Problems with President Brown's own health further complicated the situation at times, placing a considerable administrative load on President Tanner.

Hugh and Zina Brown took their last overseas trip together after the 1966 April general conference. Accompanied by their youngest daughters, Margaret and Carol, they flew to Europe on what was planned as a combined business and pleasure trip. Charles Manley and his family were living in Europe, and Zina Lou, Zola and Mary were traveling there, so the entire Brown family with the exception of LaJune anticipated a family reunion. The first week in England was highlighted by the dedication of a chapel in Norwich, where Elder Hugh Brown had spent most of his mission sixty years before. Unfortunately, Margaret became ill and her parents decided to bring her back to America, leaving Carol to travel with her older sisters.

A change of secretaries in June was an event of more than passing consequence. Norma "Mickey" Ashdown had been with Hugh B. Brown almost from the beginning of his work as a General Authority. Her replacement was — and still is — Vera S. Hutchinson. The wit who wrote that no man is a hero to his secretary should have had the chance to talk with these two capable women about their particular "boss." A sketch which Sister Hutchinson wrote after a half-dozen years with President Brown concludes: "He is a great man. Far closer to the Lord than any of us realize."

A luncheon honoring Ambassador Harriman and an extensive discussion of Mormonism with Archbishop John Wendland, the leader of the Russian Orthodox Church in America, are reported in the journal. The celebration of President and Sister Brown's fifty-eighth wedding anniversary is noted thus: "Twenty-four red roses and twelve pink roses adorned our home for the occasion."

In August, 1966, President Brown accepted Stake President Orson Millett's invitation to fly to Alaska for a five-day fishing excursion. In addition to agreeable encounters with people and salmon, he flew over the ice fields and glaciers in a small plane with an experienced "bush pilot." He described it as "the most beautiful and yet the most dangerous flight I have ever been on." A mounted Dall's sheep head, the gift of members of the Alaskan Stake, is a cherished trophy of this superb, if not entirely restful, vacation.

The homecoming was profoundly saddened by the tidings, brought to the airport by five of his daughters, that Sister Brown had had a slight stroke on August 12 that had deprived her temporarily of her speech. A major stroke eight days later required a month's hospitalization and continuing therapy. Thereafter this talented and affectionate granddaughter of Brigham and Zina D. H. Young and daughter of Charles O. and Zina Y. Card was restricted largely to her home. On their fifty-ninth anniversary, June 17, 1967, President Brown wrote:

> Even though mother is confined pretty much to a wheelchair, she keeps a smile on her face and a beautiful spirit of resignation pervades her whole being. She continues to be her old sweet self and it is a constant joy to know that she is at the door when I arrive at night and at the window when I leave. Bless her sweet heart — it is too bad she is so confined. We are so grateful she is with us.

Four months after their sixtieth wedding anniversary Sister Brown fell and struck her head. A journal entry dictated shortly afterwards states, "She has been bed-ridden since that time and, although she has no pain and eats and sleeps fairly well, it is very saddening to us to see her deprived of much association." President Brown missed her cheerful counsel and companionship, despite the efforts of his children to surround him with affection. He would sit by Zina's bedside, holding her hand, and talking to her, feeling her love even though she could no longer express it. She was to remain in this condition for over six years.

President Brown too was experiencing physical difficulties. A hearing problem was corrected in 1967 by resort to a hearing aid. In July of that year he began to have symptoms similar to the unforgotten tic douloureux, and although the trouble was eventually identified with a tooth and responded to treatment, difficulties would continue until most of his teeth were extracted in January, 1970. On June 8, 1968, he fell on the stairs in his home, and "as a result of a wreckless landing" he spent six days in the hospital. He might have remained longer, but word of the death of his oldest brother, Homer ("Bud"), impelled him to travel to Weiser, Idaho, and speak at the funeral.

The tasks and challenges of his calling did not diminish with these adverse circumstances. In addition to the calls and correspondence, personnel and fiscal decisions, committee and board meetings, groundbreakings and dedications, stake and mission visits which were required by his office, President Brown received an incredible number of requests to give advice and addresses, preach at funerals, and perform temple marriages — because he was Hugh B. Brown. His popularity among the youth of the Church continued to increase. In May, 1967, the University Stake sponsored "An Evening with President Brown" in the Tabernacle, and several thousand young men and women heard his retelling of "Profile of a Prophet." When the student leaders at BYU found themselves in competition with Idaho State University, they postponed the fast day on campus until the Sunday after the October general conference so that President Brown could be the speaker at the first fireside of the school year. Sister Brown was able to attend both of these services.

The conscientiousness of Hugh B. Brown at eighty-three is poignantly revealed in a journal entry for April 30, 1967. He had just completed a general conference, a tour of missions in the North Pacific, and a bumpy airplane trip that landed him in Denver late for the first of three scheduled dedicatory services. The journal reads: "I returned home that evening very tired, and feeling that I had let the people of Denver down because I was unable to put my all into this assignment because of my fatigue."

A two-week trip to the Far East took President Brown and Elder Gordon B. Hinckley into Hong Kong, Taiwan, Korea, and Japan. In dedicating a chapel in Hong Kong, the first counselor told the universally applicable story of the "Unsentimental Cuss" and "warned the saints to live in peace and not to criticize one another." At a missionary meeting in Taipei, according to his journal, he "was impressed to tell them that there was sitting in that room some young man who would one day stand in the Council of the Twelve, but before that day he would pass through the very fires of hell, but this great honor would come . . . if he lives worthy of it." To a congregation in Japan he sounded the theme of the entire tour and added another word of prophecy:

> Brother Hinckley forgot to tell you that I am an old man. He told all the other congregations that I am an old man. But the older I get the more sure I am that the thing that I am teaching is the Gospel of the Lord Jesus Christ. . . .
>
> I come to you tonight representing a peculiar church in one way. . . . It is not an American church, or English or German church. It is the worldwide church of Jesus Christ, and someday it will fill the whole world. . . .
>
> Somehow I feel the spirit of prophecy on me tonight, for I am looking into the future and I am telling you that you are going to live to see some marvelous things in connection with this Church of Jesus Christ of Latter-day Saints. You will see the time when men from all nations will send to the Mormons to get leaders and you young people must prepare yourself to fill these calls . . . and we will prepare the earth for the coming of the Son of God. . . .
>
> Some of you listening to me tonight will live to see the day when there will be a Japanese man in the Council of the Twelve Apostles. I do not know when it will be. I will not live to see it. Some of you young people will see it, and then you will realize that God loves the Japanese people, and you will join with other nations in forming a great and united Church all over the world. . . . I feel this in my heart tonight and I dare to make this prediction in the name of the Lord. (Unpublished magnetic tape transcript.)

Concern about former missionaries who were drifting toward Church inactivity is reflected in a project conducted in May, 1967. Special meetings in the Salt Lake, Logan, St. George, and Los Angeles Temples brought President Brown and others of the General Authorities together with several thousand recently returned elders. He wrote, "I feel sure these experiences will have a tremendous influence for good upon the lives of our young people."

A tour of eastern Canada and Montreal's Expo '67, accompanied by Zina Lou, and a few days of yacht-based salmon fishing in the Columbia River, accompanied by Mary, were the recreational highlights of President Brown's summer. In between was a pleasantly exciting breakfast visit with the English historian, Arnold Toynbee, of whom he had "long been an avid fan." Also exciting in a quite different way was the Sunday in August spent in close consultation with the local police following receipt of a report that "four carloads of negroes armed with machine guns were reported coming to Salt Lake City for the purpose of inciting a riot and particularly to destroy property on the temple block." Because of the recent rioting elsewhere in the country, security precautions had to be taken, but nothing happened to give substance to the rumors.

The services of the general conference, September 29-October 1, 1967, were the first transmitted over color television. Although Hugh B. Brown had prepared a message on another subject for the Sunday morning session, he later noted in his journal: "I felt that there was a need to review to the very large TV audience, as well as those attending, the account of my visit with the prominent English gentleman which has been published as 'The Profile of a Prophet,' and which has been used on tape by many missionaries. . . ."

The journal entry for the day following the conference was in a different vein. "Seems I must have bragged a bit about catching a 30-pound salmon and to save face I decided to display the 'big fish' at a dinner for my friends." Hugh and Zina Brown, along with all the children and their partners except LaJune's husband, greeted 235 guests for dinner in the Empire Room of the Hotel Utah. Although the guests of honor, President and Sister McKay, were unable to be present because of the death that day of the President's sister, most of the General Authorities, the governor, Utah's two senators, various civic and church leaders and their partners participated. According to the journal of the evening's master of ceremonies, everyone "satisfied their hunger for food and fish stories" and enjoyed "good company, good food, good entertainment and a wonderful feeling of fellowship." A special tribute was paid to the McKays "and they were able to listen to the program by wire."

President Brown celebrated his birthday working at the

office, with a quiet family gathering in the evening. He journalized: "It doesn't seem possible that I am 84. It should be more like 62, but Zina tells me I don't count very well. . . ." While on a conference visit in California shortly afterwards, he enjoyed riding with a nephew, Heber Brown, on one of his Arabian horses and, according to the journal, "I even tried my skill again at the pool table." In January he flew with Marvin Wallin, Paul Cox, and Paul Green to a fishing location on the west coast of Mexico. Of the sail fish which now hangs on a wall in his home, he wrote:

> It is a fighting fish and fought every inch of the way to the boat, took a little over 40 minutes to land and proved to be 8 feet 6 inches long and weighed 95 pounds — the best fishing experience of my life, thus far, but I still have an ambition to catch a marlin sometime.

The year 1968 produced some complex problems because of the impact of President McKay's deteriorating health on Church policy-making and President Brown's own health problems, coupled with the traumatic incapacity of Sister Brown, but the journal shows no reduction in the volume or variety of matters which were brought to his attention.

While in Washington, D.C., on Church business in March, President Brown met with Vice President Hubert Humphrey, who gave him "a fine pair of gold cuff links with the stamp of the Vice President," and with Secretary of State Dean Rusk, who "made the significant remark that some things could only be solved when one was on his knees." Later in the year he found two official visitors from France to be "very much interested in the fact that in the Church, though we can be either Democrats or Republicans, we can meet together in harmony. . . ." He introduced them to Elder Thomas Monson "to illustrate the relationship of Democrats and Republicans."

Presidents Brown and Tanner conducted the April general conference, at which "all of the Brethren responded magnificently," according to the journal, and "the messages from President McKay were read by his son and well received by all the people." Immediately afterwards President Brown dedicated the LDS exhibit at the San Antonio HemisFair. A series of special meetings for college-age women, sponsored by the LDS Student Association under the direction of Elder Paul Dunn, took President Brown and other leaders to the Tabernacle, BYU, and other campuses in the spring. The sacrament was prepared and served by General Authorities and stake presidents to the large congregations of young women who had been asked "to come in the spirit of fasting and prayer." The phrases "a most inspiring occasion" and "a glorious time" describe these events in Hugh B. Brown's journal.

Following the October conference, which illness kept him from attending, President Brown spent an agreeable weekend in Hawaii with Zina Lou, handling some Church appointments, visiting the Polynesian Cultural Center, and enjoying the hospitality of LaJune and her husband, Jerry Hay. Two days after his return Sister Brown's disabling fall occurred, and the change in her circumstances inevitably took some of the zest out of the following winter for him.

The flavor of Hugh B. Brown's last year in the First Presidency can best be suggested by a few random items from his daily journal:

> Met with First Presidency, after which held a meeting of the Expenditures Committee which took the balance of the morning.
>
> Went to Cardston to attend Gold Wedding of my sister, Roumelia. . . .
>
> I gave the baccalaureate address at Ricks College. . . .
>
> Went to Nauvoo, Illinois, with my daughter, Mary, for the groundbreaking of the Visitors Center. Harold and Joan Lee were also with us.
>
> . . . met with four young dissenters from the B.Y.U., including one Negro boy. . . .
>
> First Presidency meeting with Presiding Bishopric. . . . Held a Zions Securities meeting the same day.
>
> Performed a wedding for Richard Poll's daughter. . . .
>
> . . . a secluded spot among the lakes out of Anchorage where we had the most fantastic fishing experience of my life. . . .
>
> . . . was privileged to give the opening prayer in the U.S. Senate, at the instigation of Senator Edward Kennedy and Chaplain Edward L. R. Elson.
>
> Talked with Eugene England regarding the magazine *Dialogue*. . . .

It was our old Church History group and we had a glorious time together.

. . . met with Llewelyn R. McKay regarding some matters having to do with his father.

Had a long interview with Lowell Durham regarding music in the Church.

. . . spoke at the groundbreaking of the Ogden Temple and turned the first shovel of sod.

. . . spoke at the groundbreaking ceremonies of the Provo Temple and turned the first shovel of sod.

Had a visit from President Wilkinson of the BYU with reference to the difficulties that have arisen between the Y and Stanford.

. . . went to the [Calgary] Stampede and had a wonderful experience with an up-to-date rodeo.

. . . was a holiday celebrating the landing on the moon of the astronauts.

Met with the members of the Council of the Twelve and the First Presidency in the apartment of President David O. McKay on his 96th birthday.

Following the October conference President Brown and his daughter Mary flew to Germany for a week-long servicemen's conference at Berchtesgaden, formerly the retreat of Adolph Hitler. Meetings in London, Ipswich, and Maidstone followed; "It was good to be back with the English saints again." The tour finale was a luncheon with Lord Thomson of Fleet and approximately forty guests, including members of the House of Lords, the .Chief Justice of England, a former Lord Mayor of London and, as guest of honor, Governor Ronald Reagan of California. The occasion must have brought back memories of dressing up for a Lord Mayor's ball more than thirty years before.

The 1969 October conference was the last held under the personal oversight of President Hugh B. Brown. In addition to sharing the conducting responsibilities with President Tanner, he presented the names of the General Authorities for the sustaining vote of the conference and spoke briefly at the general priesthood meeting. His major address at the Sunday morning session was on the subject of "Faith." On the eve of his eighty-sixth birthday he still saw religion in terms of questions as well as answers. He declared:

> But every discussion of faith must distinguish it from its carica-
> tures. Faith is not credulity. It is not believing things you know are
> not so. It is not a formula to get the universe to do your bidding.
> It is not a set of beliefs to be swallowed by one gulp. Faith is not
> knowledge; it is mixed with lack of understanding or it would not
> be faith. Faith does not dwindle as wisdom grows. . . .
>
> *Faith is not a substitute for truth, but a pathway to truth. (Vision
> and Valor,* pp. 43-44, 47.)

On Sunday morning, January 18, 1970, President Brown
received a call from David Lawrence McKay informing him
that the President of the Church had passed away. He spent
most of the next four days making arrangements for the funeral
at which he had been asked by members of the McKay family
and the Council of the Twelve to conduct the service and to
speak. Tens of thousands witnessed the service at noon on
Thursday, January 22, in both the Tabernacle and the Assembly
Hall on Salt Lake City's Temple Square and by radio and
television.

Of the man whom he had known so long and intimately,
Hugh B. Brown wrote in his journal, "President McKay was a
very popular and wonderful president for 19 years — much
loved by all who knew him — A very effective and inspired
leader." And of their relationship over the almost seventeen
years that he had been a General Authority, President Brown
wrote: "I have served him as best I could. We had many
experiences, some intensely interesting and inspiring, and some
slightly frustrating, but all in all it has been a wonderful experience." Three years later he told his son Charles Manley,
"David O. McKay has done more for me than any other man in
my life."

On Monday, January 19, events took place which abruptly
changed the life of Hugh B. Brown. At the meeting of the
Council of the Twelve, to whom authority passes when the
Church President dies, it was unanimously decided to recommend Joseph Fielding Smith, President of the Council of the
Twelve, to be the new President of the Church, with the
designated calling of "prophet, seer and revelator." He was
set apart by Elder Harold B. Lee, who now became the senior

member of the Council of the Twelve, and he in turn set apart Elder Lee as his first counselor and N. Eldon Tanner as his second counselor. The custom of making the ranking apostle a member of the First Presidency was well precedented, and these actions were also unanimous.

President Brown recorded: "I am very happy to be relieved of many of the duties heretofore devolving on me. From now on, I shall be a member of the Council of the Twelve, take such appointments as they make, and be relieved of many onerous duties."

As he and President Lee, his friend from the first LDS Servicemen's Committee, exchanged offices in the Church headquarters building, Hugh B. Brown's memorable years as a member of the First Presidency came to an end.

18. Adviser to LDS Youth

A colleague at Brigham Young University, Dr. Sidney B. Sperry, once enumerated what he called the "extraordinary talents" of Hugh B. Brown:

> One is his power of speech. . . . Another is his gift to inspire. . . . [Another] is his ability to be both leader and companion of young people. He is at once sympathetic and sensitive to their points of view, and they trust and respect his judgment. (*Continuing the Quest,* p. x.)

Those who over the decades have turned to President Brown because they "trust and respect his judgment" have, of course, represented all ages and walks of life. Their number prompted this mildly plaintive note in his journal in September, 1967: "If my secretary did not send some of those who call at my office to others the deluge of people with their problems would overpower me." The journal is salt-and-peppered with such notes as "met with Miss . . . and discussed her problems," and "spent some time with . . . trying to straighten out his thinking." The secret of Hugh B. Brown's attraction for the troubled was described by his close friend in the Council of the Twelve, Richard L. Evans, in these words:

He is an uncommon man — approachable, lovable, human; courageous, forthright; dedicated to uplifting lives with a warmth that comforts, that encourages, that gives real and solid hope to the repentant, the wayward, the wandering; to those who have made mistakes, and to those who are sincerely searching and seeking. (*Ibid.*)

Yet it is for Mormon youth that Hugh B. Brown has possessed a special aura from his days as stake and mission president through his careers as military coordinator and university professor into his callings as a General Authority. As tennis competitor, fireside counselor, and closed-door confidante — as leader and companion — Hugh B. Brown has been seen in heroic dimensions by two generations of LDS young people. One of them attended the special service for college-age women at Logan, Utah, in 1968 and then wrote to her family in New York; part of the letter found its way back to Utah with a postscript, "A Mother's thanks, dear President Brown." It reads:

. . . Then the most wonderful was Hugh B. Brown — he's 85 now, and hardly needed a microphone. He taught us about talking with God and told us a wonderful missionary experience of his when he first talked with God. He emphasized the importance of holding His hand, and to me and many of the girls I talked with later, it was apparent that he was holding the Lord's hand and that He was present with us. President Brown spoke of the women in his life. His mother, who taught him to call for God, his wife, who was an angel, and whom he never heard raise her voice! And then of his 7 sisters, his 6 daughters, his 12 granddaughters, and his 13 great-granddaughters.

At the conclusion he held out his arms as I have often imagined Moses to have done and blessed us — and indeed I had the feeling hands had been placed upon my head. There were few dry eyes and much sobbing! He blessed us to endure to the end — to be mothers of sons of Israel — to be virtuous and clean and to live close to the Lord.

United with this charismatic Hugh B. Brown, who sways congregations by the force of his personality and testimony, is the thoughtful counselor described by Richard L. Evans thus:

His power to touch intimately and unforgettably the hearts and lives of young people includes encouragement to question, freely and sincerely— but with faith and with respect for facts, and for authority, and for the eternal truths. (*Continuing the Quest,* p. x.)

His empathy for the perplexed stems at least partially from his own experience. Reminiscing about his maturing years, he acknowledged without apology, "I questioned all the things that men question." His own "apprenticeship of doubt" — which extended intermittently into his middle and later years — has led him to a special affinity for those who resist answers which rest on authority alone. His technique of handling problems, like the solutions which he offers, gives wide latitude for individual choice. He prefers to persuade rather than prescribe, and to leave open the questions which do not require definitive answers.

A sampling of President Brown's responses to letters which have come to him since his appointment to the apostleship reveals these characteristics. Some were written at the request of President McKay to people who were seeking authoritative answers. The tenor of these responses is similar:

> . . . the Presidency is not disposed to undertake to enlarge the wording of the Word of Wisdom as contained in the Doctrine and Covenants.
> . . . it is not the policy of the Church to define precisely for each tithe-payer what a full tithing would be for him.
> The President has not indicated that the end of the world is near and has repeatedly said we should all continue with our regular work. . . .

The letters which dealt with personal problems Hugh B. Brown answered with counsel and consolation. The woman who complained of her financial predicament was referred to her bishop; for her lament about her childlessness he offered assurance that this was "no evidence that God has forsaken you." With parents grieving the loss of a daughter he could, of course, share the feelings which he and Zina often had that Hugh Card was very close. Yet he advised against assigning specific explanations to such tragedies. "God works in a mysterious way and he has his own reasons for not revealing to us his purposes with respect to individuals. . . . "

To a guilt-ridden correspondent President Brown replied that "the only thing we have found helpful in such matters . . . is to fill our minds completely with good thoughts by meeting with the right kind of people, reading the right kind of books, and turning off the switch whenever evil thoughts come into our minds." He added, "I am wondering whether you have ever consulted a good psychiatrist with respect to this matter. They sometimes are very helpful. . . . " The young man who believed, like the distraught woman whom Hugh B. Brown once defended in an Alberta court, that he had sinned beyond forgiveness, received this assurance and advice:

> As you say, I do not have the right to forgive, but I can and do speak authoritatively when I say, God will forgive whenever there is true repentance. . . .
>
> Worrying, fretting, crying, praying over past mistakes is largely a waste of time. The past is past; the present is ours and the future can be made worthwhile if we bury the past and move on into the future with faith in ourselves and in our heavenly Father.
>
> My advice is that you do not communicate to anyone the matters that you enumerate in your letter — put them out of your mind and out of your life. . . . You have not committed the unpardonable sin, nor can you.
>
> The world is yours. Life is sweet, challenging, and very much worthwhile for all of us who devote ourselves to building character, to helping others to understand the gospel and to making the gospel a part of our lives.

Letters from or about people with real or fancied grievances against the Church are fairly common. A representative reply from President Brown is this:

> . . . He is a good man but spends too much time pondering some difficult situations which he has encountered, and because of holding these things too close to his eyes is unable to see the large area of good and meritorious accomplishments of the Church. . . .
>
> I think we should all keep our eyes open for the good and beautiful in the Church. Obviously some mistakes have been made in the past and will be made in the future because we are all human, but in the main the Church is divinely guided and the Prophet Joseph Smith saw and heard the things of which he has made record.

Hugh B. Brown has received considerable correspondence from Latter-day Saints who are disturbed about the exclusion of Negroes from the priesthood. His replies consistently support the policy of the Church without condemning the critics. After affirming his conviction that God is just, he wrote to a young student, "I fear sometimes we are wont to regulate His program by our wrist watches."

A young woman received this advice, written a few months after Hugh B. Brown left the First Presidency:

> In my own life I have found it desirable to lay aside some things that I do not fully understand and await the time when I will grow up enough to see them more clearly. There is so much that is good and true that I can and do approve and accept with all my heart that I can afford to wait for further light on some of these disturbing questions. . . .
>
> I suggest it may be profitable for you to read this letter with your husband and then together kneel and pray to God for the faith that will carry you through the wilderness of doubt and bring you out on the mountain peaks of hope, sustained by faith. . . .
>
> If at any time you think I can be helpful on any question, please do not hesitate to write as I too have had my struggle with some problems, but they have, I am glad to say, been worked out in my more mature years until I have no hesitancy in bearing testimony to you that the Church, the whole Church, is right and true. . . .

From his sermons, writings and courses at BYU, it is clear that Hugh B. Brown has had only moderate interest in the more abstract points of LDS theology. The fifteen radio lectures delivered in 1947 reveal that he was very well informed on the structure of Church doctrine and the scriptures which support it, and missionary conferences have generally found him equal to the kinds of questions which elders like to ask. But his sermons and writings are heavily conduct-oriented, and the authorities cited cover a wide range of secular as well as sacred literature and experience. Further, though the perils of contemporary life are frequently underscored, the tone of the messages is almost always affirmative and optimistic. The titles to his collected messages — *Eternal Quest, Continuing the Quest, The Abundant Life,* and *Vision and Valor* — are keys to the man and to his popularity with young members of the Church.

Here are some of his words to the BYU studentbody on March 25, 1958, a few days before his ordination to the apostleship: "As I look out upon this audience of young Latter-day

Saints, what I behold is potentially grander and greater and more precious than what the psalmist saw in the starry heavens. He saw the handiwork of God; I see His offspring." The message which he gave them is entitled "What Is Man and What May He Become?" The following excerpts show how he appealed to both the minds and the emotions of the ten thousand students and teachers who heard him:

> I have mentioned freedom to express your thoughts, but I caution you that your thoughts and expressions must meet competition in the marketplace of thought; and in that competition truth will emerge triumphant. Only error needs to fear freedom of expression. Seek truth in all fields, and in that search you will need at at least three virtues: courage, zest and modesty. The ancients put that thought in the form of a prayer. They said, "From the cowardice that shrinks from new truth, from the laziness that is content with half truth, from the arrogance that thinks it has all the truth — O, God of truth, deliver us. . . ."

> The Latter-day Saint view of man's potential is in the vanguard of religious or scientific thought. Before the Gospel was restored, no one was heard to say, "As God is, man may become," and yet Jesus said, "Be ye therefore perfect, even as your Father which is in heaven is perfect. . . ."

> If any of you have been bothered about the subject of evolution, I submit that here is an inspired concept of evolution which exalts rather than debases man. It relates him to a divine Creator both as to origin and to destiny. Here is true evolution, to which you can subscribe with absolute safety. . . .

> Scientists and teachers of religion disagree among themselves on theological and other subjects. Even in our own Church, men take issue with one another and contend for their own interpretations on subjects which we do not have too much information. But this free exchange of ideas is not to be deplored as long as men remain humble and teachable.

> For example, there are various opinions on the subject of the time involved and the method employed in the great and continuing drama of creation, the biblical account of which is compressed into a few lines of print. It seems obvious that the scriptures were not intended as texts in biology, anthropology, geology, or any other of the sciences. . . .

Having quoted Psalms, Matthew, John, Will Durant, David Sarnoff, and J. Reuben Clark, Jr., in support of this exalted concept of man, Hugh B. Brown next cited the apostles James E. Talmage, Joseph Fielding Smith and John A. Widtsoe on the length of the creative process and continued:

> I call your attention to some words by Elder Anthony W. Ivins. He said: "I do not argue with the men who say the earth is only six thousand years old, or those who say it is six hundred thousand years old, or those who say it is six million. I know we are here on earth, and I know the Lord has told us why we are here. The time will come when we will know all the rest. . . ."
>
> Neither fear of consequences nor any kind of coercion will be used to secure uniformity of thought in the Church. However, we must also be careful never to teach anything as Church doctrine which may be our personal interpretation of a subject. There are some fundamental teachings of the Church on which all members should agree and to which they should subscribe.
>
> Let us never lose sight of the fact that the Church is led by revelation, that the Lord has one agent through whom He speaks to the Church, and that is the President of the Church. President David O. McKay said recently, "Whatever the subject may be, the principles of the Gospel of Jesus Christ may be elaborated upon without fear of anyone's objecting, and the teacher can be free to express his honest convictions regarding it, whether that subject be in geology, the history of the world, the millions of years that it took to prepare the physical world, whether it be in engineering, literature, art — any principle of the Gospel may be briefly or extensively touched upon for the anchoring of the student who is seeking to know the truth. . . ."

After thus emphasizing the broad range of legitimate inquiry which is associated with his topic, Elder Brown restated the core elements and then challenged his listeners:

> From modern revelation we learn that the spirit of man consists, in part at least, of intelligence, or the light of truth, which is coeternal with God — which means that it has always existed. We also learn that the elements are eternal. This eternal, immortal spirit was, pursuant to plan, tabernacled in a mortal body which was organized out of eternal elements which are not destroyed by the dissolution which we call death. When eternal spirit and eternal elements are joined again, man, then an immortal soul, may receive a fulness of joy. . . .
>
> May you ever strive to be worthy of your source, equal to your opportunities and be constantly preparing for your destiny. (*Continuing the Quest,* pp. 199-210.)

A unique opportunity for students to express both their concerns and their curiosity came when the institute of religion at the University of Utah sponsored a session with President Hugh B. Brown called "Questions from the Floor." On that occasion, two weeks before his eighty-sixth birthday, the white-haired apostle told several hundred young people that they were free to ask any questions they wanted to. "I'll probably answer most of them by saying I don't know," he cautioned. "I'm not binding the Church by what I say, but I shall try to be frank, honest, objective, and, I hope, inspired."

The transcription of the interrogation shows that the questions ranged from elementary to esoteric, and some may have been phrased to ensnare. They tended to include some of the same questions which have provoked letters over the years, and which students in other institutes and universities constantly ask of the religious "authorities" to whom they have access. The responses illustrate the wisdom and style of President Brown's interactions with inquisitive LDS youth, and some of them also illustrate that his training as a laywer had not been forgotten. From the transcript comes these excerpts:

> Question: What about the generation gap which exists in the Church, mainly between the General Authorities and students like us?
>
> I'm not old enough to know what to do with that. I think, however, it is overemphasized. . . . I think we're closer to you than you think we are . . . and you're closer to us than you're aware of. . . . I'm inviting young people every day to come to my office and talk over their problems. . . . By sitting down and talking it over there'll be an understanding grow up between us, so that the young person or the older person can both make some adjustments. We older men can learn a lot from you boys and girls. . . . So let's not be worried about the generation gap. I think it's closing. . . .
>
> Question: Why does the Church discourage inter-racial marriage?
>
> I'm a farmer by nature. . . . I know the wisdom of selecting the future parents of future generations of animals. The Church takes the position that we ought to be as careful, at least, when we select our mates as we are when we select the future parents of our animals. . . . There are enough problems in married life without introducing some fundamental problems such as a difference of race or color or so on. . . . That doesn't mean that you're better than someone else, but marry someone who thinks as you think, who will aspire as you

aspire, and teach the children of both of you things that both of you agree upon. . . . Be careful in your marriages.

Question: Will people for whom work is done in the temple have opportunity in the next world for advancement?

Yes. Very definitely. We're eternal beings, and pursuant to the instructions given by the Master himself certain ceremonies must be performed by, or in behalf of, each of us and all people. . . . And they for whom the work is done are placed on an equal basis with those who do the work for themselves.

Question: Are men such as Billy Graham, the great evangelist, inspired?

God is no respecter of persons. All good men who are doing good are accepted of him. . . . The Holy Ghost is available to all men. But the gift of the Holy Ghost comes by direct imposition of hands. I would not presume to say whether or not the Holy Ghost prompts remarks made by men like Billy Graham, or any other. . . . We agree with much that is said and taught by other churches and by leaders of other churches, but when it comes to representing the Lord it's necessary that the man speaking have the authority to speak. We do not say we're the only church. We do not say we have all the truth . . . but we do say that we have the right directly given through Peter, James and John, . . . to speak and act in the name of God, and that right is limited to men who hold the Melchizedek Priesthood.

Question: Why do some people feel that they have received personal revelation concerning the person they marry, while many others do not?

I think that as a rule the Lord does not come down and take us by the ear and turn us around and lead us to somebody and say, "This is your future husband or wife." . . . He gives us our freedom. He makes it possible for us to have contact with various individuals, and sometimes we get a very definite impression that this particular person is to be our companion for life. That may not be a revelation. . . . It may not be right. I think we have to be very careful in selecting our companions. . . . I believe that our Heavenly Father was responsible through some impressions that he saw fit to give me, that that was to be my wife. Now, that's an exception. . . . But it's available to you. Get on your knees and plead with Him for guidance and then have the courage to follow His guidance. . . .

On questions probing for differences of opinion among the General Authorities, President Brown's replies gave little satisfaction to the interrogators. Sex education in the schools was at the time a subject on which there were public disagreements in

Church circles. He prefaced his reply, "I'm glad to speak on
that question because I don't know much about it." Then he
went on to express a preference for sex education in the home,
but in an afterthought endorsed the schools and universities as
additional resources.

The perennial question about birth control elicited an answer which is particularly interesting, since the First Presidency
had issued an official statement six months before which strongly
discouraged artificial contraception:

> I'm speaking now for myself, and I think the Brethren would
> agree, we feel that we'd better not make any sweeping pronounce-
> ments such, for instance, as the Catholic Church has made, because
> of the difficulties which result. There are so many different condi-
> tions in the homes, different people to deal with, that this whole
> question of birth control becomes very much involved and very com-
> plex. But, as a general rule, we say to our young people, the purpose
> of your marriage is to have children. If you wish to regulate or
> space those children, that's up to you. We're not going to follow any-
> body into their bedroom. I think freedom in this matter ought to
> be understood. . . . I think as man and wife we owe it to each other
> to take a reverent view of all these matters, and then act accordingly.

For the Vietnam War, then at its height, President Brown
offered to his draft-conscious auditors no solution, but a strong
preference for getting out somehow. To an inquiry about "second
endowments" he simply replied, "That is one of the things we
do not discuss publicly." The standard question about the
Church's position on two-party politics produced the traditional
response that "every man is absolutely free to choose his party,"
but the still-active partisan could not resist the exaggerated
boast, "I'm about the only Democrat up in the Church offices."
As for the vintage question about the nearness of the Millennium,
Hugh B. Brown's response this time was, "If I knew I'd mend
my ways."

The national agitation against BYU athletic teams being
at its height, it is not surprising that the racial issue was introduced:

> Question: Is there a consensus among the First Presidency and
> the Council of the Twelve that the Negro ought not to hold the
> priesthood?

The question as to whether or not the Negro should hold the priesthood . . . is constantly arising. That has been decided for many years and will remain decided, I presume, until such time as the President of the Church himself shall indicate that a change should be made. I think we should make it clear here that the Negro will be in as advantageous a position as anyone else when the time comes for judgment. . . . As time goes on changes will undoubtedly come, but when they come they will come from the President of the Church. As to the consensus, the Brethren are all united now that the time has not come until the President speaks on it. When he does we'll be united in our response to his expressed wish.

A question with a somewhat similar thrust, couched in terms of the position of "liberals" and "conservatives" in the Church, gave President Brown an opportunity to emphasize both the importance and the limits of freedom of opinion:

I had a man in my office the other day questioning me as to why there is some difference of opinion between some members of the General Authorities on the question of the John Birch Society. I told him, and I tell you now, that the Brethren are united on all principles and doctrines of the Church, all principles of the gospel. There is no division whatsoever. When it comes to expressing an opinion on some other organization or some political or quasi-political question, each one is entitled to have his own opinion and to express it. . . . I have been all my life advocating to all people, in and out of the Church, that they should think through every proposition that is presented to them, making it theirs by digesting it, finding out what is fact with respect to it, and then coming up with a positive position on it. Let that position be modified as time goes on by discussing it with others. But there is no question but that both liberals and conservatives have their freedom in expressing their opinions.

To the fervent testimony which he conveyed to these young collegians, President Brown added in conclusion an expression of President McKay's love and blessing. He mentioned that the President was not well and that the doctors' report was not encouraging. This was October 10, 1969, but if Hugh B. Brown was concerned about impending changes in his own role in the First Presidency, he disclosed nothing in his response to this earlier query:

Question: What are your views on the succession in the Presidency of the Church? Do you see it as some of the Church leaders have that the President of the Quorum of the Twelve automatically becomes the President of the Church?

It's not automatic in the sense that it's instantaneous. You know in the British Empire when the King dies we say, "The King is dead. God save the King." That simply means that the authority of the King carries on. When the President of the Church dies, his counselors will step back in their places in the Quorum of the Twelve; and the Quorum of the Twelve, as a Quorum, becomes then the presiding authority in the Church with the President of the Quorum as the senior member. However, the Twelve may decide on who is to be recommended to the people to be the next President of the Church, and then the matter is presented to the people in conference assembled. But, there is no automatic changing of authority to any particular man.

Three months later the President of the Church died, the counselors in the First Presidency stepped back into their places, and the President of the Quorum of the Twelve was selected, set apart, and later sustained as President of the Church — not automatically, but in accord with precedent, the collective decision of the Twelve, and the voice of the people in conference assembled. In his new situation, Elder Hugh B. Brown continued to be in heavy demand as a counselor to LDS youth, along with their parents and the membership of the Church at large.

19. Husband and Father

The most important element in the history of President Hugh B. Brown, with the possible exception of his testimony of Jesus Christ, is his family. During their eventful life together, Zina Card Brown was his stabilizer and lodestar. As the six daughters and two sons came along, their problems and accomplishments were his paramount concerns. When Zina's long illness ended, the children and their families filled the void with affection and attention. At this writing (July 31, 1975) they number seven children, twenty-five grandchildren and fifty-nine great-grandchildren.

President and Sister Brown were married for sixty-six years. Every wedding anniversary was celebrated with words of affection and tokens of appreciation. The custom started with the first day of their marriage and it was extended from anniversaries to birthdays, Valentine's Day, New Year, Christmas, Thanksgiving, and the birthdays of the children. Even washdays were brightened by symbols of endearment, and the fact that they were usually chocolates meant that they had enduring impact upon the petite Zina.

Roses were the particular symbol of this romance. Earlier chapters have noted their regular appearance on anniversaries, even that depression summer of 1940 when Hugh Brown eked out funds to buy four dozen roses for Zina and then took her to a fifteen-cent double-feature movie. The roses which for years adorned the picture of Pilot Officer Hugh C. Brown were reminders that the circle of the parents' love fully encompassed their children.

Special as it was, the marriage of Hugh and Zina Brown was not without its stresses. Frequent and prolonged separations were difficult for both of them, and many of these left Zina with heavy responsibilities for managing or disposing of property, making moving arrangements, and caring for the children. She was alone much of the time, even as her mother had been often alone. That she should remain heavily involved with the children's affairs throughout her life is not surprising.

More than one of his children has observed that, for all his outstanding qualities, Hugh B. Brown was not the easiest man in the world to be married to. His mercurial temperament produced periods of soaring optimism and times of gloom and despair. (As a girl, LaJune fancied she could predict her father's mood by noting whether his hat brim was up or down.) The optimism, coupled with a penchant for business speculation, led Hugh Brown into ventures which Zina did not endorse and which rarely proved profitable. The same optimism, coupled with a liking for the limelight and an interest in public service, led him into political and governmental undertakings which did not work out well. Then his sensitivity compounded the effect of the disappointments and gave Zina a challenge to which she was always ready to rise. Zola remembers of her father:

> He didn't have the temperament to be a public man. He was too sensitive and could be hurt so deeply. Mother really bolstered him up when he would lose confidence in himself sometimes when things would go very wrong. He would think, "Well, maybe I can't do it," and Mother would always say, "Yes, you can, Hugh." He would always say about Mother that she believed in him when he didn't believe in himself.

To help Hugh B. Brown fulfill his destiny was Zina Card's mission from the day she took his name. Shortly after Mary's birth she wrote a note to her soldier-husband which began, "Hugh, I just nearly worship you." Because this was so nearly true throughout their lives together, she could usually cope with the challenges and frustrations which were part of her chosen calling. These tested Zina's mettle during those early years when she sometimes played second fiddle to Hugh's mother and sometimes watched while other women showered attention on the man she loved. They were associated with the several "prunings of the currant bush," when the comfort Zina administered might or might not be solemn and sentimental. Mary remembers a note which her mother once taped to her father's mirror: "Your crowns are greater than your crosses, my darling." And the challenges and frustrations included the times when Zina proved that she had a temper. According to Charles Manley: "The only times I saw her get upset about anything, when you could really recognize that she was upset, was when someone would say something unfavorable about Dad. Then she was a tiger."

President Brown has always known that he married a prize, and it has been pointed out in many chapters that he delighted to tell her so, sometimes in ingenious ways. A box of candy, a new car, a poem, a surprise check for five dollars or a hundred, a tribute in a conference address, an electric refrigerator, a trip to Waterton Lakes or Paris, or a note on the envelope of a letter might convey his love. And into a newsy letter he wrote in 1947 when Zina was away at the home of a married daughter he slipped a sentence that summed it all up: "We miss you in the morning and at noon and in the evening and through the night and when people call and when they die — we miss you all the time."

Reminders of his love were in every letter to Zina, usually in an original form. (Example: "One news item which is not on the radio is a real scoop, viz., I love Zina Card.") One of the expressions of love and gratitude is in a treasured letter he wrote to Zina in May, 1945, while in New York waiting for a berth on a ship which would take him back to England to resume his interrupted presidency of the British Mission:

> In the hurry of getting away and of details here I had little chance to do or say anything on Mother's Day. It means more to me each year as travel and time tend to adjust and focus the lens

of my eyes through which my heart looks with wonder and amazement at a beauty which I fear was not appreciated until age provided the telescope through which to look. And now amidst all the glorious constellations in the firmament of human relationships the "Pole Star" known everywhere as "Mother" is the most luminous and the one which has guided my little bark since it was launched. Until I was twenty-four it was my own mother and since then you who kept the needle of my soul pointed heavenward. I can pay you no greater compliment than to say, and mean it, that the lustre of that star did not dim when she resigned to you the task of generating that light. For what that steady light has meant to me, and to eight others, I thank God — and you.

Nor did their mutual loving attention diminish with the years. Mary recalls:

They had a romantic ritual which they called their "Sentimental Seventies," and which they followed almost every morning. He would kiss her as he left the breakfast table and she would tag along behind him as he descended two steps on his way to the basement garage. He would pause and turn back to her. "Did I kiss you goodbye?"

She would shake her head in mock-innocence and lift a puckered mouth in joyful anticipation. After this second kiss he would finish his trek to the garage and she would bustle off to the dining room window to watch the maroon car (they were always maroon!) come up the driveway. Blown kisses were exchanged through the windowpane. Then she would hurry to the front porch to wave him on his way for the day, and stand and watch until he blinked the brake lights three times — for "I - Love - You"— as he turned out of sight.

Even after Mother became an invalid and could no longer watch his goings and comings from a window, he used the auto horn to say a last goodbye and a first hello. During the six years she was bedfast, at times when it was necessary for President Brown to fill assignments out of the city she would seem to fade like a little flower out of water. But as soon as he returned to her side his presence was like a magic potion, bringing the color back to her cheeks and the sparkle to her eyes.

During this sad time he commented:

My darling companion, Zina Card Brown, is the epitome of patience, faith, and an almost supernatural serenity. Whatever may be my summation of life's vicissitudes, I have been more generously blessed in my marriage relationship with Zina than in any other one activity of my life. And for this, I thank the Lord.

What Hugh and Zina Brown wrote to each other and to their children is part of the cement that has held them all together over the years. Typical families of today, for whom the telephone and the printed greeting card are gradually eliminating the writing of personal messages, must stand in awe (or envy) at the mountain of manuscripts which documents the relationships of Hugh and Zina Brown and their children. That the husband and wife, so often separated, should correspond frequently is less remarkable than that they should sweeten so many of their newsy letters with protestations of affection and supplement them with spontaneous love notes even when they were together. Often their expressions were in poetry. One of her loveliest messages to him is titled "Hugh":

> Hungry is my heart when you're away.
> Until I hear your voice again
> My thoughts all stray your way.
>
> Glad is my heart on your dear return.
> How strange it is that life's lamp
> Does so slowly burn!
>
> Life's lamps so brightly burn
>   When you are at my side.
> 'Twas ever so, my Darling,
>   Since I was first your bride.
> Now I call you Daddy,
>   Instead of saying "Hugh."
> Eight times you've answered to that call,
>   But now, alas, we're through.

The poetic range of Hugh B. Brown extends from frivolous doggerel to carefully crafted verse. An undated example of the latter is called "To Mother":

> As years ago we carried to your knees
> The tales and pleasures of eventful days,
> Knowing no deed too humble for your praise
> Nor any gift too trivial to please,
> So still we bring with older smiles and tears

What gifts we may to claim the old dear right;
Your faith beyond the silence and the night,
Your love still close and watching through the years.

Corresponding with the children must have been a major activity of Zina Brown's life from the time when Zina Lou first went away from home until sickness stilled the mother's pen four decades later. From her they learned the day-to-day minutiae of their parents' lives, and through her they learned a great deal about the activities of one another. Her letters also contained, as has been noted elsewhere, frequent reminders of the greatness of their father and assurances of his love for all of them. During some of the difficult times of separation or adversity, she complained a little to the older girls, but her concerns were generally with the children's problems and her faith was irrepressible.

Hugh Brown wrote with less regularity to his children, but the aggregate volume of letters is impressive. Sometimes he wrote hastily on a train or in a hotel room, but he rarely forgot birthdays or failed to express thanks for gifts or remembrances. He was particularly supportive in their times of trouble, sometimes offering suggestions and always expressing admiration for their courage in facing their problems. He was particularly pleased when he could lend a helping hand, and, as has been mentioned in other chapters, he pursued through much of his life the goal of sufficient wealth so that he could assist his children and grandchildren with their educational and other plans.

Many of the letters for birthdays and other special occasions have become cherished possessions. Hugh Brown wrote to Zola for her tenth birthday:

> As I sit here I can hear the sweet notes of a canary. . . . How nice it would be if we could all try and see the pleasant things in life, look out through the cage like the canary does and see only the sunshine, never noticing the bars of the cage. . . . We can live our lives in the sunshine if we will but try to see the pleasant things in life. . . .
>
> May the Lord bless you, my dear girl, that with each passing year you may grow in body and mind and be a worthy daughter of your blessed mother, for no girl ever had a better mother than you have. . . .

A three-page letter from a Portland, Oregon, hotel, typed in Hugh Brown's non-professional style and dated October 19, 1930, offers love and counsel to his firstborn son on his eleventh birthday. As he often did, despite Zina's preference for other metaphors, President Brown made his points by drawing parallels to horses. "Men and horses are a lot alike," he told young Hugh Card. "Some are all for show and make-believe but cannot be depended on to do a real job." Bell, the handsome and erratic bay mare, and Dan, the plain and dependable grey gelding, came through impressively in this letter, and the wild ride through a Canadian blizzard on Dan's back makes a point about integrity which an eleven-year-old can handle. These points are spelled out in conclusion, and their seriousness is emphasized by the closing, "Your devoted father, H. B. Brown":

> Now my son, it is not my purpose to write you a long letter of instructions but your Daddy is expecting you to be a great and good man and he knows that much depends on what kind of a boy you are. A good colt usually grows into a good horse and a bad colt into a bad horse. So good boys make good men, and bad boys, bad men. Just tell yourself that you are going to be a fine man and then think of that every time you are tempted to do anything you should not do and you will be surprised what you can make yourself do. . . .
>
> There is another thing you must remember and that is that those of your brothers and sisters who are younger than you will follow your example and will do what they see you do, so you must be very careful what kind of example you set them. I had five brothers younger than I and four sisters and I always felt that I must not lead them away from the right path in life so I refused to smoke or drink or swear or steal or lie because I did not want them to do those things, as if they learned them from me I would be responsible.
>
> You have a fine mind. The Lord has given you much natural ability and He expects much from you. He wants you for His servant, so prepare yourself for His service. Keep your body clean and fine and keep your mind bright and active so you may do the work He has for you.

Impending marriages were the occasion for letters spelling out many of the points which were later incorporated in *You and Your Marriage*. Indicative of his continuing concern for his children and their families is "A Letter to My Children," dated May 29, 1957. It begins: "Sometimes I have experiences which I should like to share with you and occasionally I read things which I wish each of you could read. . . . " A recent public dialogue in Salt Lake City by Harry and Bonaro Overstreet, "outstanding scholars in the field of psychology and psychiatry," is described as "one of the best joint lectures I've ever heard." Four single-spaced pages of quotations follow — notes which Hugh Brown had taken, plus excerpts from the Overstreets' book, *The Mature Mind,* especially the chapter called "The Home As a Place for Growing." The letter ends:

> I hope the above quotations and observations may be helpful to you who are still in the business of raising families. I wish I had had this material before me when I started raising you folks, but somehow we muddled through. My love and blessings. . . .

Gifts were usually accompanied by personal greetings. When Charles Manley received a worn copy of Albert J. Beveridge's *The Young Man and the World* for Christmas in 1946, he received also this note from his father:

> When I make a present of a book which I have just purchased, I am liable to give it as I would a hat, a pair of gloves, or some other remembrance. . . . But when, as seldom happens, I give a book from my library, one which I have read and liked and gone back to again and again for inspiration and guidance, when I part with what has helped to make me, I give of myself and thereby identify the receiver as more than a friend — he becomes a mind relative, and we will thereafter think the same thoughts and fashion our lives out of the same material. . . . I send it on to you now, not because it is no longer useful to me, but I wish to share a treasure with my son and with his son. . . .

As they came along, the grandchildren, too, began to receive evidence of affection and concern. Here Hugh B. Brown sometimes indulged his fancy for atrocious puns and parody. LaJune's two daughters received a Christmas greeting in 1947 which began, "It's a few days before Christmas and Grandfather's house, without any children, is dead as a mouse." It ended, "Have fun while you're children but just you remember that Spring and the Summer will lead to December."

Of course, before the letters to the children and grandchildren and the talk of houses "dead as a mouse" came the years when the eight Brown children were growing up together and the parents were testing the principles which they also preached. Zina later wrote to Mary: "What is so important to us as the eternal welfare of our own children and their happiness and well-being in this life?" It is clear that the Hugh B. Browns were in full accord on their answer to this question.

The most vivid memories of the children's growing up are set in the family home in Salt Lake City. There the space was ample after the remodeling, the decor was pleasantly conservative, and despite some depression-imposed economies the style of living was comfortably middle class. When the Browns moved early in 1927, Zina Lou was seventeen, Zola was fifteen, and LaJune, Mary, Hugh and Charles Manley were twelve, ten, seven and five respectively. Margaret was a baby and Carol's arrival was almost two years in the future. The variety of activities which took place within the walls and on the tennis court and grounds at 1354 Stratford Avenue during the next ten years can be imagined.

Zina Brown conducted an organized but not tightly disciplined household. Her husband provided an allowance for her personal and household expenditures, but Hugh liked to shop for clothes and he often bought hers. The girls enjoy telling of the time he returned from a business trip with outfits of appropriate size and style for Zina and the four older daughters. (In a Relief Society Conference address in 1969, President Brown claimed to be "somewhat a specialist in the matter of women.")

Charles Manley remembers his mother as being an excellent cook. "She always served a beautiful, well-prepared table with a variety of foods, and she was very good on desserts. . . . " Everyone in the family remembers when President Brown brought President Grant home for dinner between sessions of a Granite Stake conference, just after Zina had had a painful session with the dentist. Little Margaret volunteered to the Church leader, "My mother sure didn't want you to come today." (President Grant did not help the situation by passing up the dinner which Zina had laboriously prepared in favor of a bowl of bread and milk.)

Zina's approach to family discipline was consistent with

her calm and amiable attitude toward life in general. Ida Archibald Brown, a sister-in-law, remembers that Zina was "exceptionally easy with her children." Zola remembers being provoked by her younger brothers and appealing to her mother. "Can't you ever scold them? Can't you get mad at them once in a while?" Her mother just turned to her and smiled and said, "Now, Darling, this is the way I want to bring up my children. When you have children, you can bring them up just the way you want. . . . "

President Brown acknowledged that he "had enough of my father in me to exercise control," but he did not use physical force other than an occasional thump on the head with his fingers. It was called "thimble pie." It should be noted parenthetically that he had strong fingers from many years of milking cows and doing other farm work; when he thumped the children on the head it was something more than a love pat. A brief passage in *You and Your Marriage* suggests recognition by the author that he may not always have measured up to the high standard of controlled and loving discipline which he set for himself. "Some children are cowed into silence by unwise display of authority and the curtailments of any show of independent thinking," he wrote; "the eager child is tapped on the head or forced to draw into a shell, as the final word of authority is spoken in anger." (P. 134.)

The children were required to attend Sunday School, both for their own sakes and because their father was the stake president. Zina accompanied them until their number reached seven. Thereafter, as it is felicitously stated in a biographical sketch by Nellie O. Parker, "she worshipped as she remained at home to catch her breath and put things in order before their return." LaJune remembers being permitted to stay home sometimes to baby-sit Margaret and Carol. Asked if their status as the children of the president of the largest stake in the Church affected his sons and daughters, President Brown acknowledged that both he and Zina had said, "You must do so and so, because of your father's position." He believes that "this suppression was not a good thing for my children in some respects. They felt that they were not individuals in their own right and they looked upon me as someone rather removed from them. . . . "

In his dictated memoirs Hugh B. Brown stated: "Every man has his troubles raising a family during their early period and during their teen-age life, and we had the usual amount of that, but all in all we feel grateful now, as we look back. . . . " He added: "I do not remember any of my children at any time wilfully disobeying my orders."

Schoolwork was not permitted to be shirked in the Brown family, but there was no heavy pressure for grades. Both parents loved and wrote poetry and several of the children tried their hand at it later in life. The girls learned domestic skills, the boys went into scouting, and all were encouraged to develop talents and hobbies. The tennis court helped prepare the father for the missionary matches at Gordon Square even as it provided a space for many family activities. Zina Lou learned to play golf with her father, and LaJune sometimes caddied for President Brown when he played with such dignitaries as Senator Reed Smoot. Horseback riding was the delight of many in this family whose presiding authority once wrote, "I have never had an automobile, no matter how expensive, that gave me as much real satisfaction as I have had with a good horse."

All of the living Brown children prize the fun-filled times on Stratford Avenue. Zola remembers the family get-togethers in the evening around the piano, the phonograph, and the radio. "Sometimes we would listen to "Amos and Andy" or "Myrt and Marge," and during the commercials Mother and Dad would say, 'Why don't you go down and get a bottle of pears or peaches. . . . " She also recalls that her father was a great storyteller. "We would sit on the floor around his knee and he would tell stories that he would see in the fire and that he would make up."

A letter from Zina to Mary in August 1945 suggests that the spirit of Stratford Avenue was still flourishing when four members of the family — father, mother, Margaret and Carol — were reunited in the British Mission headquarters. It reads:

> We all got gay tonight and had fun at tea time. Daddy [just back from his tour of the Continent as servicemen's coordinator] had told us a long tale at noon at dinner re the French girls and their "hair-dos" piled high on their heads, etc. So just before supper (tea) we all put our hair up and some put in flowers or feathers. Made

up our faces. Even got Sr. Dunn to (the girls did her hair). When
Daddy came in we were all seated waiting for his comment. He rose
to the occasion and we had a gay time around the table.

Charles Manley remembers that he and his brother would
watch their father shave, using a shaving brush. The boys would
taunt, "Big ears sticking out, Big ears sticking out." He would pre-
tend to ignore them and then turn quickly and dab their noses
with shaving cream. Mary's memories of her father as a tease go
back to Canada and a high cabinet on which, when she was
quite small, he would sometimes place her. "Well, goodbye,
Darling, I have to go to work," he would say, leaving her with
visions of her bones being found up there years later. After the
first time it became a game. Zola recalls that President Brown
would often tease his wife.

Concerning family prayer, the family remembers kneeling
at the table before the evening meal. They always enjoyed their
father's prayers, and they recall their mother saying that she
fell in love with Hugh Brown the first time she heard him pray
at 146 4th Ave. "Talking to the Lord" was a trait which the
children early noted in their father. (When asked to pray in
one of their homes in later years, he said, "I thank Thee, Lord,
that we don't have to make an appointment to gather before
Thee.") When President Brown was gone, as was often the case,
Zina called the children together for family prayers.

Filled as it usually was with the love of a vivacious mother
and a generous and fun-loving father, the Hugh B. Brown home
was a pleasant place to be. It was especially nice at Christmas,
for which family rituals evolved with the years. In Zola's words:

> There was a large stairway that came down to a landing, and
> beyond the front room there was a little music room where we had
> the Victrola. Daddy would put on a record. . . . Then we would line
> up at the top of the stairs, "littlest by littlest," and Mother and Daddy
> would stand at the foot of the stairs. . . . It makes me cry every time
> I think of it. They would be looking up at us with sweet smiles.
> Mother had been up till 4 a.m. just finishing things. Then we would
> traipse down and we would see them both standing there with tears
> in their eyes and smiling and watching us as we opened the presents.
> . . . Another thing I remember about Christmas was Daddy telling
> us not to eat our candy until we had finished our oatmeal. We always

had to have the oatmeal. . . . Some of those Christmases Grandma Card, Brigham Young's daughter, was with us and then she would come down the stairs. . . .

In December, 1936, when Hugh B. Brown had an idea that there might be a change of house and vocation, he suggested that the family go "all out" with decorations because that might be the last time they would all be together. The house and the trees around it were a blaze of lights, as the business depression and the problems of the liquor commission were forgotten in the last big Brown family Christmas. President Brown's premonition proved to be true; a year later the three married girls celebrated in their own homes and the rest of the family did so in London.

Nine years later, when Hugh C. was gone and only Margaret and Carol were at home to celebrate another English Christmas with their parents, President Brown — the self-styled "sage stuffed with turkey" — wrote a family letter to the five couples in the United States and their children. It reads in part:

> You know, as I see the average people here and elsewhere and come to know how they live, with love and kindness and happiness seemingly rationed because of the shortages . . . , I feel very grateful for our own abundance and for the blessings we have had through the years of having in the home one who is a genius at mixing life's ingredients so as to produce an almost perfect family life. Mother's tenderness and love have carried us over many rough places and sweetened many a mixture which without them would have been bitter indeed.
>
> We were talking the other morning at 3 a.m. of the events of our lives — of the coming of each of you and what your coming has meant to us, and how each addition has somehow changed the whole and modified it for the better. Each has brought something that no one of the others has had, like adding a new pane to a beautiful stained glass window. Someday you'll all know how much more beautiful the window of life looks in the mellow softness of the evening. One gets a certain effect when he looks through the window at the moon and a different one at midday. . . . But I think I like the quiet evening light the best. Perhaps the dimness of one's eyes adds something which is blurred a bit when there is too strong a light, and perhaps what one sees on any occasion depends largely on what is in one's heart and life as a purifying process.

President Brown's living children assemble in his home on his ninety-second birthday: (l. to r.) LaJune Hay, Zola Hodson, Zina B. Brown, Charles M. Brown, Mary B. Firmage, Margaret B. Jorgenson, Carol B. Sonntag.

In assessing the total impact of the family experience enjoyed by the children of Hugh B. and Zina Card Brown, two further points are appropriate. The first was made by one of the girls in reminiscing. Speaking of her parents' love and affection for each other, she said, "I thought that everyone was like that." As the children grew up and established their own homes, they found that everyone was not "like that," and adjustments had to be made. The second point is that the activities of the parents, the father in particular, took them away from the children at times or took the children away from home situations which seemed to be stable and secure. This, too, required difficult adjustments.

As their children moved out in the world and experienced both joys and disappointments, President and Sister Brown were always concerned and supportive. They were affectionate to the partners their children chose, and they became very loving grandparents and great-grandparents. Their pride in the accomplishments of their expanding family was boundless, and their attitude in times of trouble was once expressed by Zina in a letter to one of her daughters: "If .... makes the decision — *no matter what* — we'll stand right back of her and help her in every way possible."

Previous chapters have noted how President and Sister Brown took advantage of many opportunities to visit their children and do things with them. Trips, sometimes extended, were shared as the family circumstances of one or more of the children permitted. When Zina was no longer able to accompany her husband on his assigned journeys, one of the children was usually ready, willing, and able to be a traveling companion. Suggestions from children and grandchildren have often been incorporated in President Brown's sermons and writings. This contribution as well as the years of loving support from the whole family received symbolic recognition when Zina Lou and Mary were asked to sit with their father on the stand during the session of the 1969 Relief Society Conference at which he spoke on "Service." The affectionate, close-knit family group has been a comfort and support to President and Sister Brown in their old age.

The events of the years subsequent to Hugh B. Brown's release from the First Presidency were shared with Zina through the visits of family and close friends, the daily one-sided conversations (due to her loss of speech) which he had with her when he was in town, and the extended reports which he gave, holding her hand and noting the responses in her eyes, when he returned from longer absences. His trip to the Washington, D. C., Temple dedication was the last adventure to be so shared. On December 19, 1974, in her eighty-seventh year and the sixty-seventh year of her marriage, Zina Card Brown died. An impressive service in the Bonneville Stake Center on December 23 recalled the highlights of her life of service. Principal speakers were Presidents Spencer W. Kimball, N. Eldon Tanner and Marion G. Romney, and Elder Marvin J. Ashton.

It was another Christmas, and what the parting meant to Hugh B. Brown can be inferred from a letter which he wrote following the Lord Mayor's dinner in London in 1937. After assuring his children that Zina was the prettiest woman in the British Empire, he continued:

> I can only hope we can both live until the last one of us dies. That's Irish. And when we go, we can go hand in hand. That is the only way I will be able to get through the pearly gates, to hang on her hand and slip through on her record. And then when you kids come up there, Mother will have a big harp and I with chin whiskers will have a banjo and we'll play and march as you come, "littlest by littlest" as we used to say on Christmas morning. . . .

20. Oldest General Authority

The life of President Hugh B. Brown has spanned almost two-thirds of the history of The Church of Jesus Christ of Latter-day Saints. The two stories have been entwined since the name of the son of Homer Manley and Lydia Jane Brown was placed on the records of the Caanan Ward of the Salt Lake Stake in 1883. Of the twenty-four men who served as first or second counselor in the First Presidency prior to the death of President McKay, it is doubtful that any held a greater variety of callings of responsibility in the Church than President Brown. (It is interesting to note that Joseph F. Smith and David O. McKay were second counselors immediately prior to their appointments as president, but that Harold B. Lee was the first man to hold the positions of first counselor and then President of the Church.)

In October, 1883, the world's Mormons were organized into twenty-seven stakes and eleven missions; the Salt Lake Stake encompassed the entire Salt Lake Valley and its conferences were held in the sixteen-year-old Tabernacle. The Church's approximately 170,000 members were concentrated in the Territory of Utah and its immediate neighbors. Missionary work was concentrated in the British Isles, Scandinavia, Germany, Switzerland, The Netherlands, the eastern United States, and the island kingdom of Hawaii. Converts were still responding by the thousands to the appeal to "gather to Zion," even as colonies of refuge for polygamous Mormons were being planned for Mexico and Canada. As noted in an early chapter, the latter effort created the opportunity which drew the monogamous Homer M. Brown family to Alberta at the end of the nineteenth century.

The British Mission to which Elder Hugh B. Brown was called in 1904 was one of twenty-one in a church which numbered its members at 312,172. The Church President then was Joseph F. Smith, who was six years old when his uncle Joseph Smith was killed, and the generation which "knew the Prophet" was disappearing. The Church leadership was adjusting to the impact of the Woodruff Manifesto, the suspension of the doctrine of gathering, and the abandonment of a public role in politics, and the word *Mormon* conjured up such negative images as to limit the success of the 698 missionaries who were Elder Brown's contemporaries.

When Hugh Brown and Zina Card exchanged marriage vows there in 1908, the Salt Lake Temple was the newest and largest of the four temples in operation, and the Cardston Ward, in which he had just been sustained as a bishop's counselor, was one of 660 wards in the Church. The Lethbridge Stake was the 101st to be organized since the founding of the Church in 1830, but was the 86th of those then functioning. When Hugh B. Brown became the stake's first president in 1921, the world total of living Latter-day Saints had passed 548,000. Aggressive anti-Mormonism was on the wane, but proselyting efforts were still largely confined to the same areas that produced the flood of convert migrants to the American West in the days of Brigham Young and John Taylor.

The long presidency of Heber J. Grant spanned Hugh B. Brown's two stake presidencies, his successful law practice in Salt Lake City, his less successful ventures into Utah politics and government, his second British mission and part of his third, and most of his career as servicemen's coordinator. It witnessed the centennial conference of the Church, April 6, 1930, at which President Brown of the Granite Stake and eight thousand others voted in the Tabernacle to sustain the General Authorities and joined in the "Hosanna Shout" which LDS custom associates with very special occasions.

President Grant reported to the conference that the membership of the Church then numbered approximately seven hundred thousand, organized into 104 stakes with more than one thousand wards and branches, and 29 missions with 800 branches. Two thousand full-time and nine hundred stake missionaries were the preceding year's totals, and 6,511 convert baptisms were the rather modest fruits of their labors. Also reported for 1929 is the fact that "the Church expended from the tithes of the people for education more than $918,000.00."

As stake president, public official, and mission leader in the 1930s, President Brown faced many of the problems which led to the establishment of the Church Welfare Program. This widely heralded activity, like the radio voice of the Tabernacle Choir, helped to change public impressions of the Latter-day Saints, especially in the United States. During both of his assignments as head of the British Mission, Hugh B. Brown had to cope with the disastrous effect of World War II on the regular proselyting program, but his military work promoted that religious enthusiasm among LDS soldiers, sailors, and airmen which contributed to the upsurge of missionary activity when the conflict ended. An earlier chapter has noted that many young people who heard "Major Brown" in the camps of America and Europe heard him again when they sat in the classes of "Professor Brown" at Brigham Young University. The one-time Canadian cowboy was just moving from the university to the oil and gas fields of Alberta as LDS membership reached one million in 1950.

President Hugh B. Brown's service as a General Authority coincides with phenomenal worldwide growth in the Church. Earlier chapters have highlighted his role, but the thousands of hours spent on trains and planes, in meetings and interviews, and dictating correspondence and speeches can only be imagined. The following statistics reflect some of the results with which he has been prominently associated since that tempestuous night in Edmonton in 1953 which preceded his call. The data are from April conference reports for the years in which he was

appointed Assistant to the Council of the Twelve, member of
the Council of the Twelve, and first counselor in the First Presidency, and then released from the Presidency:

	1953	1958	1963	1970
Number of LDS Stakes	211	269	384	533
Number of missions	42	47	77	92
Number of full-time missionaries	1,750	2,778	5,781	7,590
Number of convert baptisms	16,436	33,330	105,210	79,126
Total Church membership	1,246,362	1,555,799	2,117,451	2,930,810

Although he wrote in his journal that he was happy to be
relieved of his responsibilities in the First Presidency, it is understandable that Hugh B. Brown experienced an emotional let-
down in the weeks which followed his release. The limelight
which he had enjoyed passed to others, and in the excitement of
installing a new First Presidency his notable service seemed to be
forgotten. The combination of circumstances made him more
conscious of the fact that he was in his eighty-seventh year.

Actually, President Brown's life continued to be exciting,
and, according to his journal, when he finished decorating his
new office on the second floor at 47 East South Temple it was
"better looking" than the one he had before. Of the meeting of
the First Presidency and the Twelve on February 12, 1970, he
wrote: "Many important matters were discussed and I felt
quite at home in my old place on the Council of the Twelve."
A few days later he was invited to meet with General William
Westmoreland, the former commander of United States forces
in Vietnam, and he enjoyed the award dinner at which the Utah
National Guard honored the general.

In March, 1970, Hugh B. Brown was assigned to fly to
Japan and help with the dedication of the Mormon pavilion at
the Osaka World's Fair. Zina Lou accompanied him, and in
Honolulu LaJune joined them. At the fair they met Elder
Gordon B. Hinckley and Elder and Sister Ezra Taft Benson for
the dedicatory exercises; the cold of the unheated pavilion and
the warmth of the Japanese version of "Man's Search for Hap-

piness" were particularly memorable. The same cold weather kept President Brown from seeing the emperor and empress formally open the exposition, but he made note of the fact that the first pavilion visited by the royal family was the Canadian.

Stops at Taipei and Hong Kong combined mission touring, sightseeing, and shopping. At the close of the visit with the scenery and Latter-day Saints in Bangkok, Thailand, LaJune returned to Hawaii. But President Brown and Zina Lou decided that there would never be a better chance to see the Taj Mahal, so they converted their return trip into a flight around the world. The poverty of India, plus the discomfort of an upset stomach, made a bleak impression, but the Taj was a delight. "It is a very beautiful jewel," he wrote, "so peaceful, majestic, and thoroughly complete." Homesickness took over while the touring partners were in Teheran, so plans to fly to London and go from there by ship were abandoned and two days later they were at home.

A missionary meeting at Monroe, Louisiana, on April 27, 1970, prompted one elder to write, "The Zone Conference was the greatest experience I have ever heard, seen, or felt in my entire life." Oma Wagstaff, the wife of the Gulf States Mission president, wrote to her friend Zina Lou Brown:

> The things President Brown said, his great testimony, the respect the elders had for him, all created a deeply spiritual atmosphere. In addition, President Brown prophesied that some young man sitting before him would one day stand where he now stands as a member of the Council of the Twelve. Hardly a breath was drawn, but eyes were full of tears and a few elders began to openly sob. He went on to give them such wonderful instruction. None of us wanted to have him quit talking. When he did, I pinned one of our Gulf States Mission pins on his lapel, but my eyes were so full of tears and my hands were shaking so hard I could hardly do it. He eased the tension by saying, "Aren't you supposed to earn this?"

The invitation to speak at the seminary graduation exercises at the American Fork Training School was particularly gratifying, and President Brown has maintained contact with this institution for handicapped children. The opportunity to speak at the dedication of the restored Wilford Woodruff home at Nauvoo was also satisfying, since Hugh B. Brown had admired the fourth president of the Church ever since seeing him at the Salt Lake Temple dedication in 1893.

A special Appreciation Dinner on May 28, 1970, gave spokesmen from many walks of life opportunity to acknowledge the contributions of Hugh B. Brown. Sponsored by Utah Governor Calvin Rampton, with the assistance of Milton W. Weilenmann, the affair was attended by approximately 450 "prominent citizens" who, according to the journal, "paid $15.00 a plate." Charles Manley Brown told the group, "As his son, I can say tonight what others perhaps could not, that here is a prophet who is with honor in his own home." Other speakers were Judge Aldon J. Anderson, Wendell J. Ashton, Roy W. Simmons, and President N. Eldon Tanner. Telegrams were received from former President Lyndon B. Johnson, Treasury Secretary David F. Kennedy, former New York governor W. Averill Harriman, and others. Music was provided by groups from the Utah Symphony and the Tabernacle Choir. Following the speeches Governor Rampton gave President Brown an official declaration of appreciation for services rendered to the people of Utah, and Mrs. Rampton presented him an original painting by the pioneer Utah artist, Carl C. A. Christensen. The guest of honor recorded in his journal: "All of my family, except my dear wife, were in attendance at this dinner. It was an enjoyable occasion, but I felt somewhat like they were giving my funeral a bit prematurely."

Assignments continued to come. In August he toured the Northern States and North Central States missions, accompanied by Zina Lou and James A. Cullimore, the Assistant to the Twelve who shared with President Brown the oversight of the missions in the central United States and Canada. While they were in Minneapolis, a phone call to say hello to Hubert Humphrey brought the former Vice President to the mission home for an amiable visit. A youth conference at Rockford, Illinois, gave Zina Lou an opportunity to "brag on her Dad" and point out that there need be no generation gap.

On September 23, President Brown was advised that he was suffering from Parkinson's disease. The illness confined him to his home through the October general conference and his eighty-seventh birthday, but he was able to handle several speaking engagements and other assignments later in the year. Two hospitalizations early in 1971 punctuated a busy schedule of conferences, mission presidents' seminars, meetings and interviews. He again had the assignment of reviewing applications for the cancellation of temple sealings, and he commented in his journal that "we are trying to be reasonable and just, but certainly it seems strange that people having been so married cannot recognize their weaknesses until they are pretty well swamped by them." He continued also to serve on the boards of directors of Zions First National Bank, Hotel Utah, Beneficial Life Insurance Company, and Deseret Federal Building and Loan Company, and he found it "quite encouraging to keep contact with what is going on. . . ."

The summer of 1971 found President Brown confined to his home much of the time. He found it impossible to walk without the aid of a cane and was sometimes taken to meetings in a wheelchair. It was very embarrassing to this man who had been so vigorous and strong almost all of his life. His impatience is reflected in an anecdote from his secretary, Vera Hutchinson. Finding it necessary to leave one of the Temple meetings early and getting no immediate response to his call for the attendant who operates the underground electric car to the Church office building, he did not wait for a wheelchair to be brought but started down three flights of stairs alone. Like the earlier attempt to climb a pyramid at seventy-six, it overtaxed his strength if not his resolution.

A sad occasion in July, 1971, was the funeral of LeRoy J. Robertson, a prominent LDS musician and a very dear friend of President Brown. Dr. Robertson had recently set to music the poem, "The Prince of Peace," which Hugh and Zina Brown had sent as a Christmas message to their friends in 1970. Written by President Brown on the basis of biblical language, the original Christmas card reveals both the wavering penmanship and the unwavering testimony of the author. To Dr. Robertson "the words of *The Prince of Peace* seemed to sing when they were written," and they were later sung by the Tabernacle Choir as a Christmas carol.

Through the years that he has been a General Authority, President and Sister Brown have sent Christmas cards with a personal religious message. Original poems by President Brown have appeared on many, and even after Zina's participation in their preparation was limited to signaling assent to what her husband read to her, the names of both appeared as co-authors on several. The "Season's Greetings" for 1967 is representative:

> The real significance of the "Spirit of Christmas" is appreciated when we drop the last syllable of the word; it then becomes the "Spirit of Christ." It beckons us to the blessedness which he promised to the most unlikely people — the poor in spirit, the sorrowful, the meek, the seekers after righteousness, the merciful, the pure in heart, the peacemakers, and even the persecuted and oppressed.
>
> The Spirit of Christ will pervade the humblest cottage or gladden the palace of the king, to the degree that it is in the heart of the peasant or the king, prompting them to apply the formula of happiness — love one another.

What President Brown described as one of his "greatest disappointments" came when his name was not included in the list of General Authorities invited to attend the first area conference of the Church, held in Manchester, England, August 26-28, 1971. In view of the condition of his health, the decision may have been a prudent and considerate one. Still, the wish for one more visit to the land where he had enjoyed so many wonderful experiences is understandable, as is the disappointment.

A return trip to the Holy Land in September revived President Brown's spirits. This time Truman G. Madsen and Louis Schricker were his traveling companions, and though some of the sightseeing was done from a wheelchair, Dr. Schricker's attention to his medical needs helped to make the quick tour a very pleasant one. President Brown spoke in the October general conference and at about the same time the fourth volume of his collected works, *Vision and Valor*, appeared. A few weeks later he attended the fiftieth anniversary celebration of the Lethbridge Stake. Speaking of the experience, he commented: "Some gracious and overgenerous statements were made about my activities in Lethbridge in those early days."

Shortly after returning, President Brown suffered what was

diagnosed as a partial stroke. Elder Harold B. Lee, who had succeeded to the Church presidency a few months before, gave him a blessing. According to the journal, "At that time my daughter, Zina, was in the other room making out a proposed schedule for my funeral." The winter and spring of 1972 were largely spent in convalescence and therapy, with short intervals at the office and occasional participation in scheduled meetings, conferences, and special events. A nostalgic note in the journal records a dinner with Adam Patterson, who had served with Hugh B. Brown on the Utah State Liquor Commission almost forty years before. Sister Brown's eighty-fourth birthday and the couple's sixty-fourth wedding anniversary were spent quietly with family members.

A voracious reader all his life, President Brown now found cataracts threatening his vision. Still he managed to enjoy old friends and take occasional trips. Gatherings with "fishing buddies" now concentrated on spinning yarns rather than wetting lines. His friend Glenn Nielson took him to Cody, Wyoming, to dedicate a chapel and then, with Zina Lou, to Cardston and Waterton Lakes for a relaxing reunion with other old friends. President Brown wrote, "As long as I have friends with planes who are so gracious and generous, I am happy to take advantage of their fine hospitality." (The Nielson plane later carried him to the Washington Temple dedication.)

The latest dictation in President Hugh B. Brown's journal is dated July 31, 1972. For the next year and a half his health permitted him to go to the office only irregularly and for a few hours at a time, and only a limited number of his appointments could be kept. His eighty-ninth birthday was celebrated with a family party at home. For the first time since the World War I years he was sporting a mustache. The reporter who photographed and interviewed him wrote, "Elder Brown said that he was impressed with the scarcity of wisdom that a person can accumulate during a lifetime."

As befitted such a man and such an anniversary, the ninetieth birthday of Hugh B. Brown received considerable attention. A luncheon with the General Authorities opened the festivities on Wednesday, October 24, 1973. Interviews and visiting were

President Harold B. Lee speaks at a luncheon with the General Authorities honoring President Brown on his ninetieth birthday.

followed by a family dinner and a reception and party for close friends at the Garden Park Ward in Salt Lake City.

"He has been a model for us," declared President Harold B. Lee at the noon affair held atop the new Church Office Building. Speaking further of President Brown, he said, "Dear friend, leader, brother, we love you. . . ." Elder Spencer W. Kimball, who two months later would succeed President Lee, presented a volume of scripture autographed by every one of the General Authorities. He said, in reviewing highlights of Hugh B. Brown's career, "He's known as the eloquent one." The two counselors in the First Presidency, N. Eldon Tanner and Marion G. Romney, gave the prayers at this impressive occasion.

In his response President Brown paid tribute to the LDS leadership and declared, "The Church is in great shape and is on a solid foundation." He challenged all people to recognize the fatherhood of God and the brotherhood of man, and he retold once more his experience as a young bishop's counselor with the woman found in transgression. "I'm glad God is an older man," he said, as he had many times before, and this time added, "that way I'm sure to get mercy." He concluded that at ninety he was now the patriarch of the General Authorities, "so I call you my children and you have my blessing." After the applause, two of President Brown's daughters cut the birthday cake and all of his girls served it.

A highlight of the family dinner was a message which one of the Brown daughters had written on behalf of Zina Card Brown, then in her fifth bedridden year. It began, "Beloved, here are some of my tender memories of my knight with the gleaming armor of love and righteousness."

The party in the cultural hall of President and Sister Brown's home ward brought back other memories. Members of the old Millennial Chorus recalled the prewar British Mission as they sang "Stout-Hearted Men," "Smiling Through," and "I Need Thee Every Hour." Zola presented a slide lecture, "Memories of Daddy's Life," which tapped the treasury of photographs that document her parents' eventful history. Unfortunately, the projector malfunctioned; she announced that the next picture would be of Hugh B. Brown and his brothers, and instead a photograph of army horses was flashed on the screen. After the laughter was over, Zola told the story without further visual aids. She described her father's balanced life of spirituality, recreation, and desire for success. The master of ceremonies, Charles Manley Brown, illustrated his father's sense of humor and quickness of mind with a recent incident. Seeing that the elderly apostle needed help in walking, Elder Boyd K. Packer took him by the arm and said, "Let me be your cane." President Brown immediately replied, "If I am able."

A pageant written by his eighty-six-year-old brother Lawrence was presented by the Salt Lake Stake on October 24-25 in honor of President Brown. "The Key, the Vision, the Kingdom" told the story of the establishment of the Church. The local and regional newspapers, of course, gave space to biographical sketches, pictures and interviews. A KSL-TV interview included the verse which Hugh B. Brown often recited to his grandchildren and great-grandchildren:

> My bi-focals are wonderful,
> My hearing aid's a find,
> My dentures come in handy,
> But how I miss my mind!

On this memorable birthday President Brown used a wheelchair in moving from place to place, but his health improved during the following year and he was able to spend more time at his office and to attend some meetings and special events. At his ninety-first birthday he was walking without aid and his conversation continued to be both wise and witty. The *Church News* noted the milestone with a cover picture, interview, and biographic sketch; it also provided a character portrait of Sister Brown, largely drawn from anecdotes by Mary, Carol, and Zina Lou. This tribute to Zina Card Brown was particularly timely, for two months later she passed on.

In the lonely months which have followed, Hugh B. Brown has kept as busy as health has permitted, sustained by continuing Church responsibilities, the care and affection of his family and friends, and the truth which is captured in one of his favorite quotations: "God gave us memory that we might have roses in December."

In an interview in his ninetieth year, President Hugh B. Brown expressed what he perceived to be the theme of his life in these words: "I have been favored with a very special relationship with Heavenly Father. At times in my life he has taken me by the scruff of the neck and made me go in ways I didn't want to go." A letter from a Church member in British Columbia expressed a similar perception thus: "How wonderful and glorious it has been that the Lord has pruned and cut you down as a gardener does his choice trees and plants, and you have risen and been what God wanted you to be."

What Hugh B. Brown has become through the many re-enactments of the parable of the currant bush was remarkably symbolized at the dedication of the temple in Washington, D.C., on November 19, 1974. Six years previously he had participated in the groundbreaking and prayed that the Lord would spare his life to attend the dedication. Now, thanks to the revival of his strength and the hospitality of Glenn Nielson, he was back in the nation's capital, accompanied by Mary, Charles, and the Truman Madsens. Although he came to the dedicatory service in a wheelchair, President Brown required only a little assistance to approach the pulpit. It is the report of many present that, as had been the case so often during his seventy years of teaching and preaching, he seemed to draw strength from his listeners and his testimony moved many to tears. He spoke for only a few minutes, and these are some of the things he said:

> We have had an outpouring of the Spirit during these dedicatory sessions. . . . I have looked forward to this for some time. In fact, I set this as a departing point for me and thought that when this was accomplished I probably would be released or assigned to another field. It has been a glorious experience to me and I thank the Lord for it. . . .
>
> . . . I would like you to know that among the Brethren there is not one who is more close to our Heavenly Father than President Spencer W. Kimball. . . . It has been a joy and a pleasure to work with him and to see how the Spirit moves upon him in making decisions and in directing the work of the Lord in our time. I am very happy that it has fallen my lot to work with these men and to

witness their integrity, their commitment to the work, and their stalwart status among the people. . . .

On one occasion the Master said to Peter: "Whom do men say that I am?" And Peter responded that some thought He was one and some another, and then the Master said, "Whom say ye that I am?" and Peter responded, with inspiration upon him, "Thou art the Christ, the Son of the living God."

My brethren and sisters, with all the earnestness and solemnity of my soul I say to you that Jesus of Nazareth is the Son of the living God, our Redeemer, who won and made the atonement for us. . . . I am glad to make this declaration to you this day because in the ordinary course of events it will not be my privilege very long to declare these things on this earth. . . .

When Peter replied, "Thou art the Christ . . . ," the Savior said: "Blessed art thou, for flesh and blood hath not revealed it unto thee, but my Father which is in heaven." From the same source and with the same authority that he spoke, I declare unto you that I know that He is the Christ. . . .

I am very grateful that in the course of human events I have been led into circumstances and conditions where I have had to defend the truth even without wanting to save my own life. And now, rather than deny it, I would ask Him to take my life. . . .

I pray that the Spirit of the Holy Ghost may rest upon us and lead us back into the presence of our Heavenly Father. I pray that we may be able to conduct our lives in such a manner as to be worthy of His continued blessings; that we may be able, as we go forward, to walk figuratively and almost literally with our hand in His; that we can look up and feel the effect of His presence. . . .

A Mormon pioneer mother taught her son to ask the question, "Father, are you there?" Through the years he often asked, and he learned to hear the answer. Now, in the tenth decade of his life of service, Hugh B. Brown was ready to ask the question again, with the confident expectation that, still willing to submit to the Gardener's pruning, this time he would see the answer.

Index

Church Service